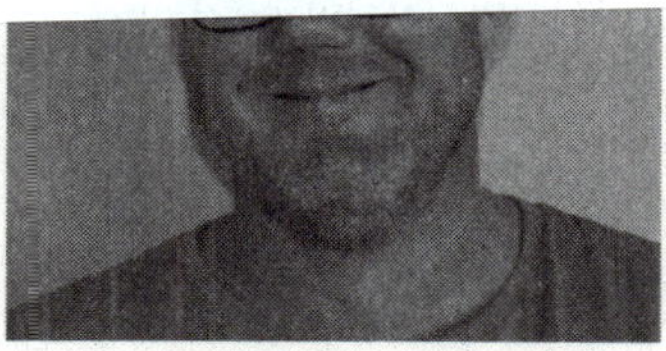

For the past decade Matt Elliott has been one of New Zealand's busiest authors, writing across genres for readers of all ages. Well-regarded for his research, several of his books have been the basis for national and international television and film documentaries. A winner of the Book of the Year and Best Non-fiction Book awards at the 2012 New Zealand Children's Book Awards, he has written four other rugby titles. Matt lives on Auckland's North Shore, and this year was a coach of the Birkenhead College fifth-grade (open-weight) rugby team.

Visit: mattelliottnz.com

RUGBY FOLKLORE

MATT ELLIOTT

HarperCollinsPublishers

HarperCollins*Publishers*

First published in 2019
by HarperCollins*Publishers* (New Zealand) Limited
Unit D1, 63 Apollo Drive, Rosedale, Auckland 0632, New Zealand
harpercollins.co.nz

HarperCollins*Publishers*
Unit D1, 63 Apollo Drive, Rosedale, Auckland 0632, New Zealand
Level 13, 201 Elizabeth Street, Sydney NSW 2000, Australia
A 53, Sector 57, Noida, UP, India
1 London Bridge Street, London, SE1 9GF, United Kingdom
Bay Adelaide Centre, East Tower, 22 Adelaide Street West, 41st floor, Toronto,
Ontario M5H 4E3, Canada
195 Broadway, New York NY 10007, USA

A catalogue record for this book is available from the National Library of New Zealand

ISBN 978 1 7755 4146 2 (pbk)
ISBN 978 1 7754 9177 4 (ebook)

Cover design by Darren Holt, HarperCollins Design Studio
Front cover image by Mark Leech / Offside / Getty Images
Back cover image by PA Images / Alamy Stock Photo
Author photograph by Melissa Elliott
Typeset in Sabon LT Std by Kirby Jones
Printed and bound in Australia by McPherson's Printing Group
The papers used by HarperCollins in the manufacture of this book are a natural, recyclable product made from wood grown in sustainable plantation forests. The fibre source and manufacturing processes meet recognised international environmental standards, and carry certification.

Dedicated to Uncle Michael (President D.M.A.S.)

CONTENTS

INTRODUCTION

In New Zealand, we have played, celebrated and commemorated the game of rugby like no other country. Men took to the game in extraordinary numbers in the late 1800s, with hundreds of clubs being formed around the country. It was a game that could be played by those of all physiques — the stout bloke, the bean-pole, the sprinting whippet, the mischievous little fella — and all occupations. Rugby has been called 'our game', and for decades, rightly or wrongly, has dominated the national landscape.

The game has a verbal history. Tales of deeds on the football field have always been shared, from the well-publicised moments of All Black brilliance, through to the achievements of provincial teams, the fables from close-knit club sides and even family stories associated with the game.

In my own family there is a story about my grandfather, James (Jim) Ford, who was watching a game from the bank at the old Athletic Park in Wellington. A cold wind was howling in from Cook Strait, and rain was lashing the ground. Jim had a hipflask inside his coat, and he and his cousin were sharing warming nips of whisky poured into the lid of the flask. A bloke in front of Jim turned around and said, 'I'll give you a shilling for a nip.'

'Fair enough,' said Jim.

He poured the nip and the bloke said, 'I wouldn't mind a bit of water with it.'

Jim tilted his head and a trickle of rain ran off his hat and into the nip of whisky, greatly amusing all around him.

Jim was once sent off in a club match, but the referee can't have viewed his indiscretion with long-lasting disdain. He later let his daughter marry Jim.

On the other side of our family, a great-uncle, Ted Searle, was a member of the Southern rugby club in Te Kopuru. Having been sent off in a game for robustly questioning the referee's knowledge of the rules, he was subsequently banned from even entering the club gates. (The referee was a local stock agent and frequent visitor to the Searle farm.) To watch a match, Ted had to sit on his horse outside the ground with his son, Ken, on the horse, too. However, when the club was in need of funds from its members, the ban was suddenly forgotten and Ted was welcomed into the fold again.

Stories such as these were our family folklore.

*

As a boy, I began to create my own rugby history stories. In my first year of Intermediate, I won a class speech competition using the All Black career of Bryan Williams as my topic.

Then, a year later, on the bus home from school one day, I had tucked under my arm my prized adidas All Black ball. (Recently bought for about $30 from a sports store in Auckland's Queen Street, having saved and saved for it.) I sat down next to an old man near the rear of the bus. He asked, with a slight English accent, if he could see the ball, and when I handed it to him he rolled it around in his big, leathery hands.

As we talked, he said, 'Did you ever hear of George Nepia?'

'Yes,' I replied. 'My grandfather has told me what a great player he was.'

'He was the best player I've ever seen,' said the elderly gent.

'Did you play?' I asked.

'I did, but then I went and played league in England. I played against George over there.' He had, he said, only recently returned to New Zealand.

I often wonder just who that man was.

A childhood friend of mine bought, at my request and payment, a duty-free transistor radio when on a trip overseas. It was a prized possession, for listening to cricket while sitting on the back lawn in summer or to rugby in my room on wintry afternoons.

I remember, a few years later, rushing out of St Patrick's Cathedral in Auckland after Sunday Mass to sit in our big Holden Kingswood and listen on the car radio to the remaining minutes of the All Blacks 21–21 draw with Argentina in Buenos Aires. The radio commentary seemed to come in on the wind, the volume and clarity fading and increasing every few minutes. The only constant was the buzz of the crowd and the hooting of horns in Ferrocarril Stadium. It was a nervous listen as Hugo Porta fired off drop-kick after drop-kick to try to win the game. Porta, with his three dropped goals and four penalties, had the highest tally for any player against New Zealand, but the question had to be asked: had his addiction to kicking kept Argentina or New Zealand in the game?

My school rugby team was, at the last minute, drafted in to be part of the opening ceremony at Eden Park for the 1987 Rugby World Cup. We were given little flags to (self-consciously) wave while standing on the field, as All Black legends Waka Nathan and Don Clarke wandered out and waved to the crowd. On the day, I think Don Clarke pulled a hamstring. The great Waka Nathan stood near us and said, 'Alright, boys.' We were then able to watch the game from the North Stand. As a couple of photographs I took at the time attest, there weren't many people at the ground for a game in which for the first time the All Blacks scored more than 50 points in a test, brought up by John Kirwan's great length-of-the-field try.

There was another, darker side to the game, too: what contact with apartheid-era South Africa did to New Zealand society. I well remember going with my father on 'No Tour' marches up Auckland's Queen Street. Exhilarating and nerve-racking!

Rugby, which for many years was always printed with a capital 'R', was very much part of the oxygen I breathed when growing up. Thousands upon thousands of New Zealanders have their own individual stories from their youth of little moments that contributed to their lifelong interest in the game.

*

There is also the material culture around the game, from the match-day programmes to cereal and cigarette cards of All Blacks, songs lauding or lampooning the game and its players, cartoons, official 'fan-wear', books, tickets, autographs, and so on. This is all part of the story of the game in New Zealand and how the game is celebrated off the field.

On a bookshelf at home I have a copy of *The New Zealand Rugby Football Union 1892–1967* by A. C. Swan. It was given to me when I was about 10 years old by Ima Batty, one of two elderly sisters we would see every Sunday morning at Mass.

Ima's husband had recently passed away. A kindly, quiet, broad-shouldered man whose face I can recall to this day, his name was Walter Batty. Tongan-born, he had played for the All Blacks from 1928 to 1931, and was famously photographed in the front row for the last match in which the All Blacks used the 2-3-2 scrum. He played for Auckland for a decade, and was awarded the Distinguished Conduct Medal during World War II.

Walter's name is written in the front of the book. It was one of the first items in my All Black ephemera collection (which my wife refers to as 'all that stuff').

*

Sport, and in this case rugby, provides the unexpected. It surprises. Leaves us bewildered. Stunned. Depressed. Ecstatic. Such moments remain in one's memory and cement themselves in the collective conscience as 'folklore', that ongoing conversation made up of the verbal and the material.

The following miscellany looks at aspects of the wonderful, confusing, famous or infamous, infuriating and exhilarating game of rugby football in this country, over more than a century. It shows how much has changed, both on and off the field, but how our love for the game and its players has (generally) remained strong.

SUPERSTITIONS

Always play with the wind in the first half. Get points on the board. The wind might die away.

Always take the wind in the second half. It takes a while for teams to settle into the game and get points.

Fergie McCormick (All Blacks career: 1965–71) would always put on his right boot — the kicking foot — first, as did Ian Jones (1989–99) and Beauden Barrett (2012–).

Dave Loveridge (1977–85) would put on the left boot — his non-kicking boot — first, as did Grant Fox (1984–93). In fact, Fox would methodically change into his clothes in the same order every time before a game.

Left sock on first for Dane Coles (2012–) and Luke Romano (2012–17), and also for Aaron Smith (2012–), who would always touch the turf as he ran out onto the ground.

Bob Scott (1946–54) always laced up his boots the same way. That is, when he wore them — he was famous for giving kicking displays in bare feet.

Making sure they packed their rugby kit bag, or packed it the same way for each match, was a superstition shared by McCormick and fellow fullback Laurie Mains (1971–76).

Maurice Brownlie (1922–28) had a favourite pair of blue dungaree shorts that he *had* to wear when playing for Hawke's Bay.

Ian MacRae (1963–70) made sure he always cleaned his own boots.

Bob Burgess (1971–73) thought that to make the All Blacks he would have to run 100 miles a week.

Stu Wilson (1976–83) put on his clothes in the same order every time — from head to toe.

Bruce McLeod (1964–70) put his shorts on last.

Allan Hewson (1979–84) always had baked beans for lunch before a game.

A number of players would have their favoured 'match undies' or Speedos, including Bryan Williams (1970–78), Simon Culhane (1995–96), Chris Jack (2001–07), Aaron Mauger (2001–07) and Sam Whitelock (2010–).

TJ Perenara (2014–) had to play in 'left' and 'right' socks.

Conrad Smith (2004–15) would always make sure he personally carried his boots and socks to the ground.

There were players who made sure they ran out onto the field in the same place in the team line or between the same players. For example, John Graham (1958–64) had to be between Kel Tremain (1959–68) and Dennis Young (1956–64).

Liam Messam (2008–15) and Ian Jones had to always sit in the same place in the changing room.

Alan Whetton (1984–91) would never put his jersey in the same bag as his boots, mouth-guard and togs. He would walk around Eden Park pre-match, stopping at each corner, imagining scoring a try there.

Starting during Graham Henry's reign as coach, when the All Blacks won a test match, the first and last song played on the bus (as the team left the ground and arrived at the hotel) was Kenny Roger's country classic 'The Gambler'.

On the team bus, management have always sat up the front.

The 'leadership group', as it is now called, sits at the back.

Ben Smith (2009–19) would have a sugar hit from a small bag of lollies just before kick-off.

Kieran Read (2008–19) would lay out his gear the same way before each game.

When taping up his wrists, Wyatt Crockett (2009–18) would always make sure the tape ended on the inside of his arm.

Colin Meads (1957–71), when he wasn't captaining the side, liked to run on last. He also had to receive a telegram from his wife, Verna, before the game. Before the fateful 1970 game against Eastern Transvaal where his arm was kicked and broken — possibly deliberately — he didn't receive the telegram, and, because he was vice-captain, he ran on second, following captain Brian Lochore.

Finally, a bit of old advice on how not to suffer from cauliflower ears: rub Vaseline into them about half an hour before taking to the field.

‘Don’t use water. He’ll turn to paste and we’ll never be able to move him!’

— referee Clive Norling to a St John Ambulance volunteer after All Black prop Gary Knight had been felled by a flour-bomb in the 1981 Springbok test at Eden Park.

‘[Bleep, bleep]!’

— Wallaby hooker Phil Kearns’s salute to Sean Fitzpatrick after scoring a try at Athletic Park in the Wallabies’ 21–9 win in 1990, which ended the All Blacks’ sequence of 50 unbeaten games. (Not enough to overtake the 52-game run of the All Blacks from 1965 to 1970.)

‘We’ll win the series 2–1 with one draw.’

— 1971 Lions’ manager Doug Smith prior to the start of a tour in which the Lions won the series … 2–1 … with one draw.

‘I’m delighted to announce the appointment of Robbie Deans as the Qantas Wallabies National Coach.’

— Chairman of the Australian Rugby Union Peter McGrath, December 2007.

‘At the moment it is like a swimming pool.’

— 1968 French manager Jean-Claude Bourrier, upon inspecting Athletic Park prior to the second test, after days of rain in the capital.

‘It wasn’t very pretty, but it came down to how much desire, how much courage the boys had.’

— Richie McCaw after winning the 2011 Rugby World Cup final.

FORESKIN'S LAMENT

Long-haired Otago number 8 Greg McGee came very close to All Black selection, having played in six of the eight tour games for the New Zealand Juniors (Under-23s) on their Australian trip in 1972. The *Rugby Annual* described him like this:

> Roaring success. The main reason so few tries were scored against the Juniors. Chased the ball incessantly in every match. Always there to cover for the backs when they dropped a pass (which was often). Ranked with [John] Callesen as the forward who contributed most to the tour.

When the Juniors had played the All Blacks at Athletic Park earlier that year (the first game on the senior team's nine-match internal tour), the Juniors forward pack was the heavier of the two sides.

Other members of the 24-man group who would go on to feature in All Black teams of the 1970s were Callesen, Grant Batty, Kent Lambert, Joe Karam, Ken Stewart, Andy Haden and Brad Johnstone. Coach Eric Watson, from Otago, would also graduate to instructing the top team.

When his rugby days were over, McGee concentrated on becoming a playwright. His 1981 play, *Foreskin's Lament*, brilliantly captures the ugly, chauvinistic, macho side of New Zealand rugby in the early 1970s. It premiered at a time when the country was divided over the 1981 Springbok tour, the South African rugby team's first visit since 1956. New Zealand had been a signatory to the 1977 Gleneagles Agreement, a declaration by Commonwealth governments that they would discourage their national sporting bodies from having contact with teams from the Republic until such time as the apartheid system was dismantled. In a statement after the signing, the collective leaders described apartheid as 'a dangerous sickness and an unmitigated evil'.

McGee actually burnt his Juniors jersey as part of an effigy in a protest prior to the Eden Park test against the Springboks, but still made it back to his flat in time to watch television coverage of the match and Allan Hewson's last-gasp penalty kick that won the match for the All Blacks 25–22 and secured a series win.

The 'Foreskin' of the play's title is a club rugby player's nickname. Foreskin/McGee pointedly muses on the fanaticism for rugby and its folklore that was such a part of New Zealand society. There were so many avid rugby fans who knew New Zealand's sporting and cultural history year by year based on where the All Blacks played (home or away), and knew our prime ministers or governors-general by which visiting rugby captains they shook hands with.

Foreskin's stream-of-consciousness monologue is spoken at the end of the play. It seems appropriate to include part of it near the start of this book.

> We were DBed, JJed, BGed, jardined, cooked, nicholled, elvidged, fred allened, otagoed in '49, bayed through the '60s, and through all of it, hot and cold wars, '51 strikes, recessions, depressions and the booms that gave them depth, hippies, yippies, and all the determined dog-paddling through our little backwater, there was one thing we knew with certainty; come winter, we'd be there, on the terrace, answering the only call that mattered — c'mon black!

'You'd better start answering your phone, fool, 'cause you're going to be in Auckland in a couple of days.'

— phone call from Mils Muliaina to Stephen Donald, who missed a call from Graham Henry to join the Rugby World Cup 2011 squad because he was whitebaiting.

'The 'Boks are weak on the short side.'

— anonymous note given to the Waikato coach Dick Everest from someone within the South African camp prior to the first match of their 1956 tour. Waikato won 14–10, scoring two tries down the short side.

WHAT DID HE JUST SAY?

When the 1956 Springboks toured New Zealand (after a visit to Australia, where five wins were notched up), the test matches were, well before the first kick-off had occurred, widely regarded as being *the* contest that would decide who would claim bragging rights to being the best team in world rugby.

The previous two home and away tours had heavily favoured the South Africans. The 1937 Springbok side that won the test series 2–1, after losing the first rubber, is still regarded as one of the best teams to play in this country. The 1949 All Blacks who went to the Republic for the next test series between the two countries are forever seen in the context of the All Blacks losing six tests in a row, including two played by different teams, half a world away, on the same day. As if losing the four-test series in South Africa wasn't bad enough.

A writer using the nom-de-plume of 'Clarence' contributed a poem to the *Otago Daily Times* lamenting those losses.

ALL BLACK BLUES — A TRAGEDY IN SIX TESTS

We'd better face the facts, you chaps,
And let the truth be understood;
So let us humbly doff our caps,
For we're no blooming good.
Since last July — forget it not —

We've played six tests — and lost the lot
At Newlands, last July, the tale
Was sad when Geffin found his mark;
Last week the final coffin nail
Was sunk on Eden Park.
Forgive if we our teardrops blink —
It's rather tragic — don't you think?
And blame the cooking, blame the chef,
The crowds (and don't forget the Press),
The wind, the weather, and the ref —
A biased linesman — Yes.
Such panaceas dim our woe
Just once or twice — but six times? No.
They say confession soothes the soul,
Then let us banish all the 'buts';
Let's own we lack the right control
And we can't play for nuts.
With our shortcomings thus confessed
Admit no flowers — by request.

The 1956 South Africans faced a New Zealand itinerary of 23 games, including four tests.

They dropped the first game to Waikato. Didn't score a point: 0–14. Hello, said the New Zealand rugby public, we've a chance here, come test time.

The Springboks won the next eight games, with three of them being by three points or less (North Auckland 3–0, Auckland 6–3, Wellington 8–6).

First test: Carisbrook, Dunedin. First blood to the All Blacks, 10–6.

During the next week a midweek win, then a loss to Canterbury, 6–9.

These 'Bok forwards don't seem to be up to much, said the rugby public.

Three more wins, then the second test at Athletic Park. The tourists come right: 8–3 win.

The public get jittery again.

A midweek win, then a draw with Taranaki, 3–3. Ferdinand the Bull nearly had kittens!

Third test: Lancaster Park, Christchurch. (Not the most straightforward of itineraries in terms of travel.) 17–10 ... to the All Blacks. Two games to one, a series win was on for the home side.

Four days later, the New Zealand Universities side beat the 'Boks, 22–15. The match of the tour so far. The students ran the ball. The tourists took them on at their own game. Rugby, as they say, was the winner.

Two more wins, including the 37–0 hiding of a very disappointing New Zealand Maori team.

Then to Eden Park on 1 September. Never had there been such anticipation before a test match in New Zealand. A paying crowd of 61,240! Many had camped out all night for tickets.

The spectators crammed into the ground witnessed what was up to that point in time the greatest and most important score in All Blacks history. Those listening on the wireless heard these words from commentator Winston McCarthy:

> In it goes. In the front of the line-out. Hemi comes through, with the ball at his toe. Going on and he knocks it out of Dryburgh's hands. Jones is coming down. He takes it in his hand.
>
> It's a try for New Zealand!
>
> Try to New Zealand. Peter Jones has scored.
>
> I'll tell you about it when the crowd stops roaring.
>
> Listen to them. Listen to them!
>
> The crowd is going absolutely crazy.

Now from that ball to the lineout, Strydom went to get it, right in the front of the lineout. Hemi kicked it away from him, took it at his toe, up about ten yards. Knocked it out of Dryburgh's hands. Jones picked it up, ten yards infield and tore up the field. He beat everybody and scored right by the goalposts. Peter Jones, a try, and the time gone, five minutes.

Now they'll argue who is New Zealand's greatest forward, for years to come, I suppose.

Dynamic is the word.

That try by our big number 8 and the conversion by fullback Don Clarke were the key scores in securing an 11–5 win. For the first time in the 20th century the mighty Springboks had lost a test series.

After the match, as thousands of fans remained at the ground, milling around the front of the main stand, they began calling for Jones and Clarke to appear.

An exhausted Jones, sitting without his jersey underneath the stand, wearily pulled on a blazer and made his way up to the grandstand balcony. Somebody from the media asked him how he felt. He replied, 'Well, ladies and gentlemen, I hope I never have to play as tough a game as today's. I'm absolutely buggered.'

Never before had that 'b' word been broadcast in New Zealand. Many laughed. Some were appalled. The New Zealand Broadcasting Corporation sent around a memo making it very clear that the Jones recording was not to be aired again! (Apparently, it wasn't until the 1980s.)

Jones later recalled: 'I realised what I had said. It came very slowly back into my head. I didn't feel startled, and I didn't think it was funny. I didn't know it was being broadcast, and it wouldn't have made any difference if I had. I went straight down again to the dressing room and sat slumped on the seat. I meant what I'd said: I did not ever again want to play in as hard a match.'

Fast-forward 50 years from that match and infamous quote. The All Blacks have *just* managed to pip a plucky Argentinian team at the José Amalfitani Stadium in Buenos Aires. Granted, coach Graham Henry had sent a second-string All Blacks side to South America due to a compressed itinerary of home tests against Ireland and then the start of the Tri Nations.

The rain- and referee-affected match saw Argentina ahead by 16–15 at the break, and the All Blacks did exceedingly well to hold on, playing the last four minutes a man down, with fullback Leon MacDonald in the sin bin. The Argies threw everything at the All Blacks in what was a thrilling finish, but the men in black won 25–19.

Captain for the All Blacks (the first of three tests he would lead the side in) was Jerry Collins. A player who expected much of himself and his team, when interviewed straight after the match he seemed a bit frustrated by his team's performance.

'It was a good workout, but that's probably not what people at home want to hear, or see on the scoreboard.'

Then he added, 'Ah, f*** it!', before covering his mouth with his hand.

There was no reaction to the use of that word as there had been when Jones uttered his swear word. After all, it was 2006 and it was a word of common usage that you could probably hear every night on television (after the watershed). It was also Jerry Collins being himself, being brutally honest, and many supporters probably felt the same way.

That wasn't the only surprise from Collins that night. Later at a post-match function he made his captain's speech in Spanish, delighting his hosts and amazing his teammates.

HIKA THE HAPPY HOOKER AND THE HAKA

The All Blacks' 1980 tour of Australia got off to a shaky start with a come-from-behind 13–13 draw with Sydney on a hot, energy-sapping May afternoon. Then came romps against South Australia (75–3), Victoria (45–6) and the Tasmanian XV (73–0). A good warm-up for the test was next, winning 12–4 in a hard-fought tussle against New South Wales (featuring 13 of the victorious Sydney team), another festival-type match against New South Wales Country (34–3) and then a first test loss in Sydney (9–13).

The stand-out player in that game had been the big Australian fullback Roger Gould. Making his international debut, his enormous touch-finders and cloud-bursting 'up-and-unders' taunted the All Black backs for much of the 80 minutes, leaving them a jittery mess in defence.

There were several stand-up brawls among the forwards, with Australian prop Chris 'Buddha' Handy suffering a deep cut on his forehead. (An event which might explain why he seemed to have such a gripe against the All Blacks when later commentating on televised test matches.)

Following the loss, the All Blacks travelled north to Townsville for the midweekers to stretch their legs in the heat against Queensland Country (63–6).

Come the second test, at Ballymore in Brisbane, and the Australians were full of confidence and up 9–0 after the first half-hour. The points had come courtesy of a Brendan Moon try, converted by Gould, who also added a penalty.

'When you're hot, you're hot, and when you're not, you're not,' philosophised ex-All Black turned comments man Grahame Thorne (soon to sport a perm that shocked the nation!).

On a sunny afternoon, the All Blacks' scrum was slowly demoralising their Australian opposites, and points finally came for New Zealand near the end of the half when Counties' fullback Brett Codlin kicked two penalties — one for a player detaching early, and the other for a collapsing front row.

Half-time: 9–6 to Australia.

Then, with about a quarter of an hour to play, came a piece of All Blacks magic.

Inside their 22, Bay of Plenty hooker Hikatarewa (Hika) Rockliffe Reid — a Ngongotaha boy who had played much of his rugby as a flanker and was now in just his second test start — burst forward after picking up the ball at the back of a ruck. He then turned the ball back to halfback Dave Loveridge, who ran across the field only metres from the All Blacks' line before lofting a pass to centre Bruce Robertson on his right.

Robertson, who played 102 games for the All Blacks, was well-known for wearing his socks around his ankles. A brilliant centre, equally adept at seeing and creating space, he could give himself and teammates a vital millisecond of time or a couple of metres of space by creating uncertainty in the defence. He would carry the ball out in front of him with two hands, offering dummy passes, or throwing a body swerve to change direction, all while running at top pace.

So it was he who counter-attacked and ran the ball up to the All Blacks' 10-metre line before passing infield to flyer Gary

Cunningham, usually a wing but that day at second-five. Taking the ball at speed, Cunningham ran to halfway, before running a scissors with right-wing Tim Twigden, who had come infield. He threw a quick pass to lock Andy Haden, who for a number of years had been the biggest man to play for the All Blacks. Several thundering strides later, just as he was collared from behind and sent crashing to the ground, Haden flicked the ball on to left-wing Murray Watts.

Watts headed infield and, on reaching the 22-metre line, passed infield to first-five Murray Taylor. He jinked, swerved and evaded gold jerseys until about 10 metres from the line. Fizzing up alongside his left shoulder was 22-year-old Hika Reid, the man who had started the movement 80 metres back.

Reid took Taylor's pass, and crossed the line as a desperate Wallaby dived to try to knock the ball from his hands. He rolled across the turf, then bounced up. Ball held in his right hand, he held it trophy-like and said, 'Yes!'

'I was running behind the backs right down the field and admiring their passing,' said Reid after the game. 'As we approached the 22, I could see the try was coming and I thought, "Boy, this is a try I'd like to score." Suddenly I had the ball and that's exactly what I did!'

It was the match-winner. Codlin's conversion saw the final score as New Zealand 12, Australia 9, and at least one New Zealand newspaper carried the headline 'Hika the happy hooker'.

There were two other major talking points in the game.

The big Australian lock Steve Williams, who in both tests had been doing his best impression of a heavy overcoat across Haden's body at the line-outs, had his jaw broken by a Mark 'Cowboy' Shaw punch. Does it lessen the offence any by saying it was retaliatory? Shaw was known to say that he had never punched a back or anybody who didn't deserve it!

Prop John Ashworth suffered a dreadful injury to his left ear that required a dozen stitches. Reportedly, there was very little of the ear still attached to the side of his head after being ferociously rucked.

The All Blacks lost the final test two weeks later, 10–26. They had been confident during the early part of the week, and had famously practised passing bricks at training. However, much of the blame for their poor showing must be attributed to the most celebrated case of All Blacks food poisoning, prior to that experienced by the team before the 1995 Rugby World Cup final.

On the Friday before the test, players started dropping like flies with dysentery and vomiting. Come the morning of the game, players were still being sick. Murray Mexted (who was so ill he thought he might actually die) and Gary Knight were both taken to hospital to have injections to stop them throwing up. Four hours later, they were running out onto the SCG.

Although the All Blacks lost that series, it really was the start of a renewed rivalry and affection for the Bledisloe Cup that continues to this day. For the All Blacks, that huge cup is the most valued prize in rugby ... after the William Webb Ellis trophy, of course.

Two years after that great Ballymore win, and having missed out on All Black selection, Reid gave selectors a reminder of his worth as part of a Bay of Plenty team that, arguably, had the greatest ever victory by a provincial team over a touring international team.

At Rotorua on 1 September 1982, in wet weather on a slippery ground and in front of a crowd of 10,000 spectators, Reid scored two tries as his side dotted down six times and humiliated the touring Australians, 40–16. This was an Australian side, coached by Bob Dwyer, that contained Glen Ella, Andrew Slack, Steve Cutler, Steve Tuynman, Stan Pilecki and rising star David Campese (who came on as a replacement).

In the Bay of Plenty side were Steve McDowall (a former national judo representative, soon to move to Auckland), All Black flanker Frank Shelford, loosie Gordon Tietjens (later our Sevens super-coach), first-five Ron Preston (who scored 20 points) and the headband-wearing wing Mark Basham.

Reid — who would end up playing 40 games, including nine tests, from 1980 to 1986 — was back in the All Blacks the following year, although he had to be content as a backup hooker to Andy Dalton. Nevertheless, he would make a great cultural contribution to the All Black teams he was part of and those that would follow.

Much of the credit for the reinvigoration and understanding of the All Blacks' haka is given to Wayne 'Buck' Shelford, who led it with a previously unseen passion and fire. However, Reid's role is also important, because he laid down a challenge to his non-Maori teammates: 'Are you going to do this properly, or not at all?' So the haka went from being something uncoordinated Pakeha players seemed to do with awkwardness to a spirited traditional challenge representing a unique aspect of New Zealand society and culture.

The first time a rugby team from New Zealand was seen doing a haka before games was in 1888–89 when the New Zealand 'Native' football team toured Britain, Australia and New Zealand. (Several British newspaper cartoons depicted them as African warriors with a leaning towards cannibalism!)

The side was a privately funded venture made up of 21 Maori and five non-Maori. They played 107 games, over 14 months, for 78 wins, 6 draws and 23 losses.

When the 1903 All Blacks toured Australia, they had a haka written for them by a Mr C. Parata, who was a brother-in-law of All Black wing Albie Asher.

Tēnā Koe, Kangaroo!	How do you do, Kangaroo!
Tupotu Koe, Kangaroo!	You look out, Kangaroo!
Mō Tīreni tēnei haere nei	New Zealand is invading you!
Au, au, auē, a!	Woe, woe, woe to you!

On the 1905 tour of Great Britain, the 'Ka mate' haka came into use, but tended to be performed only when called for by the crowd. For decades New Zealand crowds didn't see the haka, as it was only performed overseas. (Somewhat strange really, given that the haka is a challenge and surely that should have been what the All Blacks were laying down to those coming to play on New Zealand soil?)

There have been some infamous reactions to the haka, beyond just sarcastic winks and smiles.

In 1905, prior to the test against Wales in Cardiff, several Welsh players and an administrator decided to respond to the haka with the Welsh national anthem, 'Hen Wlad Fy Nhadau' ('Land of Our Fathers'). When the crowd also broke into song, it was the first time a national anthem was sung at an international game.

At Twickenham in 1979, a man ran on to the field and stood in front of the All Blacks, before dropping his pants to reveal his very pale English buttocks.

In 1989, Ireland sent their fans into a frenzy by locking arms and slowly advancing on the haka, a tactic employed by the French on numerous occasions, too. Captain and lock Willie Anderson did his own leaden-footed Irish dance towards Buck Shelford, with the two leaders ending up face to face. Prop Steve McDowall stood next to Shelford in that haka formation, and made his own advance towards the Irish line.

The 1996 Australians turned their back on the haka at Athletic Park and lost, 6–43.

At Old Trafford in 1997, feisty English hooker Richard Cockerill ended up nose to nose with haka leader Norm Hewitt.

Referee Peter Marshall briefly tried to intervene, but then seemed to think better of it. England captain Martin Johnson walked over to Cockerill after the haka and said to him, 'What the f*** have you just done?' The All Blacks won, 25–8.

The most impressive formation to receive the haka was Ireland's figure 8 at Soldier Field in Chicago in 2016. A tribute to the recently deceased former captain Anthony Foley, who wore the number 8 jersey, it caused some bewilderment among the All Blacks on the field. However, it was a signal of intent, and the Irishmen went on to record their first-ever win (40–29) against the All Blacks.

The first team to go through New Zealand undefeated on a tour was ... ? South Africa? New South Wales? Australia? No. Fiji. On their eight-match tour in September 1939 they won seven (including toppling Auckland and New Zealand Maori) and had a draw, 6–6, with a combined Nelson–Golden Bay side. Admittedly, the Fijians didn't play the All Blacks, but they didn't lose a game.

It was on this tour that Fiji first did their pre-match *cibi* (pronounced 'thimbi'). One of the players, Ratu George Cakobau — who was educated in Australia and later New Zealand, and who would go on to become Governor-General of Fiji — thought the team should have a 'war dance' to match the haka. He enlisted Ratu Bola, a high chief of the Navusaradave warrior clan, to teach the team the *cibi*.

As late as June 1939, newspapers were reporting that the tour was going to be cancelled because the Fiji Rugby Union only wanted a two-week trip with games against the New Zealand Maori. Two months later, they arrived aboard the passenger ship *Monowai*, and drew good crowds with their exciting style of play.

Fijian players had worn boots in games for the first time in 1938 when they played the visiting New Zealand Maori side in Fiji, but during the New Zealand tour a year later they often discarded their footwear to play in bare feet.

THE MAKING OF AN ALL BLACK

In 1989, television producer Ric Salizzo (who had been a sports journalist and presenter for TVNZ's nightly six o'clock news) followed the All Blacks with a camera on their end-of-year tour of Wales and Ireland. Players by this stage were becoming much more media-savvy and many of them were used to shooting promotional advertisements for companies and being interviewed in television and radio studios, and so on.

All Black John Kirwan was also a producer on the project, as he and Salizzo had formed a production company, Pasta Productions. Kirwan was the on-camera tour guide for 'The All Black Film Unit', for the behind-the-scenes documentary *The Good, the Bad and the Rugby.* (The title being a play on the famous spaghetti western starring Clint Eastwood, *The Good, the Bad and the Ugly.*)

In the third match of the 14-game tour, against Pontypool, Kirwan snapped his Achilles tendon. The sound of the snap was heard around the ground, and he collapsed to the turf. Surgery at a nearby hospital was immediate, and he stayed on with the team, making his way around on crutches.

There were some hilarious moments in the film, such as seeing the ultra-competitive Zinzan Brooke taking up Shetland pony riding.

Other such documentaries followed, including *Blood, Sweat and Touring* and *The Wyllie Bunch.* Salizzo later moved into the role of media liaison officer for the All Blacks, and then formed a new production company, Leftfield, which was responsible for the very popular *SportsCafe* television programme.

The real forerunner to these films was the New Zealand Broadcasting Corporation documentary *The Making of an All Black*, filmed in the lead-up to the 1969 home series against Wales. It was the first time the Welsh, then the champions of Europe, had visited this country.

The documentary was an extraordinary behind-the-scenes look at the All Blacks as they prepared for, and played, the test series. By way of contrast, within the team was the young and exciting centre Grahame Thorne, then a 23-year-old suit-wearing student at Auckland University, and the canny, no-nonsense veteran and farmer Colin Meads, aged 32. Thorne had made his debut in 1967, playing for the All Blacks before he had notched up even one game for his home province of Auckland, whereas Meads had already been in the team a decade.

The black-and-white film opens with images of an empty Eden Park on a rainy day, shots from underneath the stands of dripping showers and taps, then of the player and referee dressing rooms, an empty members' lounge and the commentary box. Then it cuts to the chairman of the New Zealand Rugby Football Union (NZRFU) announcing the 1969 team for the first test against Wales at Lancaster Park, followed by the notoriously nervous Thorne being asked how he felt the first time he stepped onto the field as an All Black.

'Well, I was still being sick, so I can't really remember much about it,' he says. 'I know it was at night and it was in Vancouver. It was such a terrific feeling, but all I wanted to do was get out of the dressing sheds and get onto the field and just get all my nerves away.'

'Have you managed to control your nerves?' the interviewer asks off-camera.

'They're still bad, and even in the last test against the Frenchmen I was still being sick — violently ill — about 10 minutes before the game.'

Interviewed in the kitchen of his farmhouse, big Wairarapa farmer and All Black captain Brian Lochore is asked how he learned of his first selection.

'Like everybody else in New Zealand, through the radio.'

Former coach Fred Allen had taken the All Blacks through 1966–68 unbeaten, and is interviewed in the showroom of his garment factory. He says that while the All Blacks had been playing his '55-yard football' — working to get out of their half, and attacking once inside their opponents' territory — and had 'improved', he didn't think by 'any manner of means' that they had 'reached the peak or anywhere near it'.

Like Lochore, Colin Meads is interviewed on his farm. Both espouse the virtues of 15-man running rugby, although Meads has the caveat that 'in big rugby [it will] never take away from the tight forward play. We still gotta have that.'

Standing in his woolshed, Lochore says that the All Blacks learned a lot from the 1968 French team, which had toured New Zealand the previous year, particularly the speed of their passing and the tactic of bringing an extra man into the backline. He, like most of the New Zealand spectators who saw the French play on that tour, was hugely impressed with the skills and speed of five-eighths and centre Jo Maso.

Over shots of Meads chainsawing a fallen log — no safety goggles or ear muffs in those days — Fred Allen praises the 6-foot, 4-inch and 16-stone Te Kuiti farmer and living rugby legend:

> Every player should be fit before he arrives in a coach's hands. They say probably you can't train in some areas or even in London, but Colin Meads would get all the young blokes out

early in the morning. He'd even run around Park Lane, round Hyde Park. He'd rub off on these young fellows the way they should train, how they should run. To me, he's a tremendous man from the point of view of bringing a young fellow along.

There is recorded dialogue of Meads over a long-shot of him running in his work boots, with his farm dogs swirling around his feet. Meads speaks of training four nights a week and having games on Saturdays and, early in the season, a club game on Sundays.

We see Canterbury fullback Fergie McCormick in a white coat loading a small delivery van, before well-known test referee Pat Murphy talks about the newly introduced advantage rule, anticipating that it would mean more passing, more running and perhaps more mistakes, and that referees could always use the advantage rule more.

Dargaville-born Murphy had played rep rugby for Wellington and North Auckland as a loose-forward in the 1940s before his first refereeing test appointment in 1959, the fourth test against the British Isles. He whistled all three tests against South Africa in 1965, and three of the four the following year when the British Isles visited. The two tests against Wales in 1969 would be his last international appointments.

We see Meads again, this time walking behind a herd of calves. The image of the All Black as a rural man is being further cemented. There is more voiceover dialogue from him.

Rugby's a rough game, it's a manly game, and as long as we play rugby we'll always have rough play. By rough play, I don't mean dirty play ... It's rough out there all the time, but it's all part of the game. A game that's good and hard is one that the forwards enjoy. As long as it's not dirty. You can go down on the ball and get walked all over, it does hurt you and it is rough, but as long as you know you're not going to get kicked, you have no worries about the game at all.

Thorne and Sid Going, the great All Black halfback who was also a farmer, talk about dirty play, particularly at club level, where blokes would target players who had been or were All Blacks.

Then we see three big, well-dressed men sitting around a small table. Ivan Vodanovich, chairman of selectors (the preferred way of saying 'All Black coach' in the days when the Northern Hemisphere rugby unions were suspicious of such appointments), along with fellow members of the selection panel, Les George from Southland, and Pat Walsh ('who will be involved in training the backs'). They are discussing the All Black trial that had been played that day.

Walsh had played 13 tests from 1955 to 1964, and appeared numerous times for New Zealand Maori during that period, too. A versatile and accomplished backline player, he had been selected in four different positions in tests for the All Blacks. At the time he was first chosen for the All Blacks, he was the second-youngest test player, at 19 years, 106 days. The 1969 Welsh series was his first as a national selector.

'I'd say this trial served the purpose that was set down for it,' says Walsh, somewhat stiltedly in the presence of the camera crew. 'Possession was good. Both packs went in with vim and vigour, and the seriousness of it was evident. The possession these forwards got for the backs was good possession as well.'

Vodanovich agrees: 'For a trial, it was good rugby, wasn't it?'

The Welsh team arrive in Christchurch on a National Airways Corporation (NAC) plane, where they are welcomed by some expats. Then we see them at training. Their manager, Handel Rogers, talks of emulating the All Blacks in coaching and using the brilliance of individuals for the good of the team. (There was some prescience to that, as over the next decade Wales would go through something of a golden period, with stunningly talented backs that were the envy of other rugby nations.)

The All Blacks have Thursday morning training. Meads's voiceover says: 'Pre-match training varies with different coaches ... it's always been pretty hard. You feel like doing nothing on the Thursday afternoon but go off home to bed and have a good rest.'

Retired legend Don 'The Boot' Clarke is filmed taking several kicks at goal in an empty Eden Park, using the old Sportsply-branded ball. Then he recounts how when taking a first kick early in a game he used to tell himself that it was only a practice and that he had made those kicks hundreds of times before.

In the evenings when they are all together, what do the All Blacks do to relax? They play cards, mostly the game Euchre, and talk about rugby. Depending on where they are, they might go to a 5 pm cinema screening. Says Meads, 'It's the only time I ever go to movies, incidentally.'

A suited, earnest man in a television studio reports on the build-up to the test match in Christchurch:

> Well, tomorrow is test day and today this city has been seething. Bob Deans has scored a thousand tries in a hundred different pubs. Nepia, Scott, Clarke and McCormick have been compared in tones confidential and argumentive [sic]. Players dissected, rejected, retained. Tactics analysed ... Many a try has been scored by embankment barrackers. In fact, all of the old legends have been hauled out, dusted off, added to and aired. And by this time tomorrow night there'll be a further crop of stories to add to rugby lore.

A trio of suit and tie-wearing rugby boffins in the lounge bar of a pub (no brown faces, note) give their views on the way the match will unfold and the expected result. Says one, 'There's always room for a surprise in rugby — that's why we go to see it.'

Then match day and the all-important team talk. Fred Allen gives his thoughts on its importance, and how he would prepare and deliver his famous rark-ups to his team.

> Players are naturally nervous. There's a lot of psychology comes into a team talk. You can make all sorts of copious notes. Your mind's sort of whirling round prior to the team talk, and you're trying to lift each player individually. Some you can drive a little harder, perhaps people like Colin Meads.

Meads, on the farm again, stops chopping wood to tell a rather infamous yarn from a Fred Allen pre-match talk. 'We were sitting in the lounge at the Central Hotel in Auckland. It was Freddie's first year with us as team trainer.' Then rather bashfully, he says, 'I happened to let out a yawn during his team talk, and he made me come to life very quickly with the question that if I wasn't interested in his team talk perhaps I'd better go somewhere else. So I became very interested from there on.'

Fred Allen's voiceover continues:

> Others perhaps you may need to lead a little, because they're probably younger and a little more sensitive. 'Sid,' I said to him, 'you are the man that we are going to depend on. The French quoted you as being the best halfback in the world after your performance in Paris, and I expect you to give us a repeat performance today and make every effort to score us those early points.' Well, Sid ... scored two tries and could easily have scored four. The point I make is, there again it's just a matter of lifting a man a little out of himself and letting him know what is on.

Ivan Vodanovich gives the team talk two hours before the first Welsh test. The well-dressed players (in suit jackets and pullovers) are all sitting in armchairs in the lounge of the hotel they are staying in, on the corner of Worcester Street and Oxford Terrace in central Christchurch.

Vodanovich reads his notes, which are spread on the top of a small bar. The contemplative players are like the quiet faithful at a small prayer meeting, listening to the gospel according to Ivan.

Meads: 'If you have a good man giving a team talk, it is such a great boost to the team. I think it's an essential part of rugby.'

Thorne: 'You think this is the big one. I'm always a bit scared about what he'll say. He'll probably give you a burst or something. It's a terrible feeling.'

Allen: 'Some players, you can really bully them into playing well; other players, you have to make them feel 10 feet tall; some fellas are 10 feet tall and you've got to knock them down to 5 foot 8.'

The players leave the hotel and board the bus for Lancaster Park, only a few minutes away.

Meads: 'Our idea is just to get on the bus and sit and think, "Well, what's my job?", "What have I got to do?", "Have I got all my gear?" You just meditate on what's to come.'

Thorne: 'You don't talk, you don't laugh. You haven't been taken from here to Christchurch just to laugh and joke. You're there to win.'

There are some terrific shots of the match-goers crowding around entrances to Lancaster Park. (All the more poignant for the author given that the final demolition of stands at the great ground was underway at the time of writing.)

The match begins, and we see the All Blacks score two tries on a very wet and muddy ground. By the third, players on both teams are streaked with mud.

We hear Lochore in voiceover: 'Scoring from the other team's mistakes ... is never quite as satisfying as scoring from a team move.'

A McCormick voiceover follows footage of him missing a kick at goal: 'If you miss it, you feel a wee bit downhearted because you're kicking for 14 other players and a win.'

Match over (and no footage of Welsh hooker Jeff Young's jaw being broken at a line-out), the All Blacks have won, 19–0. Under the stand, in their dressing room, the All Blacks are enjoying some bottles of fizzy drink.

Back on the farm, in a voiceover, Lochore talks about being a household name in New Zealand: 'This is a problem. You can't sneak anywhere; you can't have a quiet drink — or not very often — without being recognised. But I enjoy meeting people and take people for what they are. If they're friendly and knowledgeable about rugby, well, I enjoy talking to them.'

In Thorne's next interview he talks about juggling rugby with his university studies. We later see him in the University of Auckland library, making notes from bound law reports.

Fergie McCormick gives his view on whether being an All Black is a glamorous life: 'Financially, it's fairly hard on some people. It's not all beer and skittles. You've got training, and if you're playing two games a week, like most of the fellas do, it gets very tiring. They say it's a good life, but it's a fairly hard life all the same.'

Even before the Welsh have left the country, the All Blacks and rugby fans were looking towards the 1970 tour to South Africa, the first for the All Blacks in a decade. Lochore thinks one area the All Blacks could work on is thinking more about attack and the five-eighth not always looking to kick the ball out when in the 25.

'You're never a 100 per cent side,' says Meads.

Who have been the entertainers, the clowns and the guitarists in recent All Blacks sides?

Lochore offers Pat Walsh, Waka Nathan and Sid Going. (All Maori players.) We see Going quietly strumming a guitar.

'He's a good singer, too, but a wee bit shy,' says Lochore. 'I think he'll come right, probably, in the future.'

Going, a Mormon who didn't play on Sundays, talks briefly about a two-year stint on his mission to Canada in 1963–65. Having not played rugby while in Canada, he started playing again in his first week upon return.

Then back to Lochore's farm, where he returns to the family home after a day's work, patting his daughters' heads as he walks inside.

> If your wife's happy, I'm sure this reflects in your playing on the field, because you don't have to worry about what she's going to say if you're going away for a couple of days or won't be home early for tea. And of course there's training nights. It takes up a good deal of *your* time, and must be pretty difficult for your wife and family.

Cut to Meads's wife, Verna, sitting in the sun outside their farmhouse. Behind her a cat is enjoying the afternoon sun, while Colin sits off to one side in the doorway. When asked if the wives talk about children or rugby, Verna says:

> A bit of both. A lot of rugby really, considering people don't seem to think women should talk rugby ... [Overseas tours] have never worried me a great deal. I feel you've got to make the most of it. You could make life very miserable for yourself by sitting at home and moping about it. It's best to get out and about. The kiddies are great company now.

When asked how often her husband writes letters home when he is away on tour, she replies, 'About twice a week, which is very good for him because he hates letter writing.' Meads, head down, laughs in the background.

Meads and Lochore talk about how they started playing when they were aged only five or six. Interestingly, both think boys shouldn't be started in organised rugby until they are about 10 years old.

Former All Black and teacher Jack Kelly, who was not a fan of sideline coaching, talks about the effect of young boys watching their heroes, the All Blacks:

> With the publicity given to big rugby in New Zealand, names come out which become household names, and young players right from the beginning know these names well; they can recognise their photographs of these players in the papers. And I'm sure this sort of thing spurs them on and encourages them to be even keener.

Next we hear Vodanovich barking out coaching instructions as his team trains at a suburban field, watched by a few spectators, including some schoolboys. There are no tackle bags, no weights, no plastic cones, no resistance bands. Just a group of big men in a mix of jerseys (including several of other international sides, which were probably swapped after matches on previous overseas tours) running around the perimeter of the field.

'Sprint ... slow ... sprint ... slow ...' barks Vodanovich.

There are basic set-piece plays, with a line-out ball being sent out through the backs, and forwards running and passing unopposed up the middle of the field.

The narrator speaks:

> In this country, rugby fervour has been compared with a religion, and not altogether facetiously. Certainly its devotees effortlessly bestride the many barriers of New Zealand's egalitarian society, and the physical divisions of sex and age. A capacity crowd is almost synonymous with a big event, and this measure of public interest is an essential factor in the development of the game. Although from the players' point of view, the crowd has comparatively little effect.

Thorne talks about one unnamed Auckland rugby supporter who sits in the same seat for every game at Eden Park and yells out: 'You're just a mug, Thorne!'

The documentary concludes with footage from the second test at Eden Park: the two sides running onto the field together from under old South Stand; a huddle at half-time, complete with oranges for sustenance; McCormick kicking goals on his way to a then world record 24 individual points, made up of three conversions, five penalties and a dropped goal. (The previous record of 21, held by Englishman Daniel Lambert, had stood since 1911.) The win, 33–12, was the All Blacks' biggest against Wales and the one-hundredth test win for the men in black.

There are shots of the crowd with a group of children sitting cross-legged on the ground, close to the sideline and the action. There is nothing between them and their heroes. No barriers or officious security guards, which meant that at the end of matches the children (and a lot of adults) would stream on to the ground for autographs, to pat their favourite players on the back or walk awestruck beside them as they left the field.

We also see what were known as 'Scotsman's stands', seating erected in the backyards of houses bordering the park. Usually reserved for friends of the home-owner or occupant, sometimes tickets for them were advertised for sale in local newspapers, much to the annoyance of the national and local rugby unions. At one South Island ground, there was a Scotsman's stand erected in the backyard of the house occupied by the groundsman. (Certainly at Eden Park those behind the eastern terraces had great views and, from the author's experience in the late 1980s, they had fridges stocked with tall, cold bottles of beer, too.)

The documentary was written, directed and produced by Michael Scott-Smith, who was later to become a hugely influential administrator in New Zealand television circles, advancing the voices of independent programme-makers. Originally from England, he had studied acting at the Royal Academy of Dramatic Art in the company of Peter O'Toole and Albert Finney.

The Making of an All Black was nominated for Best Documentary in the 1970 Feltex Television Awards. When viewed today it is a wonderful encapsulation of the simplicity of All Blacks rugby in the 1960s, at a time when the team was arguably as dominant as it has been for most of the 21st century. But it also enhanced the stereotype of the great All Black forward being a rugged farmer for whom rugby, and time in the towns and cities, was but a break from the more exacting physical duties in the quiet, wide-open spaces of our rural landscapes.

'When I took over Manawatu there was still a feeling among the players that they were a minor union. They were preoccupied with what the bigger unions might do in a match. I had to get rid of that feeling, to get the players thinking about what they were going to do.'

— Manawatu coach (and pastry-chef) Graham Hamer on his side winning the Ranfurly Shield for the first time, beating Auckland 12–10 in 1976.

THAT FINAL TWO MINUTES

The final test for the All Blacks in 2013 was against Ireland, at Aviva Stadium in Dublin. The match had the most remarkable finish and showed a composure by the All Blacks that is still, on repeated viewings, utterly nerve-racking. At stake was an unbeaten year, and maintaining an unbeaten record against Ireland that stretched back 108 years.

Nearly 52,000 passionate home fans had roared themselves hoarse in delight as Ireland began with the sort of scoring onslaught the All Blacks are rarely stunned by. Within 20 minutes the Irish were leading 19–0, and the belief seemed to be growing within the players and their fans that for the first time in 28 tests an Irish win against New Zealand could become a reality.

But the All Blacks hadn't won their previous 12 tests (with an average score of 31 points) by mere fluke. This was a team that coach Steve Hansen had built a plan around to achieve the perfect season. They certainly didn't want to repeat the massive stumble at the final hurdle they had suffered when trounced by England at the end of the previous season.

The Irish put personal safety last as they tore into the breakdown and made fearless tackles, but they knew full well that an All Black riposte would come. Over the years many have joked that if rugby was a 60-minute game, Ireland would be world champions. The inspirational Irish skipper, veteran lock

Paul O'Connell, led the charge, exhorting his men on. Loose-forwards Sean O'Brien and Jamie Heaslip kept barrelling into the breakdown, and first-five Johnny Sexton had the ball on a string with kicks for territory in behind the All Blacks. Veteran centre and former captain Brian O'Driscoll — playing his last test against the All Blacks — marshalled those around him, and, in trademark fashion, shadowed his opposites and worked his way over the advantage line with ball in hand.

The All Blacks began a scoreboard claw-back thanks to a try by Julian Savea, but by half-time they were still down 7–22.

Coach Hansen calmly told the team at half-time: 'We've got to have faith that we can do this. They've scored 22 points — we can't allow them to score any more, and we've got to score 23 if we want to win the game. We're more than capable of doing that, as long as we trust each other and ourselves to do the job.'

Aaron Cruden kicked a penalty, and with 15 minutes to play Ben Franks scored a try. The gap closed to five points, 17–22. The All Blacks needed a converted try for the win. Ireland needed a penalty or a dropped goal to push them that little bit further out of reach and closer to victory.

With four minutes to go, referee Nigel Owens spotted an All Blacks' maul infringement. Penalty Ireland. Sexton placed the ball just outside the All Blacks 22, 10 metres in from touch. He took a long time composing himself for a kick that would clinch the game and be a history-maker. Too much time, perhaps?

As the ball rose from the kicking tee, the crowd behind the posts began to cheer. It looked as though it was going over. Then, it just faded away to the right.

'It was pretty tight, wasn't it?' said Kieran Read after the match. 'I was off to halfway because I thought [Sexton] got it, to be honest. I was about 30–40 metres gone and then I had to trek back to the 22. I guess we still believed and wanted to back ourselves. That was probably a game-changer, that miss, if you look back on it. It kept us in the game, and we showed how much ticker and how much fight we have got in us.'

There was still time for the All Blacks, but they had to get their hands on the ball. If the Ireland forwards got their big mitts on it, they were going to bury it deep in their collected mass.

Ireland crabbed forward, looking to run down the clock, but referee Owens awarded a penalty to the All Blacks on their 10-metre line. There was no time available for them to kick to a line-out and it was 60 metres to the try line. It was all about ball in hand and no dropped passes.

The All Blacks retained the ball for *two* scintillating minutes. Ma'a Nonu controlled a bouncing pass inside the Ireland 22. From the ruck, Aaron Smith cleared to Cruden, who had Read, hooker Dane Coles and Ryan Crotty outside him. As two Irish defenders eyed Read, Cruden threw a skip pass to Coles. With one man to beat, Coles slipped a short pass to Crotty, who scored just in from the corner.

Irish hearts were broken. The scores were tied. At best for them, it was only a draw.

But there was still more drama to come: Cruden had to make a left-hand sideline conversion to win the game.

Cruden's place-kicking style caught a few teams out during his time in international rugby. He would step back from the ball, and then, after he had set himself, readjust his feet. To those defenders on the goal line it looked as though he was about to approach the ball and kick. Many a time did opposing players run out attempting to charge his kick early, which goes against one of the oldest rules in the rugby book.

Exactly that happened on this occasion. Several Irish players ran towards him before he had begun moving into his kicking stride, which was noted by referee Owens. The kick sailed across the posts and away to the right. The Irish crowd thought the game was over and a draw secured.

Owens whistled, not for the end of the game, but for Cruden to take another kick, and this time the Irish did not have the privilege of charging the kick. Nervously, Cruden struck the ball again, only this time it flew right between the middle of the posts.

The All Blacks had won: 24–22!

The crowd couldn't believe it. Many stood looking dazed and in shock. How had they lost that game? Some booed Owens.

The players couldn't believe it, either. The All Blacks and their reserves rejoiced. O'Connell's men sank to their knees or the ground in utter dismay.

Steve Hansen made his way to the field to be with his victorious team, but first of all applauded the Irish team as they walked off, commiserating with several of the players. He told SKY Sport that the biggest thing for him had been the 'mental fortitude' shown by his team. He also said that, despite their win in that match and their record over the year, it was incumbent on his men to remain humble.

Richie McCaw gave deserved credit to Ireland for putting his team under pressure, but praised his side for their composure. He even recalled one of his first games for Canterbury, when the red-and-blacks, led by Todd Blackadder, were down 5–29. Blackadder told his team they could win the game. They did. McCaw never forgot that.

'We got one chance, and we took it.'

'My friends in the game know that I have a dent in the jaw, a crooked finger and a nose far from straight and more bones broken than I care to count, and they know that I was put out of the game with an injured knee that had to be bandaged for three years, but I have no regrets, none at all. My memories are happy ones.'

— legendary All Black fullback Billy Wallace (1903–08), 1970.

'KINDNESS ON THE FIELD'

Robert Pope was a Wellington poet and local sportsman. His playing preference was turning out in the gentlemanly cricket whites, which is reflected in this poem about the roughness of rugby, published in *The Evening Post* in the 1930s.

KINDNESS ON THE FIELD

Be kind to the hooker, or else in the scrum
Thy poor tender shins he will hack;
Or take the first chance that is offered to him
Of planting his foot in your back.
Be kind to the hooker, he's hidden from view,
And can work his revenge in the dark,
So if you insult him, as sure as you're born,
He'll deprive you of some of your bark.
Be kind to the half-back, he's nippy and sly,
And will grab you when rounding the scrum,
Or will collar you low, your heels up he'll throw,
And bang on the ground you will come.
Be kind to the half-back, that watchful young man,
If you hurt him he'll likely feel wild;
And if he should meet you again in the field,
You'd probably know why he smiled.
Be kind to the winger, or you he may prod

In the home of your afternoon tea;
He's fond of a scrap, and won't mind a rap
If your eye comes to grief on his knee.
Be kind to the winger, he's out for a go,
And promptly pays all that he owes;
So be careful to give him no more than his due,
Or he'll give you the change on your nose.
Be kind to three-quarters, they're heady and strong,
And can run like their master, Old Nick;
So if you tread hard on their corns beg their pardon,
Or limp off the field with a rick.
Be kind to three-quarters again let me say,
For their hatred of roughness is such
That, if you should fend them, or neatly upend them,
You'll travel henceforth on a crutch.
Be kind to the full-back or, when in his grip,
He'll handle you roughly for sure.
He's a virtuous fellow, and hates fast young men,
So take care that your language is pure.
Be kind to the full-back, 'tis kindness well spent,
Don't approach this stern player with vim;
If to score you must try, put your collarbone by —
A collarbone's nothing to him.

WELL, IT *IS* A WINTER GAME

Before the professional era, rugby was primarily a winter game, played in the cold, the wet, the wind. Occasionally snow and ice added to the testing of players. Before the advent of multi-million-dollar underground drainage systems and scientifically developed turf, fields cut up quickly in wet conditions, especially when the long, bolt-like sprigs of the forwards were churning the ground at scrums and mauls. Unions hosting big games would be loath to move curtain-raisers to outside grounds or call them off altogether. The managers of some teams touring from the Northern Hemisphere would express frustration or bewilderment that games were played on the No. 1 ground before an international game.

All Blacks on end-of-year tours to Great Britain and Ireland were used to seeing piles of straw lining the edges of fields, having been laid over them the night before to stop frost settling on the pitch. On a couple of occasions in Twickenham in the 1950s, it was so cold that, as the straw was being raked off, the frost quickly settled and players' boots crunched through the icy surface as they took to the field.

*

When the first All Blacks side to tour the British Isles played Scotland at Inverleith on 18 November 1905, things were frosty all round. The Scottish Rugby Union (SRU) had originally refused to guarantee the NZRFU payment of £200, instead offering a share of gate-takings. What a miscalculation that proved to be, as 21,000 passed through the gates for the game! Then they starting cribbing at the fact the All Blacks were paid a per diem on tour, albeit a miserly three shillings a day. This made the All Blacks professionals, grumbled the haughty administrators at the SRU. They did not recognise professionals, so their players would not be awarded caps.

Hay hadn't been spread across the ground the night before the match, and All Black manager George Dixon was advised by the SRU that due to the weather conditions the game would probably be called off.

Dixon and tour captain Dave Gallaher quickly made their way to the ground from their hotel, and, despite finding a pitch more suited to ice-skating, steadfastly declared they would not agree to a cancellation.

The All Blacks' insistence on playing the game, with a match ball that was curiously over-inflated, nearly backfired on them. With about five minutes to play, Scotland were leading 7–6. Gallaher steeled his men, who then ran in two quick three-point tries. The first was a real beauty, a set move from a scrum near halfway. Final score: 12–7 to the All Blacks.

Fullback Billy Wallace had to leave the field during the game due to a sickening fall, with a late charge sending him crashing to the ground, his head slamming into the icy pitch.

The coolness in all quarters remained after the game. At the final whistle, the only cheers came from a number of expat Kiwis and Australians. There was no SRU-organised after-match dinner, and a refusal to let the New Zealanders keep the match ball.

*

The third and deciding test of the three-match series against the 1921 Springboks, the South Africans' first visit to New Zealand, was played at Athletic Park on 17 September. On a dismal day, the attendance was still 18,000, and the game became known as 'the umbrella test'.

The night before the game, heavy rain had lashed Wellington and vast pools of water collected on the pitch and surrounds. Rain continued to fall throughout the day and while the match was being played, expanding the shallow pools across the ground.

In spite of the conditions, those who saw the game said it was a good one, with both sides creating chances as they splashed and sloshed about the field. The final score? Nil-all.

During the game, the local referee, Mr Neilson, had started to feel unwell, and immediately after the game was taken the short distance from the ground to Wellington hospital. Word quickly spread among those wetting their insides with whisky and warm beer in Wellington's taverns that he had died. Fortunately, this was not the case.

Athletic Park seemed to have been situated so as to perfectly funnel the howling southerlies that would blow in across Cook Strait and drive from one end of the ground to the other. When France played the All Blacks there on 5 August 1961, the second of three tests (the home side won the first, 13–6, at Eden Park) the wind was the great foe of both players and spectators.

As had happened 40 years earlier, the night before the match the weather deteriorated. A great southerly gale began blowing, spitting icy sheets of rain across the capital and the lower North Island. The inner harbour was a frothing sea of white caps, and ships were prevented from berthing at the port. The NZRFU mulled over postponing the match, but, as it was only 'windy' and not raining constantly, the match went ahead.

The test had been intended to christen the Wellington Rugby Union's recently completed Millard Stand, named after long-time administrator Mr J. N. Millard, and built on what had been the Western Bank. It had cost £150,000 (nearly $7 million in today's money). The wooden construction's top tier was as steeply angled as the roof of a large cathedral. Just getting up there to one of the top seats had patrons making all sorts of jokes, often likening themselves to Edmund Hillary. The view of the ground may have been spectacular, but it caught the southerly perfectly. It was no place for those with hats ... or vertigo.

Come the afternoon of the match, the wind was showing no signs of abating, but nevertheless 31,000 of the 55,000 expected fans turned up. However, sections of the Millard Stand were deemed too dangerous to have people sitting up there, and no anthems were played by brass bands on the field prior to kick-off.

In his book of the tour — *Cock of the Rugby Roost* — esteemed man of New Zealand rugby writing Terry 'TP' McLean expertly evoked the Wellington chill and made the reader feel as though they were one of the thousands frozen on the sideline.

> ... an Antarctic blizzard lacking only the ice and snow. Appearance meant nothing. Comfort was all. Men wore leggings and duffle-coats, scarves wrapped about their heads, if necessary goggles to keep the wind from turning the match into a tear-stained spectacle. A photographer for *Paris Match*, one of the greatest illustrated weeklies of the world, emerged from the grandstand tunnel onto the ground covered from head to foot with windproof clothing, and as he plugged sturdily across the gale to the other side of the field he might have been one of Captain Scott's men pulling at the sledge amid the merciless wastes of the Polar plateau ... Round about halfway, on the grandstand side,

a Press photographer proved himself a Christian gentleman by dodging about after such hats as came his way and stuffing them into a large canvas bag.

The French won the toss and elected to play with the wind. The All Black forwards, wearing under their jerseys heavy woollen singlets not out of place in the shearing shed, quickly asserted their dominance, so much so that loose-forward John Graham could spend time deep in the backfield, acting as a second fullback to cover the raking, wind-driven French kicks.

Obviously, conditions were not good for the men charged with kicking the ball to touch or for points. All Black fullback Don Clarke went to clear the ball from near his line in the first half, only to see his punt slow in the wind as it went forward, rise up and then blow rapidly back over his head and over the dead-ball line. His opposite experienced the same in the second half.

At half-time, the players retreated under the stands, but the respective managers stood watch in the dressing rooms to make sure no coaching was taking place!

In the second half, Clarke attempted a penalty kick from inside his own half — his brother Ian holding the ball to prevent it from falling over — but it flew wide.

The score was 0–0 with 15 minutes to play, when France's left-wing Dupuy scored a try. Had the into-the-hurricane conversion by French first-five Albaladejo gone over, it would have been nothing short of a miracle.

The All Blacks immediately struck back, with Kel Tremain charging down a kick by the French fullback Lacaze, then falling on the ball as it was blown about in the in-goal.

Clarke's conversion attempt was from near the sideline on the 25-yard line. He lined the ball up as if to kick straight across the field, chipping it into the teeth of the gale, from where it was then carried straight between the goalposts. It was one of the most skilful kicks, with the most bizarre trajectory, that the French players and media had ever seen. Hardened Wellington spectators, on the other hand, had probably seen similar before from their rep or club kickers.

It was, nonetheless, the most memorable moment of 'the cyclone test'.

*

The Sydney Cricket Ground (SCG) was like a second home to the All Blacks when they travelled overseas. From their first appearance there in 1884 until the last, 100 years and two months later, the men in black had graced one of the most hallowed sports grounds in Australia over 50 times.

On their 13-match 1974 tour of Australia and Fiji, the All Blacks played at the ground three times: for the first and third tests, and once against New South Wales.

For the first test on 25 May, rugby journalist Bob Howitt was drenched in the process of attending the game and wrote: 'It's doubtful if any rugby test anywhere has ever been played in worse conditions.'

The mud on the surface of the field was so silty that, when it was cleared from around the area where a ball was being placed to kick, it ran like a small tide across the ground. One All Black was heard to quip: 'It's like the Manukau Harbour when the tide's half out!'

So miserable were the conditions, with hail, gale-force winds and rain, the players stayed in the dressing rooms under the grandstand until after the national anthems had been played.

If the weather was shocking, so, too, it seems were aspects of the refereeing. (But that was to be expected in Australia, wasn't it?

We copped it in cricket, and we copped it in rugby.) Fortunately, the All Blacks prevailed, 11–6, thanks to tries by Ian Kirkpatrick and Duncan Robertson.

Two weeks later, when the two sides met at that venue again, the second test at Ballymore in Brisbane having been drawn, it was a hot, sunny afternoon. Again the All Blacks won, 16–6.

*

A year after the mud-bath that was the SCG, conditions there looked to be decidedly favourable for test rugby compared with those that met the All Black and Scotland teams when they arrived at Eden Park on 14 June 1975.

The night before the game, torrential rain amounting to 130 millimetres swept across the city, with no let-up on the morning of the match. Scottish first-five, future Lions coach and rugby knight Ian McGeechan succinctly summed it up: 'It was bloody unbelievable.'

The Eden Park ground, built (as Athletic Park and Carisbrook had been) on a drained swamp, quickly reverted to its early incarnation. It was so wet that there were vast patches of the field where the grass could not be seen. The ground had hosted a lot of sports over the decades, but now it seemed that synchronised swimming and possibly even surf life-saving would be added to the list.

Nonetheless, the captains (number 8 Andy Leslie for the All Blacks and prop Ian McLauchlan for the Scots) agreed that the match should proceed, despite futile attempts by the fire service to pump water away from the ground.

Referee Peter McDavitt of Wellington told the players that, for the sake of safety, he would very quickly blow up rucks so that no one was trapped on the ground with their faces underwater for too long!

Once the match began, it looked as though the two teams were playing in different conditions to each other. The visitors could barely hold on to the ball, while the All Blacks looked as though they were playing in dry weather. Passes went to hand, and some of the running by the backs, especially wing Bryan Williams, made a mockery of the conditions and nearly the referee, when Williams went to force the ball for a try but merely placed it on the water in the in-goal rather than touching the ground, and then tried to run around behind the posts.

Even so, at half-time the All Blacks were only ahead 6–0, thanks to a try by Hamish MacDonald, the scoring of which looked like someone diving into a swimming pool. Fullback Joe Karam converted.

In the second half, the All Blacks added three more converted tries. The fact that Karam was able to convert all four tries and Scotland couldn't register a point just added to the surreal feel of the game.

After the final whistle, the dressing-room showers must have seemed quite dry in comparison with the conditions the players had experienced on the park. A bit more water was added to the Scotland changing room when captain McLauchlan reportedly cried tears of frustration at his side's poor showing. If ever a defeated side left New Zealand with All Blacks fans having some sympathy for them, it was this one.

With New Zealand being subjected to a particularly cold, wet and windy winter when the Lions toured in 1983, some members of the All Blacks took to wearing extra clothing on the paddock. Wetsuit manufacturer Neptune supplied a number of vests that could be worn to keep out the cold, and they proved their worth in the third test, on Dunedin's waterlogged, slippery and cold Carisbrook. The outside backs, including Stu Wilson — who became New Zealand's greatest test try-scorer when he overtook

Ian Kirkpatrick's tally of 15 — wore fingerless woollen gloves in the 15–8 win. There were even rumours that fullback Allan Hewson wore pantyhose on days when the icy wind would slice through a slender fullback roaming about the backfield.

*

If someone told you that the All Blacks had just beaten a very strong Australian side 43–6, you would no doubt immediately think that it must have been a game played on a dry, hard field. That certainly wasn't the case when the All Blacks thumped Australia by a record margin and a new highest total in July 1996.

The weather was, in fact, abysmal. Of course it was. It was July in Wellington, making it 'traditional' weather for an Athletic Park test. Driving wind, icy rain, soggy pitch ... Not at all conducive for running rugby?

Some say the biggest mistake the Australians made, captained by the great lock John Eales, was to turn their back on the haka. It was a decision of the Wallabies' management apparently, but Eales has since said: 'I've thought about it a lot over the years. You look back at certain things in your life and think, "Oh, I wish I didn't do that."'

The display of handling put on by the All Blacks was incredible. Long passes, short passes, grubber kicks, mauling, line-out takes ... everything seemed to work, bringing a huge smile to the face of coach John Hart.

Perhaps the epitome of the All Blacks' efforts was the moment when big Jonah Lomu, who had delighted in frequently running onto the ball to charge at the Australian inside backs or loose-forwards, slid along the slippery surface to retrieve a kick. Deftly he passed it up to Justin Marshall, who ran nearly half the length of the field to score.

In all, the All Blacks scored six tries (Zinzan Brooke, Christian Cullen, Michael Jones, Jonah Lomu, Justin Marshall, Jeff Wilson), while Andrew Mehrtens kicked two conversions and three penalties. Matt Burke kicked two penalties in the first half for the Wallabies. They ended that stanza 6–25 down!

*

In April 2005, the author sat on the Eastern Bank of the Basin Reserve in Wellington to watch the final session of the second day's play of the second cricket test between New Zealand and Sri Lanka. It had been sunny for most of the day, but as the afternoon progressed the air slowly became cooler. With a bit over an hour's play left, Lou Vincent and Stephen Fleming were grinding out a century partnership to put the hosts in front after Sri Lanka had been skittled for 211, Chris Martin taking 6-for.

Chaminda Vaas had been able to summon up some of the swing that Martin had enjoyed and had New Zealand wobbling through four quickly lost wickets.

Then the eyes of the spectators at the ground, and the television cameras, started to look south along Adelaide Road. There, rising up from Cook Strait, was a big blanket of fog. It was quite a spectacular weather event, and somewhat eerie, in a way that John Carpenter's 1980 horror film *The Fog* hadn't been.

The fog kept rising and moving closer and closer to the cricket ground. It didn't sweep in; it just eased itself down through Newtown, heading for the central city and harbour.

Reaching the southern fence and gates of the Basin, it rolled over them, shrouding the scoreboard and making its way onto the field. Measuring its speed was easy. As the umpires, batsmen and close-in fielders decided that play was likely to be halted, a Sri

Lankan player on the extremities of the field — a fine leg, if I recall — started to walk off towards the main stand at the other side of the ground. Then he broke into a jog as the fog surrounded him. Then he put his head down and ran a bit faster.

'Run!' someone yelled.

They did.

The next appearance at a major sporting event by such a weather phenomenon was the final of the Super Rugby competition in 2006, between two New Zealand teams, the Crusaders and the Hurricanes, in Christchurch.

Fans were expecting a classic encounter. The Crusaders had home-ground advantage after topping the table, suffering only one loss — to the South African Stormers in Cape Town — and their forward pack was picked to be superior to that of the men from the capital. Wellington's Hurricanes were appearing in their first final, and their strength lay in an electric backline — but the forwards would have to get them the ball first. They had beaten the Waratahs two weeks in a row, at the end of the round robin, 19–14, and in a tight semi-final, 16–14.

The day in Christchurch had been lovely and sunny, and those preparing to go to the ground were dressing for a cool, clear, dry night. But about two hours before the game, fog started to roll across the eastern and southern suburbs, and, with only an hour to go before kick-off, the ground itself was swallowed by the weather system.

The fog was incredibly thick, and was diagnosed by surprised meteorologists, both professional and amateur, as one that was likely to hang around. Thoughts went to postponing the game, but that is much easier said than done. As the general safety of players and spectators was not going to be compromised by the weather, the game took place as planned.

Richie McCaw has been quoted as saying that when he was running down the players' tunnel onto the ground, he thought the lights had gone off and was expecting them to come on again.

Just what happened on the ground, very few people actually know. If you had a seat up in the stand, you saw next to nothing. (Stadia lights don't have a fog setting like cars do.) The coaches abandoned their boxes to sit at ground level, where they could see a bit more, but even then not across the entire field. Certainly there were moments when the players lost track of where the ball was, especially when it was kicked into the thick ceiling of fog.

Television commentary became almost impossible due to the lack of vision, both from the naked eye and the multiple cameras around the ground. SKY's Tony Johnson utilised his radio commentary skills for a time to give viewers, and his colleagues up in the commentary box, some idea of what was happening.

Sports-radio host Jason Pine perhaps summed it up best when he described the game as 'like watching a stage show with the curtain down'. Never before had veteran commentator Grant Nisbett had to admit so many times in one game that he had no idea what was going on.

Final score: Crusaders 19, Hurricanes 12. A try to Casey Laulala breaking the deadlock of four penalties to each side.

There are two notable footnotes to this game. The first, which lasted several days, was the venting of the spleens of disgruntled match-goers and pay-television subscribers in letters to newspapers and on talk-radio about the game they *hadn't* seen.

The second was captain Tana Umaga's 'handbag' incident, in which he clocked teammate Chris Masoe with a woman's handbag when they were a bit worse for wear at the Jolly Poacher pub in the wee hours after the game. The handbag itself became something of a hot item, fetching nearly $23,000 on TradeMe. Masoe, who had allegedly reacted to tripping over a fellow patron's foot by turning around and punching him, was fined $3000 by New Zealand Rugby, while Umaga had to fork out for a new mobile phone for the handbag's original owner, to replace the one inside the handbag that was left with a cracked screen after being whacked against Masoe's head.

'You could imagine how I felt watching that appalling exhibition of so-called rugby. And now I find you getting the doctor to fill up socks of ice so you can say, aw, I've got a sore leg, that's why I played so poor. Sore, my arse. The only two fellas that don't have ice on them are Zinny and Fitzy. They're the only ones with any guts, the rest of you are wimps.'

— Colin Meads's post-match spray to the All Black side he managed, who had just lost 15–22 to France at Stadium Municipal, Toulouse, on Armistice Day 1995.

'What will happen now, I don't know. We've probably got a tiger by the tail.'

— Marlborough captain Ray Sutherland, after his side stunned Canterbury, 13–6, to claim the Ranfurly Shield in 1973.

'Errol, the strangest thing is happening here: you don't even look as black as you did when you started in this group.'

— one of the 1981 Springboks to Errol Tobias, first (and, at that stage, only) black player in the touring party.

100 ALL BLACK NICKNAMES

Many All Blacks players and coaches have been known to their teammates and the public by nicknames using their initials ('JK', 'DC', 'JT'), by adding a 'y' to part of their name ('Zinny', 'Woody', 'Foxy'), or by the colour of their hair ('Sandy', 'Red', 'Snow'). Some nicknames remain obvious decades later; others are topical references from a particular era, such as names of racehorses. Several stuck to the person from childhood, others once the bloke was in the All Blacks. One of them was bestowed on a player by cynical members of the media — can you work out which that is?

Harold 'Bunny' Abbott (1905–06)
Fred 'The Needle' Allen (1946–49, coach 1966–68)
Mark 'Bull' Allen (1993–97)
Lewis 'Snip' Allen (1896–1901)
William 'Robin' Archer (1955–57)
Albie 'Opae' Asher (1903)
Nelson 'Kelly' Ball (1931–36)
Scott 'Lloyd' Barrett (2016–)
Joseph James 'Wampy' Bell (1923)
Ernest 'Moke' Belliss (1920–23)
'Stormin' Norman Berryman (1998)
Kevin 'Monkey' Briscoe (1959–64)
Peter 'Bugle' Burke (1951–57)

Ralph 'Mainbrace' Caulton (1959–64)
Nau 'Brownie' or 'The Big Horse' Cherrington (1950–51)
Don 'The Boot' Clarke (1956–64)
Jerry 'Guinness' Collins (2001–07)
Anthony 'Beau' Cottrell (1929–32)
Kieran 'Colt' Crowley (1983–91)
Christian 'Paekakariki Express' Cullen (1996–2002)
Henry 'Norkey' Dewar (1913)
Ernest 'Tuppy' Diack (1959)
Craig 'Jethro' Dowd (1993–2000)
Albert 'Doolan' Downing (1913–14)
Cyril 'Scrum' Evans (1921)
Kevin 'Hayburner' Eveleigh (1974–77)
Sean 'Caveman' Fitzpatrick (1986–97)
Brian 'The Kaikoura Express' Ford (1977–79)
Arthur 'Bolla' Francis (1905–10)
Bernie 'Gabe' Fraser (1979–84)
David 'Pony' Gage (1893–96)
John 'Kipper' Gallagher (1986–89)
Andy 'Ten-four' Haden (1972–85)
Steve 'Shag' Hansen (coach 2012–19)
Edward 'Nut' Hasell (1913–20)
Carl 'Zarg' Hayman (2001–07)
William 'Scobie' Hay-MacKenzie (1901)
Harold 'Circus' Hayward (1908)
Graham 'Ted' Henry (coach 2004–11)
Craig 'Postie' Innes (1989–91)
Bill 'The Bull' Irvine (1923–30)
Francis 'Doss' Jervis (1893)
William 'Massa' Johnston (1905–07)
Ian 'The Kamo Kid' and later 'Kamo' Jones (1989–99)
Michael 'Iceman' Jones (1987–98)

Peter 'Tiger' Jones (1953–60)
Earle 'Ernie' Kirton (1963–70)
Arthur 'Bubs' Knight (1926–34)
Gary 'Axle' Knight (1977–86)
Paul 'Bam Bam' Koteka (1981–82)
Josh 'Crusher' Kronfeld (1995–2000)
William 'Dad' Lindsay (1914)
Richard 'Dickie' Loe (1986–95)
Dave 'Trapper' Loveridge (1978–85)
Fergie 'Fungus' McCormick (1965–71)
William 'Offside Mac' McKenzie (1893–97)
Paul 'Ogre' Miller (2001)
Henare 'Buff' Milner (1970)
Graham 'Goss' Mourie (1976–82)
Brian 'Jas' Muller (1967–71)
Waka 'Black Panther' Nathan (1962–67)
Harry 'Ginger' Nicholls (1921–23)
Ma'a 'Skuks' Nonu (2003–15)
Anton 'Hatch' Oliver (1996–2007)
Frank 'Five-two' Oliver (1976–81)
James 'Rusty' Page (1931–35)
Milford 'Curly' Page (1928)
Arran 'Rimu' Pene (1992–94)
Murray 'The Big M' Pierce (1984–90)
Harold 'Bunk' Pollock (1932–36)
Alan 'Ponty' Reid (1951–57)
Brodie 'Guzzler' Retallick (2012–)
William 'Cocky' Roberts (1896–97)
Scott 'Razor' Robertson (1998–2002)
Bernard 'Joey' Sadler (1935–36)
Charles 'Bronco' Seeling (1904–08)
Mark 'Cowboy' Shaw (1980–86)

Aaron 'Nugget' Smith (2012–)
Conrad 'Snake' Smith (2004–15)
Ian 'Spooky' Smith (1963–66)
Alistair 'Ack' Soper (1957)
'Smokin' Joe Stanley (1986–91)
Ian 'Nectar' Stevens (1972–76)
John 'Tuna' Swain (1928)
Hector 'Mona' Thomson (1905–08)
Reuben 'Suitcase' Thorne (1999–2007)
Kelvin 'Bunny' Tremain (1959–68)
Va'aiga 'Inga the Winga' Tuigamala (1989–93)
George 'Bubbles' Tyler (1903–06)
Roger 'Spider' Urbahn (1959–60)
Frederick 'Did' Vorrath (1935–36)
Billy 'Carbine' Wallace (1903–08)
Wilson 'Skip' Whineray (1957–65)
Andrew 'Son' White (1921–25)
Hallard 'Snow' White (1953–55)
Richard 'Tiny' White (1949–56)
Peter 'Pole' Whiting (1971–76)
Jeff 'Goldie' Wilson (1993–2001)
Nathaniel 'Ranji' Wilson (1908–14)
Stu 'Gizza' Wilson (1976–83)

‘Mate, Stirling’s off. It’s your kick.’

— New Zealand-born Wallaby hooker Jeremy Paul tells his captain, John Eales, that regular goalkicker Stirling Mortlock is not on the field, meaning Eales will have to take the last-minute penalty kick to win the Bledisloe Cup test in Wellington, 2000. The first test played at Wellington’s new ‘Cake Tin’ stadium, Australia won, 24–23.

‘Don Clarke was standing in the tunnel and he put his arm around me with tears running down his face. He said, “Sean, thank you so much for doing something so many All Black teams had tried to do in the past.”’

— Sean Fitzpatrick’s 1996 team, later named the ‘Incomparables’, became the first All Black team to win a series in South Africa.

THE LOG O' WOOD

In 1901, the governor of New Zealand, Lord Ranfurly, offered to gift a trophy bearing his name to the New Zealand Rugby Football Union (NZRFU). Initially a cup was proposed, and the union committee members made a variety of suggestions as to just what the Ranfurly Cup would be awarded for. One delegate proposed that it be played for by representative teams of the Queensland, New South Wales and New Zealand unions. An amendment was made that it be played for by the champion provincial teams of the North and South islands. This was further altered when formal rules were written up, until it was finally decided the cup would be presented to the team the NZRFU deemed 'in their opinion to be the Champion team' and then played for on a challenge basis, 'provided that the challenging union is prepared to play the holders on their own ground'.

When the London-made 'cup' arrived, it was in fact a large wooden trophy with a silver centrepiece. Closer inspection of the sport that was depicted in the silverwork concluded it was in fact association football, as there were goalposts without uprights extending vertically beyond the crossbar. A local silversmith added two thin sticks, and the shield was ready for presentation.

The NZRFU's management committee agreed that Auckland would be the first holders of the gift, based on their unbeaten record in the previous season. However, it wouldn't be until 18 months later that Auckland accepted, and played, its first Shield game, as all of their 1903 representative matches were away games.

On 6 August 1904, the first-ever Ranfurly Shield match was finally played, with Auckland hosting Wellington at Alexandra Park.

Playing at wing-forward for Wellington was Billy Hardham, who had been awarded the Victoria Cross while serving as a farrier with the Fourth Contingent during the Boer War.

The dry ground suited the visitors' fleet-footed backs, such as speedster Duncan McGregor, and the outrageous natural ability of fullback (and captain) Billy Wallace. All the points (6–3) came from tries: two for Wellington (one of them by McGregor) to a single touch-down from Auckland.

The men from the capital were cheered from the field by the reasonably sized Auckland crowd. While the spectators' appreciation sat well with the Wellington side, the actions of the host union did not: overly confident Auckland union officials hadn't even taken the shield to the ground.

According to Billy Wallace:

> I well remember that the Auckland Rugby Union were unable to present the Ranfurly Shield to us as it was locked in a bank vault in the city, and we had to leave Auckland by ship for New Plymouth on the Sunday.

The Log o' Wood, as it would affectionately come to be known, was taking its first trip.

It was only a year before Auckland reclaimed the Shield from Wellington, and the first long era of defences (23) lasted until 1913.

Wellington took the Shield from Taranaki in the last challenge before war halted the representative rugby programme, and (thanks to the four years the Shield was not at stake) ended up with a 15-game reign that spanned six years.

*

The next great era of Shield dominance began in August 1922, when Wellington lost their first defence of the season to Hawke's Bay. Between then and the start of the 1927 season, the Bay side set an astounding new record of 25 defences.

Wairarapa ended their run, but had to face Hawke's Bay again two weeks later as part of their annual home-and-away fixtures. On the day, in a fiery game (see pages 177–80), the Bay won 21–10, but then a ruckus broke out, with Wairarapa claiming that prominent Maori player (captain of the New Zealand Maori in 1926) Wattie Barclay was ineligible for Hawke's Bay as he had been playing in Auckland.

An appeal to the NZRFU occurred two weeks later, which found in favour of Wairarapa. Hawke's Bay appealed that decision, by which time Wairarapa had lost the Shield to Manawhenua anyway. They then lost it to Canterbury.

In the second defence of the 1928 season, Wairarapa were back in possession of the Log, toppling Canterbury 8–7 at Lancaster Park.

Not all were delighted with the win. The mayor of Masterton, Mr Jordan, reportedly sent a telegram to his victorious team suggesting they should drop the Shield overboard from the ship they were to sail back to Wellington on. His reason for suggesting this was that he objected to 'the subordination of the playing of the game to the team touring, spectacular rep. matches, and bog gates'.

Legend has it that after the telegram had been read to the team in their hotel lobby, two of the Wairarapa players sent one back: 'Will willingly drop Shield overboard if round your neck.'

Wairarapa's captain, the great midfield back Bert Cooke, denied to newspapermen that such a telegram had been sent, and said the mayor's message had been taken in jest.

*

One of the most extraordinary years in Shield history was 1950. The hallowed trophy started the season in the hands of Otago, who, since claiming it from Southland in 1947, had notched up 17 defences. First challenger of the season, Southland, headed back to Invercargill having suffered a 3–22 defeat.

Canterbury were up next, and kept the holders scoreless, to win 8–0. The Shield left Carisbrook and headed north to Christchurch.

Two weeks later, the Wairarapa team ran out optimistically onto Lancaster Park. For the second game in a row, the holders were kept scoreless. A dropped goal was enough for Wairarapa to win, 3–0. Never before had a dropped goal been the only score of a Shield match. The trophy was off to cross Cook Strait.

Another fortnight later, Wairarapa hosted their first defence at the Solway Showgrounds, with South Canterbury the hopeful visitors. The holder was not held scoreless this time, but the home-town team's 14 points was trumped by the visitors' 17. The Shield was carted back to the Mainland again.

The final challenge of the season was the privilege of North Auckland. Timaru's Fraser Park was in a festive mood as the game began, but a cloud of disappointment descended, with the men from kauri country winning 20–9.

What a bizarre season. Five Shield games, five different victors, with two of them (South Canterbury and North Auckland) winning the Shield for the first time. It was unprecedented that three holders would lose their first defence in the same season, and that twice the holders would be held scoreless. The Shield had never done so much travelling in a matter of weeks, twice being in both islands.

But what excitement and hope it ignited in the provinces that the 'Log' could be won by anybody.

For the rest of that decade Waikato, Canterbury and Taranaki had reigns that extended over a couple of seasons.

*

At the start of the 1960s, the Shield's home was Auckland, who had taken it from Southland in the last challenge of 1959, lost it to North Auckland and then snatched it back from their northern neighbours 11 days later. For the next three seasons, the Shield was on display at Eden Park, although it had taken a last-minute Waka Nathan try under the posts to deny Canterbury victory at the end of 1960.

With 24 defences equalling the record of the great Hawke's Bay team from the 1920s, the Aucklanders had arranged a grand gesture: the Bay would have the challenge that would determine whether the blue-and-whites could eclipse their predecessors' record.

A midweek game, Auckland played in an all-blue jersey so as not to cause confusion with the black-and-white stripes of their guests.

It was a game the visitors should have won. They had first points from a penalty, then Auckland wing Malcolm Dick scored a try in the corner to level the scores.

The Bay attacked and attacked for the last 20 minutes. Bay flanker Kel Tremain went just short of scoring a try, and a penalty attempt was on target but dropped below the crossbar. With time almost up, and the Bay with the feed to an attacking scrum near the Auckland line, all was set for Bay first-five Blair Furlong to attempt a match-winning droppie.

There was a quick heel from the scrum, and the pass from halfback to Furlong was spot on. But in the eyeline of Furlong was Auckland and All Black loosie John Graham. Captain of Auckland, he raced towards Furlong as though his jersey was on fire. The pressure of the approaching defender proved too much for Furlong, whose kick curled away well wide of the posts.

A 3–3 draw. Auckland had the new record of 25 defences, but wouldn't extend it, as four days later they surrendered the Shield to Wellington.

A couple of seasons later, Hawke's Bay were in possession of the Shield again, and extraordinarily their grip was to be as firm as it had been 40 years earlier, although it had taken a dropped goal from Furlong (who had learned the lessons of the draw with Auckland) to secure a 12–12 draw with Wellington in the seventh defence.

Twenty-one challengers were sent home disappointed from McLean Park in Napier, until the last Shield game of the 1960s and an 11–18 loss to Canterbury.

*

The Shield had stints in Christchurch, Auckland (twice) and Whangarei, before returning to red-and-black country towards the end of 1972.

Neighbours Marlborough had the first challenge of 1973, on 28 July. As you can surmise from the date of this match, this was one of those early-season challenges accepted by the holder whose eyes were on the sterner tests that awaited from the bigger provinces later in the year. But the men from the top of the South Island were confident they could cause the biggest upset in Shield history.

Marlborough were in one of those periods when everything clicked. The year before, they had beaten Auckland in Blenheim, 21–18, and also claimed the scalps of Otago and Wellington.

Coaching the side were Doug Saul and former Wellington and 16-test All Black wing Ralph Caulton. In the forward pack were Alan Sutherland (who had debuted for the All Blacks in 1968 and would go on to play 64 games in the black jersey, until 1976) and his brother Ray. On one wing was former junior sprinter Brian Ford, who had played for Canterbury and would eventually make the All Blacks.

Before they took to the field, the team was played a message from former All Black captain and legendary coach Fred Allen, whose Auckland team had held the Shield for the record 25 defences in the 1960s. Allen's message concluded with: 'Everyone must make up their mind they are going to play rugby for 80 minutes — non-stop … I expect you to play the game of your life. Spring the surprise and go out and do it.'

That is exactly what they did, in front of about 15,000 spectators, who fell more and more in behind Marlborough as their stocks rose throughout the game and Canterbury's fell, due to numerous basic errors, including being unable to complete try-scoring chances.

Canterbury did score the first try of the game, through Duncan Hales. Fergie McCormick converted it to give them a 6–0 lead. Marlborough lock Graeme Cocks got the challengers 'in with a sniff', kicking two penalties. Scores were level at half-time. Who would have guessed that?

The second half was all cut-and-thrust. As the scoreboard clock slowly wound its way towards the end of 40 minutes, the Marlborough players dug deep. The Shield was within reach, but a draw wouldn't be enough.

They forced a 5-metre scrum, and first-five Tony Goddard put over a dropped goal. A three-point lead, 9–6. They were ahead, but Canterbury could still draw the game, at the least. Surely they wouldn't remain scoreless all half?

However, with few minutes remaining, the next points came for Marlborough, and the manner in which they were scored was magical.

Ford picked up the ball that had somehow popped out of a ruck, and set off up-field. He sped past three hopeful tacklers but still had one man to beat, veteran fullback Fergie McCormick. Although McCormick's All Black days were behind him — something brought about by shortcomings in his positional play against the 1971 Lions — he was still no slouch as a tackler. In fact, his tackles could be very robust.

McCormick lined up Ford. If the tackle is made, Canterbury win. If it isn't, the Shield is gone.

Ford approached McCormick. The duo had both been in the Canterbury side a couple of seasons earlier. Did Ford have some prior knowledge from past team trainings that would see him beat this man?

The speedster slowed down. Oh, no. Was he going to bottle the chance?

McCormick closed in for the tackle. But then Ford accelerated again, through the grasp of the last man who could save the Shield for Canterbury. Off Ford sped to the try line!

The conversion was missed, but it didn't matter. Marlborough were out of reach, up by seven, and stayed that way as the final whistle blew.

Jubilant Marlborough fans raced onto the field to congratulate their heroes. Canterbury captain Alex 'Grizz' Wyllie handed the Shield to Marlborough captain Ray Sutherland. The latter's smile, and the smiles of his teammates, said it all. This was a sweet, sweet victory, and one the team and supporters celebrated with gusto.

But they only had three days until their first challenge, from Wairarapa Bush. They saw them off in grand style (36–0), then, in front of big crowds at Landsdowne Park in Blenheim, dispatched North Otago, Wanganui, Nelson–Bays, Mid-Canterbury and West Coast, before South Canterbury toppled them (6–18) in the second defence of the 1974 season.

The Shield was gone, but their stunning victory in the 350th Shield game remains the greatest win in the history of Lord Ranfurly's gift.

*

Marlborough weren't the only giant-killers of the 1970s. In August 1976, Manawatu upset Auckland, 12–10. The Aucklanders, defending for the 12th time, had snuck past Wanganui (16–9), then been held to a draw by Southland (9–9) the week before.

On the back of great displays from All Blacks Gary Knight, Geoff Old, Mark Donaldson and Doug Rollerson, the Shield went to Palmerston North for the first time. This was a golden period for Manawatu, as they were also runner-up in the inaugural National Provincial Championship that year (behind Bay of Plenty!).

The Shield stayed at the Showgrounds in Palmerston North until the end of 1978, when North Auckland won, 12–10. A year later, the Log was back in Auckland.

*

The sporting gods often send little signals to teams and players that things are going to go their way. So it was when, on 7 September 1980, Waikato began their challenge and Auckland their seventh defence. The odds were against Waikato. They were in the second division, and a challenger had never had a victory on a Sunday.

But then Bryan Williams set himself to kick off for Auckland, into the wind on a gloomy afternoon. As he was about to put his foot to the ball, it fell over. The referee awarded a scrum to Waikato, despite legal arguments from Williams. With the wind at their back, their scrum holding their own against the bigger

Auckland pack, and lock Haydn 'Hud' Rickit snaffling takes from Andy Haden in the line-outs, Waikato's confidence grew.

The passing of the backs was crisp, with Auckland's group defence routinely tested. A Doug Phillips penalty saw the challengers ahead 3–0 at the break.

'Not enough,' said old heads in the South Stand, such as Fred Allen, as Auckland felt the wind at their backs for the first time. But it was Waikato taking charge of the game, in every aspect of play, from the mauls to backline moves. While the scoreboard attendants weren't put through their paces, this was what Shield rugby was all about. Challenger and defender: show us what you've got!

Then came the movement that created another Shield legend.

Auckland were chasing the game, and started to run the ball from inside their own half. Waikato's defence herded wing Tim Twigden towards the touchline. Attempting to keep the ball in play near halfway, he looped a pass infield, but it wasn't Auckland hands that claimed it.

Waikato's curly-haired, headband-wearing 19-year-old centre, Arthur Stone, grabbed the ball and suddenly play was heading in the opposite direction.

There were two Auckland defenders in close proximity and half the field to run.

Nearly everyone in the park was on their feet and yelling, either for Stone to get to the line or a defender to get to him.

Looking like a stocky version of John McEnroe (who had lost an epic Wimbledon final to Björn Borg two months earlier), Stone somewhat in disbelief ran on and on and on, as Auckland's Lindsay Harris dived despairingly to halt him. Stone, mouth jubilantly agape, plunged over the line midway between the corner flag and the goalpost on the left-hand side of the field. Waikato had a new hero.

Said Stone after the game:

> All I could see was the goal line. I kept telling myself, you must get there, you have to score the try. I could hear one Aucklander chasing me and I could see another out of the corner of my eye. But I forgot about them. All I wanted to do was get to the line!

Stone went on to play 23 games, including nine tests, for the All Blacks from 1981 to 1986. The following year he moved to Dunedin and played nearly 100 games for Otago.

*

Waikato defended the Shield eight times before losing to Wellington in their final defence for the 1981 season. The men from the capital had only four defences, before losing to Canterbury, but in those games hometown favourite Bernie Fraser scored eight tries, with 'Bernie's Corner' officially becoming part of the geography at Athletic Park.

Canterbury's reign gained more and more momentum, until the match on 14 September 1985, which, if won, would set a new tally for the most defences. Auckland were given the honour of the challenge, as record-holders.

It's not too much of an exaggeration to say that the build-up for this game began two years earlier, as soon as the full-time whistle blew on Auckland's limp September 1983 challenge. There had been high hopes that the northerners, boasting a precociously talented and powerful 18-year-old wing called John Kirwan, would come away with the Shield. Coached by the meticulous John Hart, they had won the National Provincial Championships (NPC) the previous year, and lost only one of their previous 20 matches. Despite this, no Aucklanders were included in the All Black team for the end-of-year tour to Scotland and England, while seven Cantabs were. The blue-and-whites had a few points to prove.

Canterbury, meanwhile, had defeated nine challengers after snatching the Shield from Wellington, 16–12, the previous September. The man who had clinched that game for Canterbury was first-five Wayne Smith, who scored a stunningly memorable try in the final minutes of the match. From about 40 metres out, he went on an arcing run and scored untouched.

The rematch between those two teams was the week before Auckland's game, and just as keenly contested, with Canterbury again behind in the end stages of the game. However, a massive Robbie Deans penalty from inside his own half, and a late try to Dale Atkins, sealed it for the holders, 20–16.

Controversy swirled about after the game, with much discussion about some of the calls made by referee Bob Francis, and the fact that the dominant Wellington line-out forward Murray Pierce had to leave the field with a broken jaw, courtesy of Canterbury prop Murray Davie.

So, a week later, Auckland arrived in town. Lancaster Park was packed to capacity. The hometown heroes gave Auckland a bath, winning 31–9, scoring five tries to none.

Two years later, the return challenge was also the NPC decider.

One man in particular had learned a lot from the drubbing of '83: Auckland captain and All Black lock Andy Haden. One of the most influential players of his generation, both on and off the field, he and Hart had carefully prepared for the 1985 challenge, right down to the time they arrived in Christchurch and where they stayed.

Come the 2.30 pm kick-off, Lancaster Park was awash with 52,000 spectators, bubbling away like a massive pot of water on a stove. It was a frenzied atmosphere. (Even in Auckland — the author remembers the sound of the match commentary blaring from loud radios around the neighbourhood, amplifying the game so that it sounded as though the match was being played only a street or so away.)

Canterbury captain Don Hayes won the toss, and allowed Auckland first use of the wind. It was the option Auckland would have taken, knowing they needed points on the board as Canterbury had consistently proven themselves to be strong finishers.

The pressure was on from the kick-off, and it seemed to be affecting Canterbury the most. Fullback Robbie Deans, so often the picture of calm and stability behind his teammates, was making a mess of claiming high kicks. Others were dropping the ball, too, missing tackles and making impetuous passes. In no time at all Auckland had racked up 24 points, through tries to Joe Stanley, John Kirwan, Terry Wright and John Drake. Canterbury went into half-time with nothing on the scoreboard.

The Auckland Supporters Club members who had made the trip south were ecstatic in disbelief. The Canterbury faithful were stunned. Apparently someone threatened coach Grizz Wyllie with physical violence (which says something about the mentality of the person involved).

Come the second half, Auckland started to get the jitters, despite Steve McDowall (the man of the match) adding another try for the visitors. Canterbury roared back into the game thanks to tries by Bruce Deans, Craig Green, Wayne Smith and Albert Anderson.

The final three minutes of the game, with Auckland up by five, 28–23, were as nerve-racking as you could get, and it didn't matter what side you were on. Auckland were looking a bit ragged but hanging on by their fingernails. Canterbury were doing everything to snatch the game, as they had done several times over the past three seasons.

From a line-out inside the Auckland half, Canterbury first-five Wayne Smith punted the ball high into the stratosphere and asked the question: who will the rugby gods give the bounce of the ball to?

The breeze took it deeper and deeper into Auckland territory. All eyes were on the ball as it descended. The blue-and-white defenders were a bit like chooks in a thunderstorm as players in red-and-black jerseys raced towards their line. Where would the ball land? Which way would it bounce?

Finally, after what seemed like an age for players and spectators alike, it landed and bounced ... into the Auckland in-goal. The race was on. Kirwan just got to it and nudged it over the dead-ball line, which by this stage was lined by Canterbury supporters jumping up and down with every rotation of the ball.

As the adidas pill rolled into the crowd, referee Bob Francis blew his whistle for full-time.

The crowd rushed onto the field.

The players caught their breath.

What a stunning game.

Said Grizz Wyllie: 'I always said that when they finally lost the Shield, I wanted them to lose in style — and they did.'

It's worth noting the teams from that day.

Canterbury: Robbie Deans, Dennis Woods, Victor Simpson, Warwick Taylor, Craig Green, Bruce Deans, Dale Atkins, Jock Hobbs, Don Hayes (c), Andy Earl, Albert Anderson, Chris Earl, John Buchan, Murray Davie.

Auckland: Lindsay Harris, John Kirwan, Joe Stanley, Kurt Sherlock, Terry Wright, Grant Fox, David Kirk, Glenn Rich, Mark Brooke-Cowden, Alan Whetton, Gary Whetton, Andy Haden (c), John Drake, Iain Abercrombie, Steve McDowall.

*

Auckland's hold on the Shield went on for so long — 61 defences — that it was called an 'era'. As the challengers came and went, Auckland took the Shield on the road — and in Horowhenua in 1993, the wider rugby public had their first sighting of precocious teenage talent Carlos Spencer. Eden Park crowds dwindled, became a bit complacent and, to outside eyes, arrogant as they swapped ends at half-time in expectation of more Auckland tries.

That's not to say there weren't good games in that time. The first 40 minutes against Otago in 1990, when the defenders wiped the much-fancied Otago side off the park in scoring 39 unanswered points, remains the most dominant half of provincial rugby the author has attended.

There was also one of the most bizarre (and boring) games you would ever see: the 'no scrums' encounter with Canterbury three weeks later.

With only five minutes of the game played, Canterbury hooker John Buchan was sent off for kicking Auckland's Gary Whetton, who had been keenly rucking a Cantab. One would have expected, given the form they had been in, that with a numerical advantage Auckland would then run riot. Not so.

At the next scrum, Canterbury cannily crafted the impression to referee Bryce Lawrence that replacement Phil Cropper, coming on to take his place in the front row, was actually a loosie. Auckland hooker Sean Fitzpatrick advised Lawrence that he and Cropper had hooked against each other at Colts level. The Canterbury coaches (Frank Jack and Alister Hopkinson) later claimed the directive had come not from them, but from their players wearing the low-numbered jerseys on the field.

Unrest in the crowd grew, first at the amount of time the referee and players spent discussing the matter, then with every scrum that wasn't set. Rarely had an Eden Park crowd been more abusive. It was on the verge of its first outbreak of hooliganism.

In the end, Auckland prevailed, 33–30, although the last 10 minutes were very tense, with Canterbury scoring two tries. Grant Fox kicked seven penalties for Auckland.

The Shield finally left Eden Park in 1993 when the Waikato team, coached by John Boe, played the game of their lives to stun Auckland, 17–6. Not a good start in the coach's position for one Graham Henry.

From Hamilton, the Shield went down to Christchurch for the first time in eight years.

*

On 1 October 1994, Otago were hoping to claim the Log for the first time in 37 years. They made all the play against Canterbury, who were hosting only their second defence after taking the Shield from Waikato a month earlier. Otago scored three tries and Canterbury spent the second half playing catch-up, their revival coming from the boot of a young first-five by the name of Andrew Mehrtens, as referee Colin Hawke repeatedly pinged the tiring southern men.

With a minute to play, Otago were still a point ahead, but pressure from Canterbury near their line saw the blue-and-golds concede a force-down and 5-metre scrum. The red-and-black faithful in the ground were screaming for their boys to clinch the game, while the Otago players knew they just had to give it everything for a few more seconds and then the Shield would be Dunedin-bound.

After Canterbury loose-forward Todd Blackadder charged towards the line from the base of a scrum, it looked as though his teammate halfback Aaron Flynn knocked the ball on at the back of a fiercely contested ruck.

Hawke allowed play to continue.

The Canterbury backs had the ball, but Otago halted their advance at the advantage line, about 15 metres out and slightly to the left of the posts.

Bodies were everywhere.

The ball appeared to roll loose on the Canterbury side, slightly away from the ruck.

Otago hooker David Latta dived on it.

Hawke blew his whistle.

'Oh, it's a penalty!' screamed television commentator Keith Quinn.

Latta lay on the ground, his face in his hands. The anguish of the young man was palpable. He could barely get to this feet as Mehrtens hastily placed the ball for the kick, which he duly made.

Otago kicked off. Flynn again appeared to knock the ball on at the back of a ruck in front of Hawke. Otago regained the ball with just a few seconds to play, and attempted to run from inside their 22, but the move broke down. Ball in touch. Game over.

Canterbury 22, Otago 20.

You could see in Latta's despair just what winning (and losing) the Shield meant to our provincial players.

*

In the 25 years since that game, and the advent of the professional game, Bay of Plenty (2004), North Harbour (2006) and Counties–Manukau (2013) won the Shield for the first time. In the case of North Harbour, when they triumphed over Canterbury, one of the big discussions was over where the union should hold their celebratory parade, lacking as they were a main street.

The Shield was unquestionably one of the reasons All Black rugby was strong. Outside of a match against a touring international team, challenges had a greater intensity than any other first-class game, including the annual North versus South game and All Black trials. Shield games prior to the professional era could contain a dozen or more All Blacks, alongside some very accomplished players who were never elevated to higher honours.

Every Shield game was greatly anticipated, with excitement building all week, main-street shop windows boasting team colours and messages of support for their side, and match-day parades making their way through the centre of town.

Trains, buses and (later) aeroplanes carried excited spectators to matches. Pubs close to grounds would be full in the hours before the game, then suddenly empty as spectators walked to the match venue. It was all done in good cheer, as they used to say.

One of the disappointing aspects of the professional era, and the rise in importance of Super Rugby and the elongated international programme, is that the top players no longer turn out for Shield games. No longer is the report of a game the leading item in nightly television and radio news bulletins.

Fortunately, the Shield still holds awe for those who contest it today. There are many provincial players, especially those from the second and third divisions, for whom a challenge will be the biggest match of their playing careers. Having their names on the team lists means they join the greats of the game who have all wanted to 'lift the Shield'.

It is also heartening, when the Shield is taken to a new home, to see that the delight of supporters has not diminished over the decades. Crowds still welcome its return, filling airport arrival lounges to cheer the moment when the players, bleary-eyed from celebrating throughout the night, first raise the Log in victory on their home patch. It still means more to a young rugby supporter to touch or have their photo taken with the Shield than it does with the Super Rugby cup.

Long live the Log!

THE RANFURLY SHIELD BOARD GAME

Many of us in our youth played Subbuteo table soccer or table test cricket. In the former, little plastic men on rounded bases 'kicked' the soccer ball forward by way of a flick of a players' finger. Some became very skilled at being able to impart spin on the little ball in much the same way a snooker or billiard player could with cue in hand. Model and hobby shops would sell teams of players coloured in the livery of popular English football clubs. There were even tournaments for players to contest. Obviously the games weren't played at a great pace, but they were simple and competitive in the way they mirrored real games.

Table-top cricket was played on a picket-fenced oval of felt. Model fielders stood crouched ready to 'catch' the ball, achieved when the small silver ball-bearing was hit by the batsman into a semi-circle between the player's legs. The ball was bowled down a small, thin ramp, with the player whose side was batting swinging the bat by way of an extended arm that was controlled from behind the batsman. Again, it was a simple re-creation of a sport that could be highly competitive, but its pace also mirrored that of test cricket. Tests that lasted for days or weeks could be played, and later the then-new variant, the limited-overs match.

Rugby, of course, is a much more complicated game to replicate than soccer or cricket, so board games of footy have been virtually non-existent.

Nevertheless, in the 1960s, World Games produced the Ranfurly Shield Rugby Game. Recommended for players eight years of age and over, the rules were nearly as convoluted and complicated as those of the real thing.

The green playing field sheet was marked with small squares, and cardboard players were fitted into plastic stands. There were 12 little square pink cards to determine penalty kicks or conversions, six of which carried 'Goal' while the other half-dozen were printed with 'Flagged away'.

Forty similarly sized blue cards directed the play, with instructions such as: 'Long spiral punt bounces out, gain 40 yards'; 'Reverse pass, gain 20 yards'; 'Stiff arm tackle penalty (pick up a pink goal card)'; 'Hand in scrum penalty'; 'Drop pass, lose possession'; 'Intercepted pass, opposition gains ball'; 'Arguing with referee penalty (lose possession), (Your opponent picks up pink goal card)'; 'Mark, gain 20 yards (line out)'; 'Dummy pass, gain 10 yards'; 'Side-stepping run, gain 10 yards'; 'Grubber kick, lose possession'; and so on.

Here are some of the rules:

2. The attacking team spins the spinner to nominate a player. He then throws the dice, and moves the nominated player (forward, sideways or backwards — the attacking player must move around a defending player) the number shown on the dice (e.g. if a 3 is thrown on dice, move nominated player 3 squares — one square is 2 yards).
3. He then picks up a blue 'ACTION CARD' and follows the instructions on the back (e.g. good run, move forward 10 yards = 5 squares).

4. The attacking team repeats rules 2 and 3 until the 'ACTION CARD' states otherwise.

...

8. TRIES. These are scored when a player crosses his opponent's try line (4 points are given). Willie-A-Way, try is scored when team receives this bonus card (REMOVE CARD FROM PACK AFTER IT IS PLAYED). When a try is scored player picks up Pink Goal Card to see if the conversion is successful.
9. CONVERSIONS. These are scored by picking up a pink 'GOAL CARD'. They can only be scored after a try (as in Rule 6). After result move players back to kick-off positions.

...

13. LINEOUTS. When this occurs toss dice and the team with the highest number wins the ball.

Should the play sheet be heavily creased, place a damp cloth on reverse of sheet and press lightly with a warm iron.

When playing the game, it is a bit like chess or chequers, with both sets of players moving towards their opponent's goal line. No real strategy can be applied, so the game meanders along. If it proves one thing, it is that a board game based on a ball game really does need a ball.

Thirty years later along came the evolution of computer, and PlayStation and Xbox, versions of rugby, the best of which were in the name of *Jonah Lomu*.

The author has been also told of a simple schoolboy desk rugby game. The players would sit on opposite sides of a desk and flick a coin (lying flat) along the top of the desk. If it stopped halfway over the edge on the other side then it was deemed to be a 'try'.

A conversion was taken by placing the coin in a similar position on the edge of the desk directly in front of the player who had just scored. They would then flick the coin with their thumb so it flew through the air to the other side of the desk, where the other player was holding their fingers with the tips of their thumbs together and first fingers pointing straight up as goalposts. If the coin went through these 'digital' goalposts, the conversion was successful. (One wonders if there were many facial injuries suffered due to wayward 'kicks' of the coin.)

There was another way of playing this coin game in which a player placed their fingertips on the desk, thumbs together. They then balanced the coin on their thumb tips and flicked the coin towards the opposing goal. Apparently, these 'kicks' were even more directionless!

‘For us substitutes sitting in the stand at the Welsh test [at Cardiff Arms Park], when Wales were piling on those early points they [members of the home crowd] leant over to us and said, “What do you think of that, eh?” and gave us the two-finger sign.’

— All Black wing Robert Kururangi during the 1978 Grand Slam tour.

‘Leaving the kids at home and the family at home and the farm and all that, then you’ve got to come out and enjoy all these occasions and I am hugely honoured to have this opportunity.’

— Former Black Fern Rebecca Mahoney on becoming the first woman to referee a Ranfurly Shield match, Otago’s 49–14 win over North Otago at Oamaru, in July 2019.

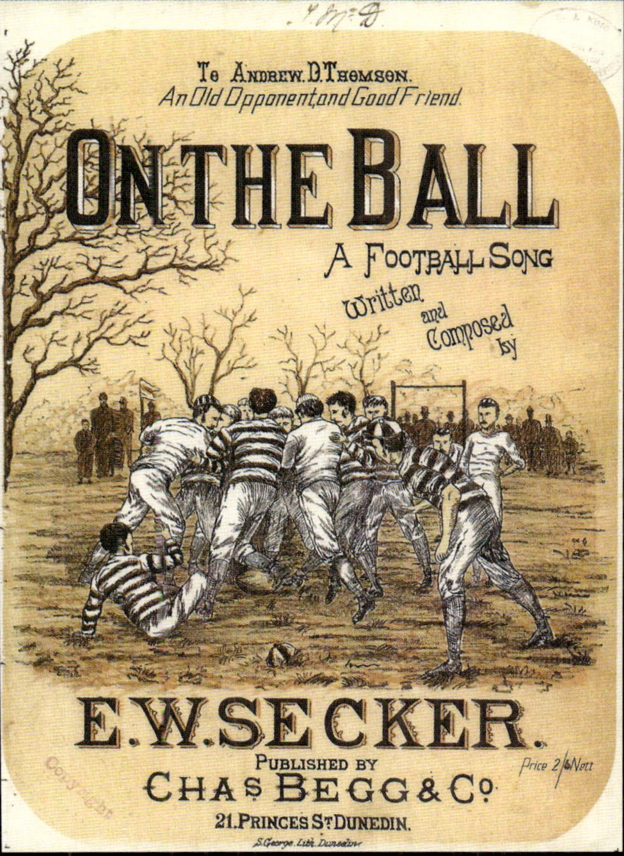

Our once well-known rugby 'anthem', composed in 1887.
(MATT ELLIOTT COLLECTION)

An extremely rare photo of the 1897 All Blacks, not yet 'all black'. (MATT ELLIOTT COLLECTION)

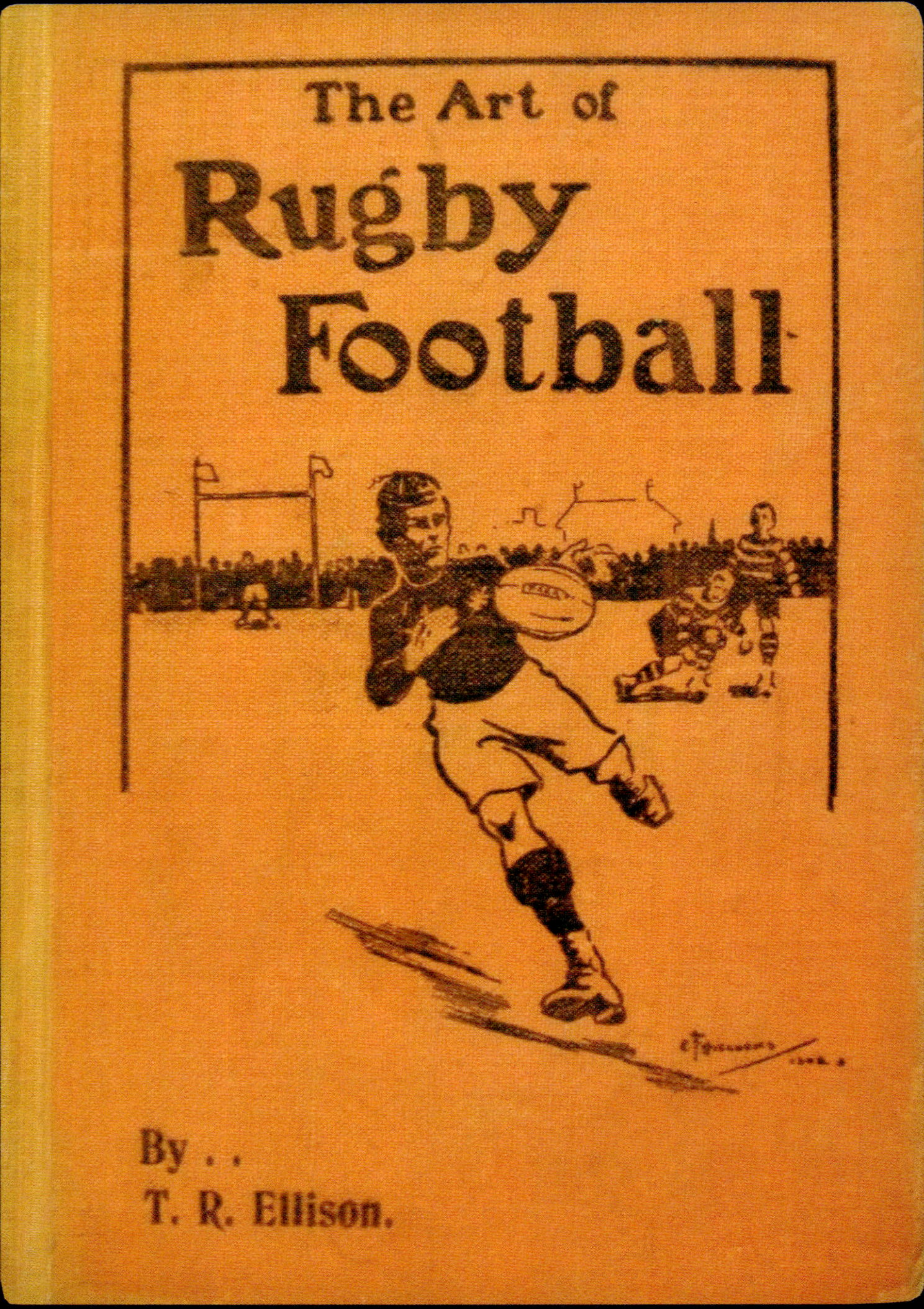

Tom Ellison's influential 1902 book, *The Art of Rugby Football.* (AUCKLAND LIBRARIES SPECIAL COLLECTIONS)

1905 souvenir programme. (MATT ELLIOTT COLLECTION)

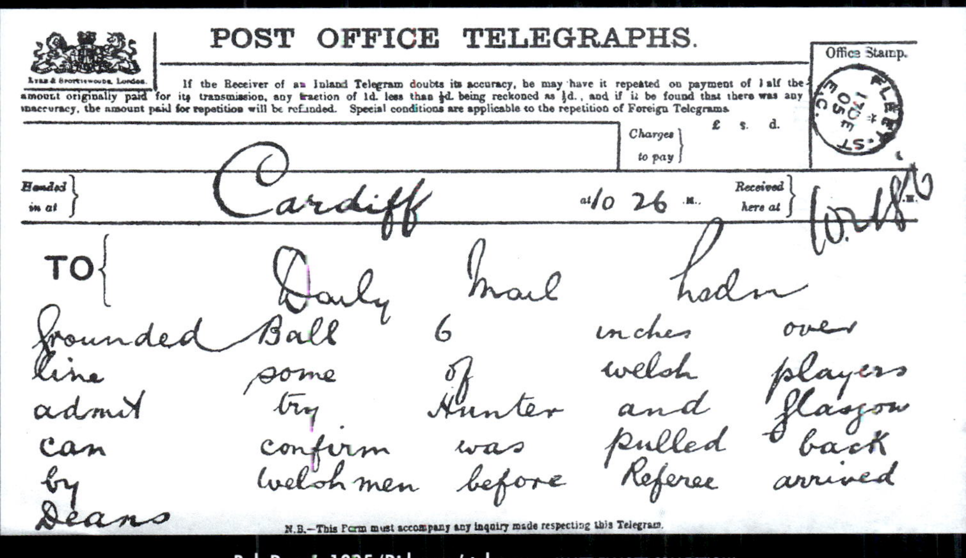

POST OFFICE TELEGRAPHS.

Office Stamp. FLEET-ST E.C. 17 DE 05

If the Receiver of an Inland Telegram doubts its accuracy, he may have it repeated on payment of half the amount originally paid for its transmission, any fraction of 1d. less than ½d. being reckoned as ½d., and if it be found that there was any inaccuracy, the amount paid for repetition will be refunded. Special conditions are applicable to the repetition of Foreign Telegrams.

Charges to pay £ s. d.

Handed in at Cardiff at 10 26 m. Received here at 10.48

TO Daily Mail London

grounded Ball 6 inches over line some of welsh players admit by Hunter and Glasgow can confirm was pulled back by welshmen before Referee arrived Deans

N.B.—This Form must accompany any inquiry made respecting this Telegram.

Bob Dean's 1905 'Did score' telegram. (MATT ELLIOTT COLLECTION)

Brian McCleary, more boxer than footballer but still good enough to be part of the 1924–25 'Invincibles'. (COURTESY DAVE CAMERON)

A cigarette card of Maurice Brownlie leading the 1928 All Blacks onto the field to play Wellington, prior to departing for South Africa. (MATT ELLIOTT COLLECTION)

Cyril Brownlie, a big man and fine footballer who will be forever known as the first man sent off in a rugby international. (MATT ELLIOTT COLLECTION)

Long-playing records of tour highlights enjoyed some popularity in the late 50s and early 60s.
(MATT ELLIOTT COLLECTION)

24 THE WEEKLY NEWS, JULY 25, 1956

Lunchtime at Carisbrook while waiting for the main match

The South African scrum-half, C. F. Strydom, sending away a dive pass

Expressions of delight on schoolboy faces

A market for test match souvenirs

B. F. Howe, Springbok inside back, being tackled by R. A. Jarden

The rival captains, J. A. du Rand (left) and P. B. Vincent

C. F. Strydom fails to charge down a kick by M. J. Dixon

J. T. Claassen and R. A. White (obscured) jumping for the ball in a lineout. H. N. Walker (No. 10) is being obstructed by M. W. Irwin

Victory for the All Blacks

Taking advantage of most of the chances which came their way, the New Zealand team deservedly defeated the South African tourists by 10 points to 6 in the first Rugby test match at Dunedin. This win has produced the tonic necessary after six successive defeats inflicted by the Springboks in test matches since 1937. A capacity crowd of 40,000 spectators filled the historic ground at Carisbrook.

The *Weekly News* captures match day as the All Blacks beat the Springboks 10–6 in the first test of the 1956 series, at Carisbrook. (MATT ELLIOTT COLLECTION)

What it was, was football.

Cartoonist Neville Lodge didn't think much of the Auckland v Springboks match in 1956.
(MATT ELLIOTT COLLECTION)

"Take a look at my teeth, will you? Here comes my boss and I told him I had to go to the dentist."

Neville Lodge depicts how slipping away from work to go to a mid-week match required all sorts of subterfuge.
(MATT ELLIOTT COLLECTION)

Despite protests, the 1960 All Blacks tour of South Africa is best remembered for having no Maori players on the side
(MINISTRY FOR CULTURE AND HERITAGE)

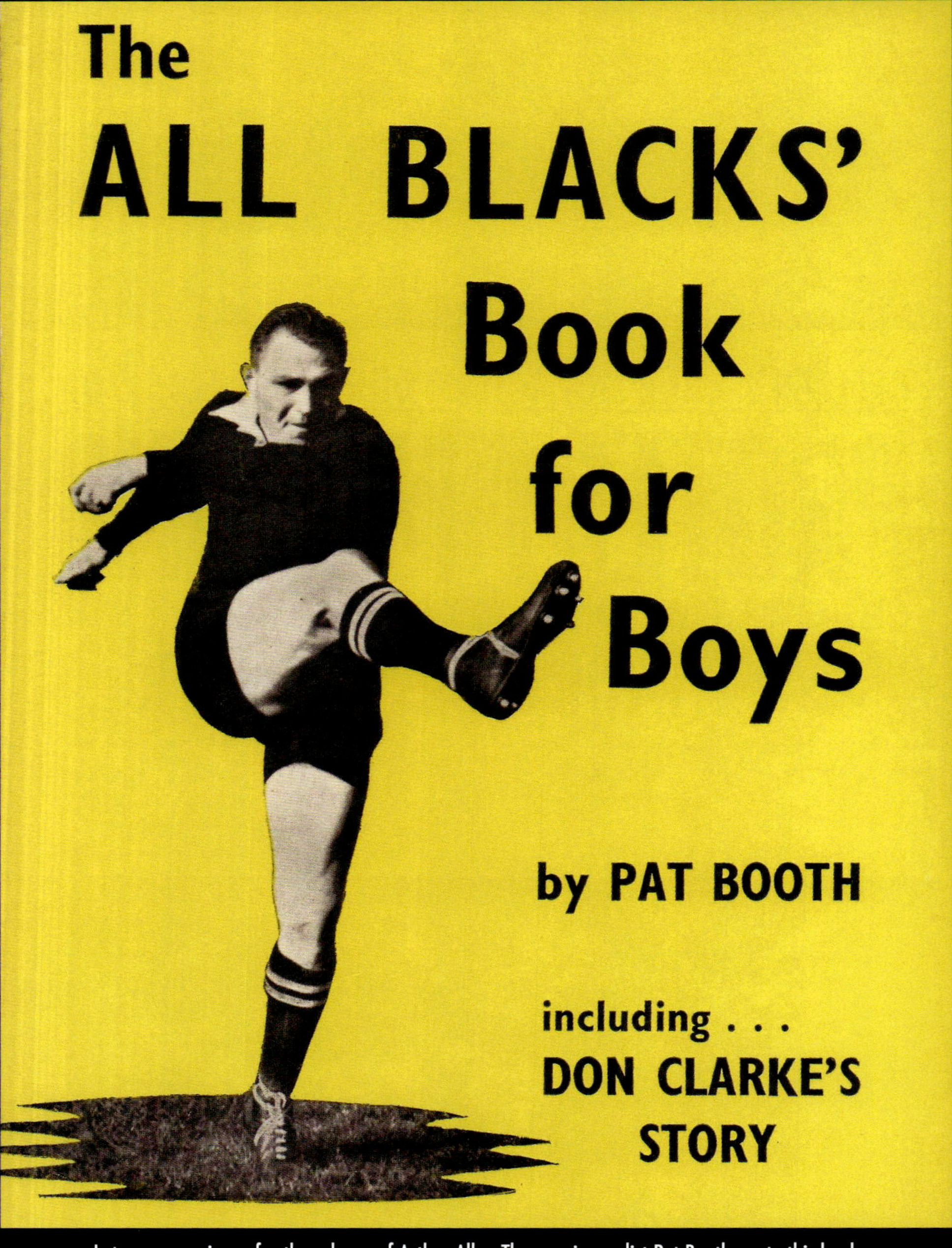

Later a campaigner for the release of Arthur Allan Thomas, journalist Pat Booth wrote this book with Don Clarke in 1960. (MATT ELLIOTT COLLECTION)

Sleeve for Rod Derrett's 'Rugby Racing and Beer' single, released in 1965 (MATT ELLIOTT COLLECTION)

The Ranfurly Shield board game (MATT ELLIOTT COLLECTION)

Fred 'The Needle' Allen, a tremendous player who captained the All Blacks in 1949. As a coach, he always got the best out of his players. Under his steely gaze the All Blacks didn't lose a test between 1966 and 1968.
(PHOTO BY S&G/PA IMAGES VIA GETTY IMAGES)

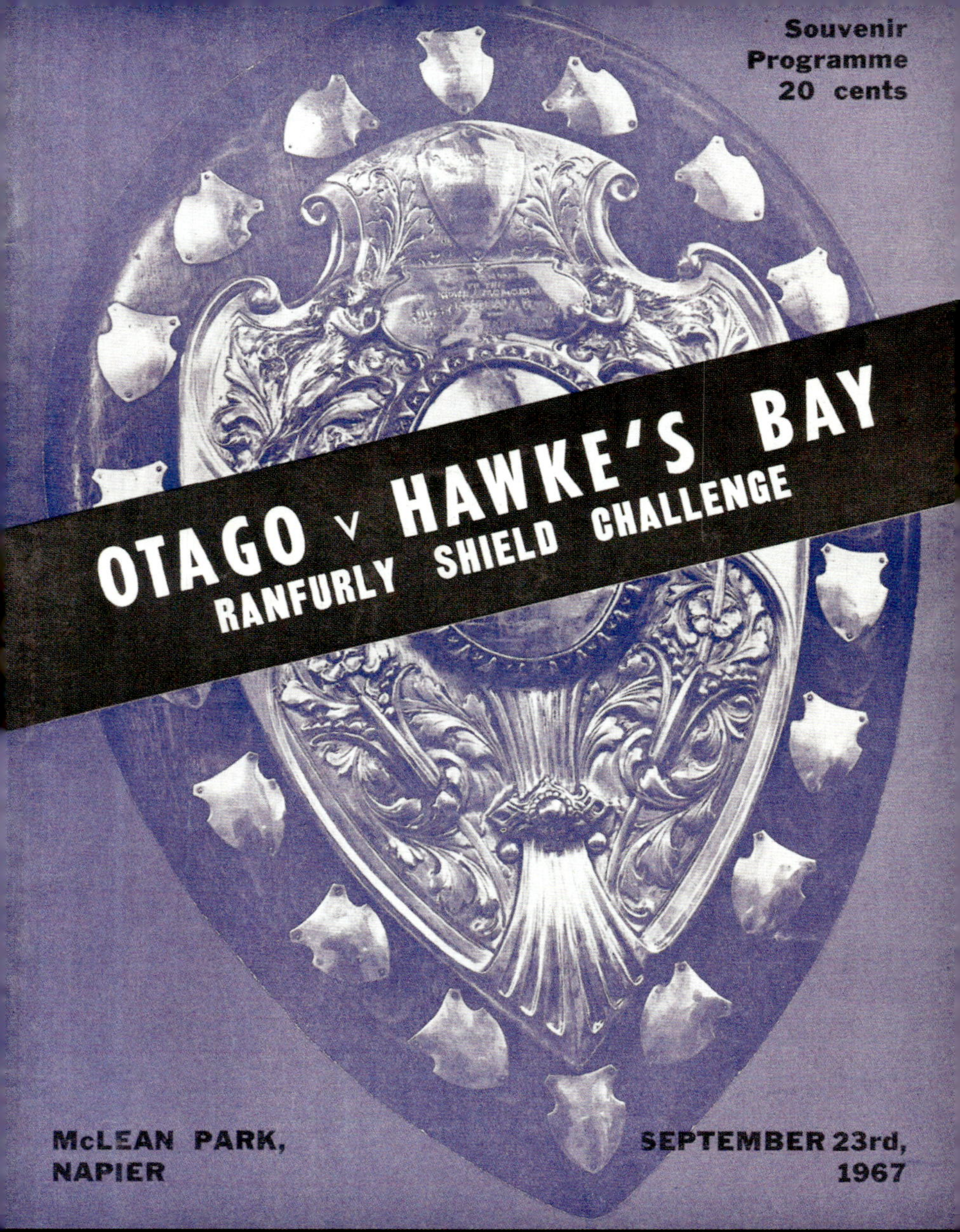

Hawke's Bay's second great reign with the Shield. (MATT ELLIOTT COLLECTION)

The long walk

He had only 25yd to go to the grandstand entrance but it must have felt like a mile with a large section of the 60,000 crowd standing up to boo.

This was the scene after the referee (arrowed) ordered Meads off in the Test against Scotland on Saturday.

It was Meads' 42nd Test and his 98th game for New Zealand.—Cable photo.

Dangerous Play Alleged

SENDING-OFF MARS ALL BLACKS' FEAT

2/12/67

From T. P. McLEAN

Edinburgh

A great deal of the glory won by the touring All Blacks vanished in a few seconds during the last international match of their tour against Scotland at Murrayfield on Saturday when the great All Black forward C. E. Meads was ordered from the field for dangerous play.

It was held by the referee, Mr K. D. Kelleher, of Eire, that Meads had transgressed the bounds of fair play by attempting to kick the legs from under the Scottish fly half, D. Chisholm, as the latter gathered a loose ball and started to run toward the touchline.

Meads and other All Blacks protested at Mr Kelleher's verdict but he had to go.

When the match ended three or four minutes later Chisholm entered the All Blacks' dressing room to tell Meads he considered the latter's action in attempting to kick the ball had been legitimate and that the decision was excessive and cruelly harsh.

Indeed, even while Mr Kelleher was talking to Meads in the process of ordering him of the television film of the incident he was satisfied as to the legality of Meads' action.

This opinion was supported by the great All Black fullback R. W. H. Scott, who also saw the runs-through.

The manager of the All Blacks, Mr C. K. Saxton, told three New Zealand journalists that he considered the referee's action to be grossly exaggerated and most uncalled for.

Incident Filmed

Subsequently he allowed himself and the coach, Mr F. R. Allen, to be interviewed on television and to comment on runs-through of the film of the incident.

These showed that New Zealand, after scoring their only try of the second half, were defending from Scotland's subsequent kick-off

Mr Kelleher, who had not previously seen the All Blacks in action, appeared to some of the players long to identify Meads with the more disagreeable aspects of the game.

In point of fact there were very few of those. Until the last few minutes, when everybody turned a little ugly of temper and some rough-house play was seen, the game was rarely more than robust.

The late touches of ill humour were probably a natural outcome of the amount of obstructive play in lineouts, to which the referee appeared on the whole strangely indifferent.

From the Scottish point of view the ill humour probably also expressed disappointment

Paid Too Great A Penalty

NZPA - Special - Copyright

Edinburgh

Solid support for C. E. Meads, the All Black who was ordered off the field in the international against Scotland on Saturday, came last night from his team manager, Mr C. K. Saxton.

Asked whether he would select Meads to play at Newport on Wednesday, Mr Saxton said: "I will play him in every game after this matter has been cleared up."

According to the tour agreement, any player ordered off under law 26, foul play, shall be reported to the secretary of the union concerned and his case be judged within 48 hours by a two-man committee.

A clause of the tour agreement reads: "A player ordered off may not take part in any further game during the visit until his case has been dealt with by the said committee and its decision conveyed to the manager."

Mr Saxton said he would be one of the committee members. The other would be a representative of the four Home unions.

Asked whether he considered any penalty was likely to be imposed on Meads, Mr Saxton said: "He has already paid too great a penalty."

Scrapbook cuttings of Colin Meads being sent off for dangerous play at Murrayfield, 1967.

(M. J. FORD COLLECTION)

Ken Gray scores a try in the 19–0 win over Wales at Lancaster Park, 1969. Colin Meads (left) is in support. (PHOTO NEWS/MATT ELLIOTT COLLECTION)

'GEAR'

Up until 1960, books published in New Zealand about rugby had been for adult male readers. Then when Waikato and All Black fullback Don 'The Boot' Clarke was at the height of his powers and popularity, he was teamed up with a young journalist named Pat Booth to produce a rugby book for boys.

The classic 110-page *The All Blacks' Book for Boys* contains over 20 chapters covering Clarke's boyhood ambitions to become an All Black, skills for forwards and backs, facts, anecdotes, stats, profiles of the 1960 All Blacks, a quiz, and even the Laws of Rugby and Ranfurly Shield rules. Throughout there is advice from Clarke that remains as relevant today as it was when the book was published over 50 years ago.

In a chapter titled 'Gear', it is stated that the old saying about the bad workman blaming his tools 'is as true in Rugby as in anything else. A kicker who muffs vital penalties may be tempted to blame the shape of the ball or the newness of his boots when, in fact, his concentration or technique have been at fault.'

Having said that, Clarke and Booth remind young readers that 'a player who neglects his gear may find that this fault affects his game'. Given the playing conditions in wintery New Zealand, Clarke cautions that you really can't be too careful about your boots. You wouldn't want to find, like one unnamed great post-war All Black hopeful, that your decision to wear short sprigs on a muddy field in a trials series loses you both your grip on the ground and your place in the All Blacks!

He continues:

> A broken lace at a vital stage of a game could cripple you as a defender and let the opposition through. See to it, too, that your socks are well gartered. There is nothing sissy about wearing your socks up. If they drag around your boot tops they could hamper you, while a layer of sock could save you from sprig cuts or minor injuries. How you look is important. The best players are those who are neat in their movements, but every player should aim to look neat, to see that his boots are polished, his jersey clean. Like other things in Rugby, this shouldn't be left to your mother, your father or some other person. Take pride in your appearance and you will find it easier to take pride in your game and your team.

In the section on 'Sportsmanship', Clarke instructs the young player to be accepting of losses and gracious in victory. 'Most important, remember that Rugby is a game.'

COACHES

For many years, rugby coaches — at all levels — were known for their fire-and-brimstone training, pre-match and half-time talks to motivate players. Invoking all manner of dread, colourful language and personal insult, even the most strident pulpit preacher would have shuddered with fear. There were rants that 'stripped the paint off the changing room walls', and verbal attacks on players that made them wish they were at home hiding under the bed.

'Young' Vic Cavanagh was a proud southern man who had played rugby and cricket for Otago. His father, 'Old' Vic, had also played for Otago in the winter game and was a long-serving administrator. Father and son coached Otago in 1936 when they held the Shield; when 'Young' Vic coached the province in his own right, the province held the Shield for 17 games, from 1947 to 1949. Both men are credited with making rucking not only a feared aspect of Otago forward play, but also something of a skill. The purpose of a quickly secured ruck ball was always to get the ball rapidly out to the wings.

Surprisingly, Young Vic was never appointed coach of the All Blacks, but that may have had something to do with his gruff personality. He was a man who made his opinions very clear. His dislike of journalists was intense, but he was revered by his players. The appointment of Alex McDonald, another Otago rugby stalwart, as coach of the 1949 team to South Africa instead of Cavanagh caused great controversy in Dunedin and surrounds.

Years after playing under Young Vic, some still had his voice ringing in their ears. 'Out you go again, girls!' he apparently once said to his players after they had played poorly in the first half.

How times change. The old insult of 'playing like a girl' could now be seen as something of a compliment! Many male players and spectators admire the skills and success of New Zealand's female rugby players, with the Black Ferns having won the Women's Rugby World Cup five times. In 2017, they were named the World Rugby Team of the Year, the first women's team from any country to receive that accolade.

*

Ted Griffin was North Auckland coach for 21 years — over 210 games — during which time the province won the Shield for the first time (1950) and claimed it on two other occasions (1960, 1971). His boys claimed the international scalps of France and Australia. In all their games against neighbours Auckland during that time, North Auckland had the greater number of wins. Griffin's team talks were legendary for how they inspired players to give their best. The great Peter Jones called him 'the Churchill of North Auckland'. The English statesman may have used a little more diplomacy than Griffin, however, who often referred to the unsatisfactory play of his charges as being like 'a bunch of old women'.

In one of his pre-match talks, he said: 'I saw [a former player] out there in the crowd a while ago. You know him. He used to play a great game of football. Used to weigh 13 stone of bone and muscle. Now he's 6 stone and can hardly stand up. In a few weeks he'll be dead from cancer. This is the last game of football he'll ever see. Make it a good one, boys.'

*

Fred 'The Needle' Allen was highly respected tactically by the Auckland and All Black teams he coached in the 1960s. But he wasn't given his nickname for nothing, and even Colin Meads would have to bow his head and mutter in obedience to Fred's criticisms of him.

Being an ex-army man, Fred had no problem with being blunt with players, and felt that this brought greater honesty from them in their dealings with him. But he could also resort to what he called 'Fred's little white lies'. Perhaps the best example of this was prior to a defence of the Shield against Canterbury. The Shield was nowhere to be seen, and when the Auckland players asked their coach where it was, he replied, 'Canterbury are so sure they're going to take it off us today that they wanted me to loan it to them so they could pose with it for a picture in the Christchurch *Press*.' The thought of that didn't half rev up the blue-and-white players.

Did the needling work? The All Blacks never lost a test while he was coach, and Auckland set a record for the most Ranfurly Shield defences.

*

Alex 'Grizz' Wyllie — who coached Canterbury during their Ranfurly Shield reign in the mid-1980s and then the All Blacks later that decade — was a man whose name and stony visage seemed to bring out the best in his players. It was the fact that he didn't say much, and wouldn't even applaud his players from the stand if they scored a crucial try, that had players wondering just what Grizz was thinking. They knew his reputation for being gruff, from his days as a hard-nosed player for Canterbury and the All Blacks.

There is a story that at half-time during the epic Shield encounter with Auckland in 1985, when Canterbury was down 0–24, Wyllie strode out onto Lancaster Park to talk to his players. With some of them not knowing where to look and wondering what sort of blast he was going to give them, the first thing he said was 'F***!' That was followed by: 'Get the [bleeping] ball and [bleeping] use it. If [bleeping] Auckland can score 24 points in the first half, you can [bleeping] score 24 in the second.' (Grizz was almost right, his side bagging 23 points ...)

*

Unlike Grizz, John Mitchell liked to speak a lot. The problem was, only he really seemed to know what he was talking about. The former Waikato captain, who had also led the All Blacks in a midweek game in 1993, had been an assistant to Clive Woodward with the England team before being appointed All Black coach when Wayne Smith had a crisis of confidence. Mitch took us all on a 'journey' to the 2003 Rugby World Cup. He also tested the shorthand and transcribing abilities of those in the media. Just what *was* he talking about?

- We've graduated Aaron's foot injury.
- No differential lies between the line of detail.
- I have to declutter their team cultures.
- Reuben is strong in his grouping on the field.
- The team is in a block-building process.
- We must cut the cake with this All Black team.
- We have to be able to win our grinds.

*

In the 2000s, a change came about in the way players were spoken to by coaches. At the All Black level, Graham Henry — whose coaching years for Auckland, Wales and the All Blacks were renowned for his gruffness, fiery half-time speeches and a propensity for criticising players even in public — found that the old ways of motivating players were no longer working. It had become 'softly, softly' rather than a kick up the backside, with the players taking greater responsibility for their attitudes on the field.

Some old rugby heads were shocked to hear, for example, that Steve Hansen didn't give the players a pre-match rocket when he coached the All Blacks; instead, captain Kieran Read did all the talking at the team hotel the day before the game and in the changing room in the minutes before they took to the field.

Giving the power to the players? What would Vic, Fred and Ted think about that?

'Remember that rugby is a team game: all 14 of you make sure you pass the ball to Jonah.'

— fax to the All Blacks during the 1995 Rugby World Cup.

'THE LAST OF THE TWENTY-EIGHT'

This poem was written by William Pember Reeves, politician and poet, hours after New Zealand's 1924–25 'Invincibles' defeated England, 17–11. They had played a man down for most of the game after Cyril Brownlie was sent off (see page 270), but managed to hold on to their unbeaten tour record.

Reeves read this poem at a function for the All Blacks hosted by the Loving Cup Presentation Committee at the New Zealand High Commissioner's office in London. Each member of the team received a copy, and others were widely circulated. Several of the verses became well-known and were frequently recited at the likes of football functions and school concerts throughout New Zealand.

THE LAST OF THE TWENTY-EIGHT

Thirty-five years on the march have swung
Since I could try to play,
Yet one old fellow to-day grew young,
I was a boy to-day.
Shouting at scrimmages stark and stern,
Cheering the triumph great
Of the sinewy sons of the Silver Fern

In the Last of the Twenty-eight.
Kia Toa! young forwards tall,
Now let the Fern Leaf shine!
Fight and fall not — until you fall
Over the English line
Kia Toa, New Zealand! See,
Nepia guards the gate;
A rock and house of defence is he,
A tino tangata great.
'A fine machine' — so the scribes repeat.
'Machine!' but when all is said
The All Black plays with his hands and feet,
But the All Black wins with his head.
Thews and sinews and brawn to boot
Had in that hour been vain
Had not dexterous hand and outspreading foot
Been tools of the guiding brain.
The lusty men of the English line,
Were they troubled about the past?
Did they waste a thought on our three times nine,
Or easily yield the last?
No! Goals were registered, lines were crossed,
But still as their race doth use
They played like men who had never lost,
And never would stoop to lose.
So from two ends of an Empire met,
Stocks of the self-same brand.
All Blacks, All White, they were twain, but yet
Sons of one brave, old land.
She'll laugh — 'Good lads!' when, as seasons turn,
Our sons to their sons relate
How the jersey Black and the famous Fern

Won through unto Twenty-eight.
Weave them a crown, for they gained it there
Winning achievement's aim
Twine them a wreath of the fern they wear,
Famed, since they gave it fame.
For the forest leaves that our champions earn
Tell best of the glory great
Of the conquering sons of the Silver Fern
And the last of the Twenty-eight.
Seven and twenty victories won!
Week upon week came tales
Of Ireland beaten, the North o'er-run,
Victories four in Wales.
Deaf to the music of Swansea's song
They had settled the ancient debt,
And stars thrice nine in a shining throng
Wanted but one star yet.
Nothing else mattered at all we thought.
Talk of the past grew tame.
Conquered provinces counted nought
In the face of that last grim game.
Twenty-seven, with that not won
Left Victory's crown to fate,
Ah, All-but-one! appeared almost none
In the pause before Twenty-eight.
They had known bad moments;
the contest, 'Black'
Feels a quiver, felt — gone again —
When an Irish pack with a gale at its back
Comes rushing in Irish rain,
When Oxford fliers whose feet have wings,
Prove slippery triers bold,

Or Cambridge Blues, when the wet mud clings,
Are desperate lads to hold.
'Twas a bath of misery, all allow,
When the hurricane loosed its breath,
And the storm above and the slime below
Were mingled on black Blackheath;
But the tightest corner of corners tight
Came after the word of fate
Left fourteen fighting a fifteen's fight
In the tussle for Twenty-eight.

'BRING BACK BUCK' AND 'WE WANT IFFY!'

No doubt the selection of the first-ever New Zealand football team in 1884 saw some observers aggrieved that their club or provincial man had not been chosen. It has been the same with the naming of every All Black side since. Over pub-leaners and Sunday lunches, with letters to newspaper editors and contributions on talkback radio, television and now social media, there have been huge discussions about the players that armchair experts thought should make the All Blacks for a coming tour, series or season.

If your man made the team, the coach and selectors were regarded as a group of learned rugby brains. If he didn't, they were a bunch of old fools who wouldn't recognise a good rugby player if he knocked on their front door wearing an All Black jersey and holding the Webb Ellis trophy.

Naturally, there have been selections that have puzzled, annoyed and shocked various groups of rugby fans over the years.

For instance, the exclusion of Wellington fullback Mick Williment from the team to tour Great Britain and France in 1967, in favour of Canterbury's Fergie McCormick. Was there any truth to the story that he had originally been selected until the selectors were told to carefully recount their selections as they had 31 players instead of 30?

Why did Canterbury utility back Shayne 'Rita' Philpott get called up to the All Blacks in Australia in 1988, when Counties fullback Lindsay Raki was the form player but missed out on the trip? Philpott hadn't even appeared in the All Black trials.

Why wasn't Waikato open-side flanker Duane Monkley ever selected for the All Blacks?

What about Graham Henry and Wayne Smith's 'special project': outside back Isaia Toeava? A phenomenal talent as an age-group player, somehow he just didn't seem to settle into international rugby, despite playing 36 tests between 2005 and 2011.

*

There has been no greater outcry by aggrieved supporters of a player than that which began with the 1990 axing of unbeaten All Black captain Wayne 'Buck' Shelford, and somewhat nostalgically it continues to this day.

Over six seasons, Buck had played 48 games, including 22 tests for the All Blacks. He was hugely respected and unchallenged as the best number 8 in the country; he led from the front and was as tough as they come (see 'All Blacks v France 1986', page 187).

One of his greatest games was against Llanelli in Wales in 1989, when the All Blacks played into a constant gale in the second half of a match where they had turned into the wind only seven points up. Conditions were so bad that there had been talk of postponing the game. Buck just kept picking the ball up from the back of the scrum, carving up big metres to keep his team going forward and preventing the home side from having much possession. The final score: 34–9. (Scottish referee Ken McCartney blew up his own storm with the whistle, penalising Llanelli 20 times and the All Blacks only three times. Home fans abused and jostled him after the game.)

Then came a two-test home series against Scotland in 1990. The dogged Scots, who came to New Zealand holding all the Five Nations and Grand Slam silverware, were outplayed by the All Blacks in the first test 31–16, but they came close to causing an upset in the second, losing only by three, 18–21.

The All Black coach, Grizz Wyllie, after repeated viewings of the match videos, was apparently unhappy with Shelford's positional play and speed to the breakdown. All Black selectors John Hart and Lane Penn were dispatched to watch Shelford play for North Harbour. They concurred that Buck hadn't played well, and the decision was made to drop him for the upcoming matches against Australia. The reason given for his non-selection was that a leg injury had hampered his form.

Shelford's own viewings of the Scotland games made him more mystified by his axing, especially as he was the only player dropped from a team that had won both tests!

The opening story on the 6 pm news was that Shelford was 'in hiding tonight after being dumped from the team'. Then the stories and contradictions began to fly: that Grizz had tried to phone Buck but only spoke to his wife, Joanne, whereas she said that Buck had phoned her to say he was 'no longer an All Black'. The All Blacks camp again blamed a leg injury; Buck publicly disagreed with that.

The public looked for conspiracy theories. Buck had punched Grizz. Buck had punched Grant Fox.

In the end, Buck was replaced by Zinzan Brooke, an equally rugged player but with a different set of skills, and he would take a while to make the position his own.

Disgruntled fans of Buck chanted for him at All Black and North Harbour matches. All around the country, even at club games, painted sheets and banners that read *Bring Back Buck* were hung in stands and over sideline hoardings.

'Bring Back Buck' remains a great compliment from the grassroots fans of rugby to a true legend of the game, one who never had to give a losing speech as All Black captain.

*

Sixty years before fans around the country started painting banners that read *Bring Back Buck*, crowds had chanted 'We want Iffy.'

Karl Ifwersen is still regarded as one of the most gifted backs this country has produced. But he played only one game for the All Blacks (in 1921), in a match where no points were scored.

Of Danish extraction, Ifwersen first caught the eye of the Auckland rugby community when playing for the College Rifles club as part of a junior side that won the Auckland competition two years in a row. He was selected for the Auckland senior team in 1912, and played in all seven matches that season, including three Ranfurly Shield defences, kicking a goal in the first match, a 6–5 win over Taranaki. The following year he was lured to 'the league code', leaving Rifles for the North Shore Albions, who played at the domain at Devonport, which was also home to the North Shore Rugby Club.

Ifwersen was one of those players whose every touch of the ball had spectators leaning forward in their seats in anticipation of some on-field magic. A natural runner with ball in hand, he possessed great vision; where other players only saw tacklers in front of them, Ifwersen saw the space between the defenders. Straight and direct running was a trademark of his play. Combining this with great pace from a standing start, jinks and swerves, and a wonderful passing action, Ifwersen made the play of an inside back look ridiculously easy.

In 1913, he played for the Auckland and New Zealand league teams. The latter went to Australia, but although Ifwersen was the top points-scorer on tour, he did not make the test selections. International honours came the following year when England visited New Zealand.

At the beginning of World War I, Ifwersen served with the 3rd Auckland Regiment as part of the Samoan Advance Party, then was discharged on account of being medically unfit. Once back to full health, he made it as far as the training camp at Moascar before becoming ill again with hookworm, and was then invalided back to New Zealand with severe dysentery.

At war's end, rugby unions were inviting former players who had turned to the professional game to return to their ranks. But Ifwersen refused to be drawn back into the union fold, captaining the national league side in three tests in Australia in 1919, and playing further internationals at home against the green-and-golds and England in 1920.

Finally, in 1921 his arm was twisted enough for him to return to union, and he joined the Grammar School Old Boys' club. It was suggested in newspapers that he was to take part in the Possible versus Probables trial match in Wellington to decide the make-up of the first test team to face the Springboks in the first-ever international between the two sides. Ifwersen could not make his way to the capital as he was away from Auckland at the time. He did captain an Auckland–North Auckland side against the tourists, scoring a try in the 8–24 loss.

A month later he was chosen for the third test, the deciding match of the series to be played at Wellington. The All Blacks had won the first test in Dunedin 13–5, but South Africa claimed the second at Eden Park, 9–5. There was a raft of changes to the All Blacks, which even saw captain George Aitken dropped from the side.

The new five-eighths combination of William Fea and Ifwersen was expected to create running opportunities for the All Black backs, but atrocious weather put paid to that. (See 'the umbrella test', page 43.)

Despite the weather, Ifwersen — who had overcome a poisoned leg in the days before the game — tried to remain inventive, and nearly created a try for one of his wings when he cross-kicked behind the Springbok outside backs, but it was knocked away in a spray of water. After the match, some rugby writers found the greatest fault in his play was his lack of desire to go to ground to recover loose balls.

Ifwersen continued to turn out for Auckland until 1924. A lovely striker of the placed ball, he became the first New Zealand player to kick eight conversions in a game (which he did against a Wellington XV in 1922, when he actually kicked nine in a game won 54–0).

Even though he hadn't been chosen for the All Blacks since that lone 1921 test, Ifwersen would probably have toured Australia in 1923 had he been available. Many in Auckland were certain he would be included in the squad to tour Britain, Ireland, France and Canada in 1924–25. However, the English Rugby Union declared him ineligible as he had previously played rugby league. The Auckland Rugby Football Union protested, on the grounds that he had played an international match since reinstatement without any protest from the South African opponents, and a number of other local unions supported them. However, the harsh edict remained.

The local hero became something of a bureaucratic martyr, which led to unique scenes when a pre-tour trial match between two combination teams (Hawke's Bay–Poverty Bay–East Coast–Bay of Plenty and North Auckland–Auckland–Thames–Waikato) met at Eden Park. During the game, Auckland inside back Vic Badeley was seriously injured, and some time was taken to remove him from the field. As the crowd waited, a replacement player from Waikato prepared to take the field. Then a chant began among a group of spectators, and it quickly spread around the ground: 'We want Iffy! We want Iffy!'

Ifwersen was sitting in the stand watching the match, and such was the volume and insistence of the chant that he was sought out by officials and ushered to the changing rooms. Wearing borrowed kit, he took to the field and was greeted by an almighty roar from the crowd.

Ifwersen's presence seemed to have a positive effect on the team he joined. Trailing 0–6 before Ifwersen took the field, they played with new zest and ran away winners, 18–9.

When his playing days were behind him, Iffy had money troubles, which led to a couple of court appearances. Proof that even in days gone by, life can be difficult when one's time as a folk hero is over.

*

This 1924 poem by Robert Pope pokes fun at provincial newspaper selections of players who their 'experts' think should make All Black trial or test teams.

THE ALL BLACKS: MY SELECTION

The Free Lance has ordained that all
Must pick a team of 'Blacks,'
That shall the stormy ocean brave
And face the British packs;
A sense of duty urged me on
To honour this decree,
But sorely was I puzzled what
The personnel should be.
I read reports by ev'ry scribe
From Auckland to the Bluff,

But very soon I learned that this
Would hardly be enough;
For there are countless players who
Are born to kick unseen;
Yet, nathless, mighty champions
Upon their native green.
The 'Oio Examiner'
Indeed was forced to scan
To see if there was a mention of
A real outstanding man;
I found at least a dozen that
'Twas held, must find a place;
While the Kawa Kawa 'Sentinel'
Had thirteen in the race.
There was seventeen from Auckland,
And nineteen from Hawke's Bay,
All positively certainties,
Whose claims none could gainsay.
Only eight I found in Southland,
Who were sure to be included;
But from Canterbury's fertile plains
'All Blacks' in scores exuded
Otago's quota to the team
Was put down as eleven,
And five of these were forwards who
Would grace a team from heaven.
The 'Times,' indeed, had qualms about
The eighteen from outside;
And wound up thus: 'Our men have claims
That cannot be denied.'
I read the Westport 'Sun's' reports,
And there I quickly learned

Of a full-back and three forwards,
Who had fern-leaves safely earned.
The 'Examiner' of Woodville
Was but sparing in its claims;
The list of men it termed 'foregones'
Comprised just seven names.
The Marlborough 'Express,' I found,
Took quite a gloomy view
Of the number of its candidates,
And put it down as two;
The Nelson 'Weekly News' complained
Of being in the cold;
Yet 'Apple Land' had five great backs,
Perforce must be enrolled.
To Taranaki's claims I then
Directed my attention,
And in the 'Herald's' columns, ten
Had honourable mention.
'These two,' 'twas said, 'must sure find place,
Let those stand out who must;
But, lacking these, we'd have a team,
New Zealand dare not trust.'
Such multifarious reading had
By now my mind perplexed;
The problem of those Twenty-nine
Was making me sore vexed.
I totted up the certainties
And found them sixty-one;
But, sixty-ones in twenty-nine —
It really can't be done.
I sat me down and scratched my head.
Now aching — when anon,

I found I'd made a blunder great —
I'd left out Wellington
Then rapidly I conned the notes,
Of 'Drop Kick' and 'Touch Line,'
And found the local certainties
A modest twenty-nine.

SECRET OF OUR SUCCESS

In 135 years of All Black rugby, the opportunities after a tour for an All Black captain to openly and freely dissect the performances of his team and their opponents have been exceedingly rare. In the modern era, player biographies reveal goings-on behind the scenes of teams, but they are often well after the fact.

Following the All Blacks' extraordinary 1905 campaign through England, Ireland, Scotland and Wales, in which they suffered just one loss in 32 games, captain Dave Gallaher was invited to contribute his thoughts to a review of the tour, 'Why the All Blacks Triumphed', published by *The Daily Mail*. It remains an interestingly relevant opinion-piece about the differing attitudes of rugby between New Zealanders and those in the Northern Hemisphere.

'SECRET OF OUR SUCCESS'

'All Black' Skipper Denies Charges of Unfair Play

Advantages of the Wing-forward and Five-eighth.

By D. Gallagher [sic] (the New Zealand Captain)

Perhaps next to our striking series of successes — which were due, to put it briefly to our superior condition, speed, and combination — perhaps the most remarkable thing about the tour was the criticism levelled at our scrum methods and formation and the much-discussed and unfortunate wing-forward. The outcry against the wing-forward assumed a very bitter tone in South Wales. People everywhere, naturally, criticised his methods, as he was an innovation, and he was occasionally accused of wilful obstruction. But on our arrival in South Wales it seemed as if the pent-up indignation of the whole race for years had been let loose on us, and on me particularly. The Welshmen have got a fixed idea in their minds that the wing-forward must be off-side directly he made a move — no matter how he went or where the ball was. The fact that he stood up close to the side of the scrum was apparently enough to disqualify him.

The controversy about the 'wing-forward' became complicated in South Wales by the introduction — mainly the work of ill-informed and irresponsible journalists, I will admit — of all the nonsense of my putting 'bias' on the ball when putting it into the scrum. The suggestion is ridiculous in the extreme. It is impossible to put 'bias' on a football when putting it into the scrum. I defy anyone to do it or to show me how it can be done. I would like to see any man — prejudiced or otherwise — put 'bias' on. If he does so, I will forfeit anything he likes to name. I am sure I could not do it — I have never tried, to tell the truth. Even if you put the ball in unfairly in the way suggested, there is nothing gained by it. The referee will simply blow his whistle, and give a free kick against you.

As to the much-abused wing-forward, a great deal of misapprehension exists, and has been fomented about him. If we had called him a 'half-back' we should have heard nothing about him — of that I am sure. But people imagined, because he was new to them, that a wing-forward was a terrible person with a double dose of original football sin. And what amused me throughout this phase of the bother was that nearly all of our opponents themselves played wing-forwards, although they called them 'halves.' They had one half who put the ball in and took it if it came out his side, and another half on the other side who did ditto if it came out there. That is practically playing two 'wings' but they were above suspicion, apparently, because they were called 'halves.'

Quick scrum work

No referee could accuse me throughout the tour of putting the ball in unfairly, or of putting 'bias' on it. I would be quite content to accept the verdict of such referees as Mr. Gil Evans or Mr. Percy Coles on the point. When I have been penalised in this connection, it has simply been due to the unfamiliarity of the referee with the quick work of our 'hookers' and 'heelers.' There were times when the scrum work was done so neatly and expeditiously that as soon as the ball had left my hands the forwards shoved over the top of it, and it was heeled out, and Roberts was off with it before you could say 'knife.' It was all over so quickly that almost everyone — the referee sometimes included — thought there was something unfair about it, some 'trickery,' and I was penalised. But directly a referee grew accustomed to the quickness of our scrum, he frankly admitted and realised that there was no 'trickery' and that the ball had not only been put in, but passed out fairly. People here have been accustomed, when the ball was put into the scrum to see it bobbing and wobbling about, and frequently never coming out in the proper way.

How can a man possibly put 'bias' on a ball if he rolls it into the scrum? The only way to put any screw on a ball would be, I should say, to throw it straight down shoulder high, on to its end, so that it may possibly bounce in the desired direction. I have never done that — in fact, it can't be done in the scrum

— and if I had ever attempted it I should have expected to be penalised immediately.

Another charge made against me in the Welsh press was that I threw the ball in against my own forwards' inside foot, so that it would bounce out and I could thus get it. Now, I deny that absolutely and emphatically. The ball certainly does frequently come out, on both sides, without having been properly in, and if it comes my side, I catch it and throw it to my half in a mechanical way, knowing full well that the referee's whistle will go. It is a bit of by-play that deceives no one, and in our case is accounted for by the fact that in New Zealand we are taught to play to the whistle. Until it sounds, the ball, technically, is in play.

It may, of course, conceivably happen that the whistle does not go under such circumstances, and in that case, we should enjoy a slight advantage, but it is also quite conceivable that, if I did not take the ball as it was kicked out, and my opposing half did seize it, the referee's whistle might just as easily remain silent, and where would the advantage rest then, do you suppose?

I have been jeered and hooted at over and over again for doing that which every other half in the country does every other day. Does the English or Welsh half, under similar circumstances, stop dead and wait for the whistle to go? It is conceivable that the referee — either through incapacity or inability to see properly (which frequently happens) — may be of opinion that the ball has properly entered the scrum, and decline to blow his whistle, although obviously he ought to have done so. What would my position be, then, if I had failed to gather the ball as it came out, and pass it? It is for the referee alone to say whether the ball has properly entered the scrum or not, and I play to his whistle, as every footballer ought to do. I am always one of the first to recognise the whistle and bow to it. And why should I be accused of 'dirty tricks' in doing this merely because I am called a wing-forward and not a half-back, I am at a loss to understand.

Advantage of the wing-forward

A great advantage of the wing-forward is his power, due to his upright attitude of immediately stopping play among the opposing backs — of nipping in the bud a hostile movement. He can watch the progress of the ball going out of the scrum much better, and directly it is out it is his province to pounce on the opposing half before it can get it away. It was this procedure — a perfectly legitimate one — which is practised more or less successfully by the ordinary half — which made the wing-forward unpopular more than anything else. Every time I sprang around the scrum to collar the opposing half, I was greeted in Wales with ugly, menacing cries of 'Play the game.' It is the wing-forward's constant care to keep behind the ball while doing this, and I need hardly say that, with such angry eyes continually upon me, and the referee's whistle always on his lips, I scrupulously tried to avoid any irregularity in this respect. Of course, I may sometimes have made a mistake in this respect, like any half-back frequently does, and overrun the ball. If I did so, and tackled the half before he got the ball, I was always the first to admit my mistake, and that I ought to be penalised. But this overrunning of the ball happens every day in the case of the ordinary Welsh or English or Irish or Scottish half. He also sometimes gets in front of the ball, in the mistaken belief that it is out of the scrum. There is this difference between us however: my mistake is supposed to be wilful, and is received with hoots and cries of 'Dirty game!' In the other case, the mistake —

in both cases due to over-eagerness — is allowed to pass without comment by the crowd; and the penalty kick is taken as a matter of course, and as an ordinary incident of the game.

I must confess that the unfair criticism to which I have been subjected, while in Wales especially, has annoyed me. For instance, what is one to say about the remarks of Mr. Livingstone, an ex-President of the Welsh Union, who is reported to have said that I played an 'absolutely dirty and unfair game'? The demonstrations against me at the Cardiff International and Swansea were altogether uncalled for, and were directly attributable to the utterances of presumable responsible officials, such as I have quoted. However, I shall try to forget them. I shall doubtless have a complete revenge if I ever visit England again in seeing that the Welsh Union has adopted the wing-forward game in all its nakedness, as they have already modified their back and scrum formation in keeping with ours — perhaps the greatest compliment that the New Zealanders have received during the tour.

I can quite understand how the wing-forward seemed an unnecessary sort of excrescence to the home players. The wing-forward, as we play it, is the embodiment of an idea, a system of play, which is new here. They stick to the style of the old halfback, who puts the ball in the scrum, and then runs around and picks it up as it comes out at the back. That antique method would be impossible with us. The New Zealand half (or wing-forward) after putting the ball in, could not possibly get round to the back of the scrum in time. Our scrum heels out too quickly for that.

The five-eighths formation

From what I have heard, wherever the New Zealand five-eighths formation has come under the notice of good judges of the game, it would not surprise me if some of the more progressive clubs and unions were to adopt this system over here. It has long been obvious to us in New Zealand that the five-eighths innovation affords two advantages — one of attack and the other of defence. In attack you have two men behind the scrum-half who can run round either side of the scrum, and thus develop an attack from either side through being so near to the scrum. They also are able to draw the defence before our three-quarters really get to work, and it frequently happens that the five-eighths have disposed of, say, two or even three of our opponents before the three-quarters are fairly in their stride. The centre-half may go right up to the opposing three-quarters before he gets rid of the ball. He draws one of the three-quarters and if he passes to the five-eighths they always have a chance of cutting through. If not, they can pass out to the three-quarters. With the ordinary three-quarter formation, there is scarcely sometimes enough room to work in the field. They jam each other onto the touch line.

The advantage of the double line of defence which the five-eighths and three-quarters supply is too obvious to need any elaboration.

Our opponents

Our hardest matches were the Scottish and Welsh Internationals. The Scottish match was played under exceptional circumstances — on hard, desperate ground, and it was a hard, desperate fight — a 'tough go' from start to finish. There was nothing much in the game either way, though I think we had just the best of it.

The only criticism that I feel at liberty to make with regards to English teams is concerning their three-quarters. The average three-quarter does not run straight enough. Instead of him running straight up to his opponent, he passes the ball before he reaches him, and his colleagues do the same, with the result that the spectacle is often seen of a beautiful exhibition of passing between the whole three-quarter line right across the field without a yard's advantage having been gained.

It seems to me that the three-quarter is much more dangerous, even if he fails five times out of six, when he tries to pierce the defence, by running straight. Even if he sees his way effectually barred five times, and he has to pass out, the sixth time he gets through, and a try ensues.

But this I will admit: the generality of the teams we have certainly dribble better than we do, especially the Scottish and Irish forwards. They keep the ball closer to their feet, and have more command over it. The loose passing rush also spelt danger to us.

The line kicking of the generality of the backs is also very good, and the Welsh teams shine particularly here. Winfield and Nicholls are models in this respect, and the former, especially in the International, saved his forwards a tremendous amount of work. They got into our territory almost every time by their splendid long kicking into touch.

I think that British teams generally might devote a little more time to training. In New Zealand we players go into the 'gym' two or three times in a week, purely for the love of the game, so that we can keep fit. We argue that if a game is worth playing, it is worth training for. A man cannot last a hard game out if he does not train. He must either train or crack up.

So far as the social side of the tour is concerned, we have been right royally treated, and we cannot say too much about it. It has been most agreeable wherever we have been — and nowhere more so than in Wales — and I only hope that I may be a party to a return of the abundant hospitality that we have received here when the Old Country sends her next fifteen to New Zealand.

Lying on the ball

I think the British Rugby Union might, with advantages to the game, alter or remodel some of the laws bearing upon the actual play. For instance, the law respecting lying on the ball in stopping a rush. In New Zealand, a 'penalty' is awarded if the player falls upon the ball and does not immediately take steps to get rid of it. He can go down to gather it, but he must not lie upon it.

In my opinion, the majority of cases of injury in this country are owing to a player deliberately lying upon the ball. He sustains his hurt through the opposing team rushing over him, and in the endeavour to get the ball away from him. Besides, lying on the ball stops the play and makes the game slower, as a scrum — and there are plenty already — nearly always ensues on these smothering tactics. There are times, of course, when you must go down to stop the ball; but in New Zealand, if after stopping the rush, the player does not immediately get away from the ball, the whistle goes for a free kick. It makes the game so much brighter.

‘Four more years, boys.’

— Wallaby halfback George Gregan’s sledge to All Blacks replacement halfback Byron Kelleher during the 2003 Rugby World Cup semi-final in which the Wallabies beat the All Blacks, 22–10.

McCAW, CARTER, COCKSEDGE

New Zealand Rugby's highest accolade for a player is the Kelvin R. Tremain Memorial Trophy, named after the outstanding Hawke's Bay and All Black flanker of the 1960s, who, when he had packed his big boots away, was a noted administrator (as Hawke's Bay Rugby Union chairman and an NZRU council member) and team manager.

Tremain's rugby-playing days began at Northcote Primary on Auckland's North Shore, and at secondary school he spent two years in the Auckland Grammar First XV. Upon leaving school he became an agriculture field cadet, studying at Massey and Lincoln universities. His provincial career is best known for his time in the great Hawke's Bay sides of the 1960s, but he also turned out for Southland, Manawatu, Canterbury and Auckland prior to that.

In 1959, he debuted for the All Blacks against the Lions, and went on to play a further 85 games for the men in black, including 38 tests in all.

Tremain was a naturally gifted player, with a great set of all-round skills that made him look almost omnipresent on the field. A prolific try-scorer, he dotted down 136 times in 268 first-class games.

Sadly, he succumbed to cancer in 1992 at the age of just 54, and the annual award for the best rugby player in New Zealand was named in his honour.

In 1971, an award for the New Zealand Rugby Personality of the Year was instituted by the Ponsonby Rugby Football Club. The first award dinner was held at the newly opened Mandalay cabaret in Newmarket, Auckland. Guest speakers included Des Connor (former Wallaby and All Black halfback), Tom Pearce (former NZRFU president), John Pring (who refereed the four tests against a touring Lions side in 1971) and J. P. R. Williams (the sensational Welsh fullback who starred for the victorious Lions).

Part of the proceeds from the evening went to the St John Ambulance Brigade, whose volunteers have very much been a part of Saturday rugby in New Zealand for decades. Tickets for the event were $10.

On the night, the first recipient of the award (voted for by a group of local rugby writers) was North Auckland, North Island, New Zealand Maori and All Black halfback Sid Going.

That same year the inaugural *New Zealand Rugby Annual* named its first Five Players of the Year (three of whom were Lions tourists — Mike Gibson, Barry John and J. P. R. Williams — along with Going and Colin Meads). The *New Zealand Rugby Almanack* has also named an annual selection of outstanding players since the 1930s, and continues to do so to this day.

*

In 1989, the first team of New Zealand women chosen by a national selection panel took to the field. Yet to be given the moniker of 'Black Ferns', they were called a New Zealand XV. Their opponents for the match in Christchurch, which they won 13–7: the California Grizzlies.

In the early 1990s, Laurie O'Reilly — a wonderful man who had coached the Canterbury women's team, was national selection convenor of the women's game in New Zealand, and held the position of Commissioner for Children — had the trans-Tasman women's trophy named after him. In the first few years of competition between the Wallaroos and the Black Ferns, the New Zealand women were utterly dominant, and interest in the trophy waned until picking up again in the mid-2000s.

The New Zealand domestic game continued to grow in terms of the overall playing numbers of women and thus teams representing their provinces. Players such as Anna Richards, Farah Palmer, Regina Sheck, Annaleah Rush, Louisa Wall, Monique Hirovanaa and Vanessa Cootes became nationally known as outstanding rugby players.

In 2016, Palmer, who captained the Black Ferns from 1997 to 2006, including three Women's Rugby World Cup (WRWC) titles, became the first woman on the New Zealand Rugby board. Palmer's was a hugely significant appointment given that the all-male governance of the game, stretching back over 120 years, was being increasingly questioned and criticised. That same year the Women's Provincial Championship was renamed the Farah Palmer Cup.

The following year the Fiao'o Fa'amausili Medal, named after the prolific try-scoring hooker who became the first Black Fern to attain 50 test caps, was introduced to the Farah Palmer Cup competition, with players earning points through the season to become player of the year.

Then 2018 saw one of the most momentous happenings in New Zealand rugby. The four nominees for the Tremain Trophy were announced and they included Black Ferns halfback 30-year-old Kendra Cocksedge, who had been World Rugby Women's Player of the Year in 2015, and is the highest points-scorer in New Zealand women's first-class rugby. The three men nominated were All Blacks Brodie Retallick, Richie Mo'unga and Codie Taylor.

Cocksedge wasn't the first woman nominated for the award. That honour had gone to the Black Ferns Sevens captain, Sarah

Goss, in 2017. That year the Black Ferns were crowned Team of the Year following their fifth WRWC triumph.

But when the 2018 winner was announced at the glitzy televised function held at Sky City, it was Cocksedge whose name had been added to a list that in recent years had included Andrew Hore, Chris Jack, Richie McCaw, Dan Carter, Jerome Kaino, Kieran Read, Beauden Barrett and Sam Whitelock.

An understandably stunned Cocksedge, who grew up in Taranaki but moved to Canterbury (don't they all!), later said that the award and recognition:

> ... means the world. The blood, sweat and tears that goes into putting on any type of jersey — when you win awards like this, it pays off. It's stepping stones that we are making here, and going forward we are going to keep paving the way in the women's game. I'm hoping that there is a young me out there somewhere watching and wanting to aspire to want to win an award like this in the future.

Acknowledgement of the women's game and the publicity generated by Cocksedge's honour reflects the continued rise in the women's game, as player numbers, particularly in schools, continue to rise, while player numbers in the men's game have been on a downward trend for some years.

International unions still seem to have some fiscal difficulty funding the elite female game and acknowledging those women as 'professional'. England, for instance, funded their top female players for one season, then claimed they couldn't afford to the next.

However, there is no doubt that other deserving female players will join Cocksedge's name on the Kelvin R. Tremain Trophy making a truism of the oft-quoted saying that rugby is 'the game for all New Zealand'.

'So for my mind, we just take the win — be happy about that because test wins are to be valued, be positive about the fact we didn't get any more big injuries and then flush the dunny and move on.'

— Steve Hansen after the 27-6 win against Italy in Christchurch in 2019, where the All Blacks really struggled to beat the determined visitors.

LETTERS TO THE EDITOR

In the 1970s, arguments over sporting contact with South Africa were a constant, but they became more passionate as the brutal suppression of anti-apartheid protestors in the township of Soweto became a major human rights issue and the focus of much international attention. Despite an unofficial but widely recognised international sporting embargo, rebel rugby and cricket tours from a number of nations were undertaken, and individual players were invited to be part of World XVs for exhibition matches or to celebrate anniversaries of South African provincial teams. Tanzania boycotted the 1976 Montréal Olympics, pointing to the All Blacks' controversial tour of apartheid South Africa as one of the reasons for doing so. Twenty-seven other African nations followed suit.

The following letters, both for and against players visiting the Republic, are from the *8 O'clock* newspaper, August 1977:

> We asked readers whether they think the All Blacks invited as individuals to play in South Africa should go there in view of Tanzania's latest athletics boycott threat. Here's what they say ...
>
> 'Many men from NZ fought in the two world wars for individual rights. Thousands gave their lives, many others their health. Are their efforts just to be brushed aside? Rugby players have as much right as anyone else to go where they

want to. Because they're All Blacks, they're being singled out by Tanzania to put more pressure on the government. I truly admire Tane Norton and the other players — they want to play only football, not politics.'
— Mrs B.A., Mt Roskill (Best letter winner, $10)

'Bruce Robertson [who had toured South Africa with the All Blacks in 1976 but returned disenchanted with the bias of referees and appalled by the apartheid system, so much so he refused to play the 1981 Springboks] spoke for thousands of Kiwis when he flatly refused to accept the invitation to South Africa. Every sportsman or sportswoman is being put on the line for the few who are supposedly just exercising their human rights. Seeing that South Africans can live with apartheid, why don't we just leave them to their own consciences?'
— Mrs S.R., Mt Albert

'The government has no right interfering in sport and less right to interfere with the affairs of other countries, especially South Africa. Instead of being concerned about a lump of leather being booted around a park, what about doing something about the rapes, murders, robberies, road deaths, vandals and housing shortages here in NZ?'
— T.M., Herne Bay

'I cling to the belief that friendship and world peace can be achieved only by the intermingling of ordinary persons of all countries in culture and sport. Sport should be divorced from politics — the rights and beliefs of the individual are paramount.'
— Mrs E.T., New Plymouth

'Since Rob Muldoon did a left wheel at Gleneagles the Africans won't let us off the hook. They'll always want us as their pet bunny. So my answer to Mr Sarakikya of Tanzania is that Kiwi citizens have rights, too — as well as black Africans.'
— A.M., Matamata

'It is not the Government's place to tell these rugby players where to play, but the Rugby Union's. It's a lot of bunk that players will be going as individuals. They'll still be classed as NZ representatives. NZ people are not one-eyed as many Rugby followers are.'
— Mr A.C., Newton

'Our young men should be allowed to go to South Africa to play the game of their choice. They should not be blackmailed again by the black African nations — not now that what they were squealing about, integrated sport, has been introduced.'
— Mrs G.G., Lower Hutt

'Sport is something we do well at. When it comes to meddling in other countries' affairs we run a poor last. Let our sportsmen and women travel freely without intervention from Government or protest groups. We shouldn't lose any sleep over Tanzania's boycott threat. Their only path to fame was carved out by a bloke called Filbert 'Whatshisname'.'
— T.G., Henderson

'On tour, All Blacks become a complete side through eating, drinking and thinking rugby and as a consequence, in my time, most of our finest rugby has been played overseas. That's why I was so delighted on this occasion. I cannot recall any All Black team sustaining a level of performance like that for a full 80 minutes.'

— All Black captain Graham Mourie after his side had beaten Australia 33–18 in front of 52,000 at Eden Park, September 1982. Fullback Allan Hewson scored a then world-record 26 points, including a massive dropped goal from halfway

RUGBY AND RACING

Rugby players and coaches have been well-known for their interest in horse racing, be it popping into the TAB with a copy of the *Best Bets* tucked into their back pockets to lay a few bets, or actually owning horses as part of syndicates.

Steve Hansen grew up in a family that bred and trained gallopers. When a boy, Hansen dreamed of becoming a jockey. He has had financial interests in a number of horses over the years, including being part-owner (1/15) in a lightning-fast horse named Nature Strip and another called Theanswermyfriend. Just like rugby players, horses have their good and bad days, which can delight and frustrate their coaches and trainers.

Similarly, former All Blacks coach John Hart has had interests in gallopers and pacers, although there was some notoriety attached to his horse Holmes D. G. running in the New Zealand Trotting Cup at Addington in 1999. The All Blacks had just lost their Rugby World Cup semi-final to France, after which Hart resigned, but some of the reactions to that loss by All Blacks fans were appalling. According to Hart, 'One guy spat in my face. They threw beer cans at my horse when he went out on the track.'

Taranaki wing, farmer and 1914 All Black captain Dick Roberts was well-known around the country as a racehorse owner, as was his teammate Thomas Fisher, who had been Buller's second All Black.

Bill Hazlett, a fast and strong loose-forward for the All Blacks in the 1920s, was the first gallops trainer to clock up 1000 wins as an owner. The Southlander's horses dominated the winners' lists (by owner) in the late 1960s.

Another Southland identity, Robin Archer, who played for the All Blacks in the mid-1950s, was honoured with Life Membership of the New Zealand Thoroughbred Breeders' Association, and his silks were based on his Pioneers club's colours.

Canterbury front-row forward Jack Bond, a one-test All Black in 1949 after having played with the 'Kiwis' army team at the end of World War II, was an owner and breeder. So, too, Manawatu's Alphonsus 'Phonse' Carroll, who hooked for the All Blacks at the start of the 1920s, and five-test Canterbury lock from the 1950s George Dalzell. (The Whitelock brothers — George, Adam, Sam and Luke — are his grandsons.)

Proud product of Patea in south Taranaki, loose-forward Alistair Scown played five tests for the All Blacks from 1972 to 1973 and later had a racehorse stud farm.

Ten-test second five-eighth of the late 1980s and early 1990s Bernie McCahill was known to like a flutter on the horses. No surprise really, given that his Irish-born father, Barney, had interests in a number of horses that were punters' favourites, such as Castletown, McGinty, Mickey's Town and Irish Rover.

The small Canterbury All Black wing of the early 1920s, William Ford, was given the nickname 'Jockey', but champion All Black wing and holder of sprint titles in three countries at the start of the 1900s, George Smith, had actually been a jockey prior to his rugby career. As a teenager he had ridden the winner of the Autumn Handicap at Ellerslie, a horse called Impulse.

Hohepa Jacob, the All Black and New Zealand Maori loose-forward of the 1920s who had made his first-class debut for

Horowhenua aged just 16, was custodian at Otaki race course for many years.

Then there are the horses that have been named after All Blacks. Pinetree was a popular galloper in the early 1970s, and Christian Cullen (named, with permission, after the super-quick All Black fullback) was one of the greatest pacers this country has produced, winning an incredible 22 of 31 starts.

Former champion driver-turned-trainer Mark Jones has had several pacers with All Black-influenced names: Saveapatrol (Julian Savea), Zacspatrol (Zac Guildford) and Izzy Dagg. Israel Dagg and his wife, Daisy, joined the world of ownership syndicates when Jones found the right horse for them. The horse was just starting his career as the World Cup-winning fullback was winding down his, due to ongoing injuries.

‘Was it a punch? Did he hit the ground with his jaw? Did he hit the corner flag with his jaw? We don’t know. We didn’t see it. Your Waka Nathan had his jaw broken twice in British tours. It was an accident, certainly, when it was broken against Llanelli, so this is an accident now.’

— 1969 Welsh manager, Handel Rogers, after his team’s hooker, Jeff Young, left the field with a broken jaw during the first test. Privately, there were mutterings that Young’s jaw had hit Colin Meads’s fist after the Welshman was holding back Ken Gray.

‘We’re not playing tiddlywinks here, mate.’

— Hurricanes captain Tana Umaga to referee Peter Marshall during the 2003 semi-final against the Crusaders. Umaga had, incorrectly, been adjudged to have made a high tackle on Dan Carter.

DEATHS AND INJURIES

There can be no argument that rugby union is a dangerous game, and has been from its very inception. The sport involves the collision of bodies, which in all positions are now vastly bigger than the physiques of players when the game was first played in New Zealand in the 1870s.

Broken bones have always been a by-product of rugby. For many years, when the game was based around forwards dribbling the ball, shins were cracked and snapped. Shoulders, too, were dislocated frequently. Lifting a tackled player and dumping him on the ground was seen as an example of fine, strong tackling. Many are the artistic representations of action during football games where players are depicted held aloft, about to be thrown to the ground.

Newspaper readers around the country, but particularly those in Auckland, closely followed the 1877 inquest into the death of a Parnell player by the name of Pilling. He died as the result of 'concussion of the spine' suffered in a game against Ponsonby on one of the fields at the Auckland Domain.

Pilling, ball in arm, had driven head-first into a group of Ponsonby players and reeled back, collapsing on the ground. Teammates immediately tried to lift him up. On the advice of a doctor he was taken, not to the nearby Auckland city hospital, but to his residence in Parnell. (The house, strangely enough, was owned by a woman with the very rugby name of Mrs Ruck!)

Pilling's condition seemed to stabilise, although he complained of having no feeling in his legs. Then, when someone tried to move him in the bed, to which he protested loudly, 'he fell into a fit, which lasted about three minutes, at which he then expired'.

Newspapers reported that following his death 'many spoke strongly in reprehension of the dangerous game which had cost a valuable life'. Injuries to players such as broken collarbones, shins and even thigh bones were noted. Suggestions made by the inquest panel included that the rules of rugby should be changed to be more in line with association football (i.e. soccer) to prevent such deaths in future.

*

This societal discussion and concern about the roughness of the game was not restricted to New Zealand. In 1889, the famous English humour and satire magazine *Punch* published a poem about the injuries that can be sustained playing football using either an oval or round ball. It was reprinted in many New Zealand newspapers.

FOOTBALL À LA MODE

A manly game it is, I think,
Although in private be it spoken,
While at a scrimmage I don't shrink,
That bones may be too often broken.
I snapped my clavicle last week,
Just like the rib of an umbrella;
And sprained my ankle, not to speak
Of something wrong with my patella.
Last season too, my leg I broke,
And lay at home an idle dreamer.

It's not considered quite a joke,
To contemplate a broken femur.
And when, despite the doctor's hints,
Again at football I had tussles,
I found myself once more in splints.
With damaged gastronemic muscles;
Some three times every week my head
is cut, contused, or sorely shaken;
My friends expect me brought home dead,
But up to now I've saved my bacon.
But what are broken bones, my boys,
Compared with noble recreation,
The scrimmages and all the joys,
Of Rugby or Association?

Some businesses in New Zealand threatened to fine workers who had time off as a result of football injuries. A Christchurch footballer reportedly died as the result of 'over training'.

There were off-field dangers, too. Workplace accidents in the late 1800s claimed many lives each year, and it was not unknown for football teams to fail to field teams due to the death of a player. In 1891, a club team from Thames, the Wanderers, were due to travel to Auckland to play Ponsonby, but they had to cancel the match as their fullback had died.

*

Three All Blacks have died from injuries received on the footy field.

The first, in 1899, was Otago's Alexander 'Barney' Armit. He was paralysed after being tackled by his 1897 All Black teammate Taranaki's Alf Bayly. He passed away three months later.

In 1932, Bert Palmer, a front-row forward from Auckland (who had played 18 games, including three tests for the All Blacks, since debuting in 1928), died in hospital the day after breaking his neck in a club game.

Nicky Allen only played nine games including two tests for the All Blacks, all in 1980. But he remains regarded as one of the most naturally gifted five-eighths New Zealand has produced. The greatest of the players who have worn the number 10 jersey seem, like the greatest batsmen in cricket, to have a lot of time with which to kick, pass or run. Allen was one of those multi-skilled players, and those who saw him playing for the All Blacks on the centenary tour to Wales, and especially the test match at Cardiff Arms Park, wondered just which planet he had arrived from.

From his rugby days at Auckland Grammar School (where he first began to have issues with concussion), he had been marked for a great future, although some thought his left-arm pace bowling might see him have a long career in the summer game.

Allen opted for rugby, but, for one reason or another, wasn't a player who seemed to settle in one place for very long. He was chosen for the All Blacks having played for Counties, after moving south from his home province of Auckland, for whom he had notched up two seasons.

Then with the rugby world at his feet and great expectations falling on this new superstar of the All Black game, he shuffled off to Australia after sitting out all of the 1981 season due to a knee injury.

Allen returned to Auckland in 1983 and was chosen for the blue-and-white hoops in their centenary year, but then went back across the Tasman the following year.

In 1984, playing club rugby in Wollongong, Allen was tackled and his head crashed against the hard, dry surface. Rushed to hospital, he had a brain bleed and remained in a coma. Tragically, his life-support system was turned off on 7 October and his body returned to Auckland for burial.

*

There is also the sad story of Aaron Hopa, the dynamic loose-forward with a 'mullet' haircut from Waikato. He made four appearances for the All Blacks on the 1997 end-of-year tour to Britain and Ireland, and was in the wider training group preparing themselves to compete for selection for the 1999 Rugby World Cup.

In December 1998, Hopa was with a small group of Waikato Chiefs players and another man, completing their diving instruction on the eastern side of Slipper Island, off the Coromandel coast. Having been successfully practising an emergency ascent, upon resurfacing Hopa lost consciousness. He passed away shortly after the boat they were on reached the wharf at Whangamata. The big prospect was aged just 27.

The coroner's inquest into his death described it as 'bad luck', with speculation that Hopa may have had a weak lung as the result of a sporting injury.

*

It is somewhat remarkable to think that it is only this century that rugby's lawmakers and governing bodies have become united in their concern about head injuries. Mind you, it was the 1980s before the All Blacks had a doctor or physiotherapist travel with them. Even having ice available to be applied to the knocks and sprains that players suffered was considered something of a luxury.

Many are the stories of rugby players, at all levels, being knocked out or dazed and carrying on playing once they had been revived by sniffing smelling salts or having cold water splashed on their face. But when the 1913 All Blacks played in North America a player died as the result of a head knock.

During the match against Victoria British Columbia, the home side's fullback Peter Ogden was knocked out early in the first half. Attempting to stop an All Black forward rush, he copped a knee to the side of the head and flopped lifelessly to the ground. It was several minutes before he regained consciousness and was able to stand up. A number of those attending to him suggested he leave the field, but he insisted that he could play on.

At half-time, he obviously wasn't 'right', so the All Black captain Alex McDonald urged the Victoria captain to replace his injured player. Ogden again resisted any attempts to have him retire from the game. When play resumed, he was concussed again. He continued to play, but to all observers he did look decidedly dazed.

Two minutes before the game ended, he was tackled by All Black loose-forward James Douglas and both men crashed to the ground. Douglas quickly got up and followed play, but Ogden lay prone on the ground for the third time. He was taken to the dressing room where a medic diagnosed 'severe concussion of the brain'. The enquiring All Blacks were told he was slowly coming around again. On the contrary, he was slowly dying.

At 7 pm, All Black manager George Mason was advised that Ogden had died. According to one All Black: 'All festivities were, of course, abandoned, the sad and sudden calamity casting a gloom over the whole city.'

Jim Douglas was particularly disturbed by the news, and had the very unnerving experience of having to remain in the city for several days to attend a coroner's inquest into Ogden's death.

*

In June 1917, at a Christchurch club game between Marist and Linwood it was reported that *eight* players had been knocked out in a ferocious match.

Seven years later, in 1924, future All Black captain Jock Richardson copped a boot to the head early in the North versus South game at Athletic Park, which noticeably affected his play. For example, at one point he fielded the ball and then just stood still. This allowed the chasing North Island winger to make an easy tackle on the big loose-forward from Southland. After the match, Richardson told a member of the press that he could remember his captain, Arnold Perry (who later became a rugby doctor), giving him a quick check. 'From then on till the bell rang out at half-time my mind was a blank. The bell brought me back to life, and when I looked and saw the score was 25 to nil against us, I was the most surprised man on the field.'

Only since 2012 have there been strict protocols for team doctors to follow when treating players who have suffered head knocks. Increasing numbers of top-level players are having time away from the game to recover from repeated concussions. Sports writer Dylan Cleaver of *The New Zealand Herald* has written a number of articles highlighting the suspected links between head knocks suffered in rugby and the onset of dementia and depression later in life.

*

In the third test against the 1950 Lions at Wellington, there was a uniquely unfortunate occurrence. Both the All Black captain and vice-captain sustained serious injuries that not only saw them out of the match but out of top-class rugby completely.

All Black prop and vice-captain Johnny Simpson — a World War II veteran and member of the Kiwis army team — suffered a serious knee injury with less than a quarter of the match played. Known as 'Iron Man', he reluctantly left the field, leaving his team, in the days before replacements, a man down.

Then, with about seven minutes left to play in the first half, Dr Ron Elvidge, the outstanding midfield back from Otago who was captaining the side, suffered a serious cut to his face and injured his ribs and collarbone. He looked distinctly uncomfortable as he, too, left the field aided by a zambuck. ('Zambuck' was the nickname for St John medical staff and volunteers who would be present at rugby games. Their uniforms and ambulances were black and white, the same colours as a brand of ointment called Zam-buck.)

As the match progressed, the 13 remaining All Blacks were hanging on for dear life, but the score was only 3-all. Loose-forward Peter Johnstone moved out to the wing to provide cover in the backs, meaning a two-man advantage for the Lions in the forwards.

Then around the ground the crowd rose to their feet as Elvidge returned to the field, head bandaged, one arm visibly very limp. He made his way to the wing and, looking in pain and somewhat disoriented, seemed to be there acting merely as an All Blacks scarecrow, hoping that the mere sight of a man in a black jersey might be a deterrent to any attacking play from the Lions wings.

Then the All Blacks went on the attack. The ball was sent along the backline. There to take the last pass was Elvidge, a few metres from the line. In a tackle that made most of the crowd wince, he barrelled over the line for the winning score. Had an All Black captain ever suffered so much for his team before?

Elvidge's time in the black jersey ended after just 19 matches, including nine tests, and he then devoted himself to his medical career. At the time of his death aged 96 in March 2019, he was the oldest former All Black.

Simpson's injury brought an end to his All Black career after 30 matches, including nine internationals.

Both men are considered among the best to have played in their respective positions, and for years after they retired, punters and journalists would wonder how different things might have been had they not been injured and continued playing the game at the highest level.

*

There weren't many players naturally fitter than William Ngataiawhio Gray. Bill, as he was known, had been a New Zealand Maori junior tennis champion, and first played for Bay of Plenty aged 17. He made his debut for the All Blacks five years later, and was a key backline figure in the 1956 series against the Springboks, in which he played all four tests. In that series, he tackled his heart out and was also the subject of some very bruising tackling from the visitors, who had initially thought that the All Blacks' inside backs may have been a weak point to exploit. Gray certainly proved that wasn't the case.

In 1957, he toured Australia with the All Blacks, and was back across the Tasman the following year with the New Zealand Maori. On that tour he badly broke his leg. The medical specialists' prognosis in the days after he sustained the complicated injury were not good, with amputation a distinct possibility. Playing rugby again would be highly unlikely, they said.

There was no way Bill, only in his mid-20s, was going to say goodbye to the game he loved. To keep fit and rebuild the strength in his leg, legend has it he went deer-stalking — while he still had the leg in plaster!

In 1959, he was back on the field, not just for his club, but also playing rep football for the combined Bay of Plenty–Thames Valley team that gave the Lions a hell of a fright before being pipped 24–26.

After his injury, Gray didn't add to his tally of 11 games for the All Blacks, but he did turn out for the Bay until 1966.

*

Bryan 'Beegee' Williams (now Sir) was the poster player for the All Blacks in the 1970s. (Indeed, the author had a poster of him on his wall.) He was later named Player of the Decade. Williams had pace, determination, a much-imitated side-step and powerful thighs, the sight of which apparently made women swoon!

A constant presence in the All Blacks since first selected to tour South Africa as a 19-year-old in 1970, in 1977 he badly dislocated his hip in the second test against France at Toulouse (won by the hosts, 18–13). Ankle-tapped as he headed for a try near the corner-flag, he crashed into the turf causing the ball of his femur bone to pop out of the hip joint.

The medical treatment offered at the time was far from satisfactory, Williams being told by a French medic that he would probably still be able to run on it! It was through the repeated insistence of his wife, Leslie, and teammate Lawrie Knight (who was a doctor) that the great winger was taken to hospital to be operated on. Had he been taken back to the team hotel, as the French liaison officer had suggested, the worst-case scenario was that he would have lost his leg due to the lack of blood flow.

Fortunately, Williams returned to play for the All Blacks on their 1978 Grand Slam tour, finishing with 113 games for his country, 38 of them tests.

Later a co-coach of Auckland (with Maurice Trapp) and coach of Samoa, Williams was a key figure in the Pacific Islanders securing their first-ever test match against the All Blacks, in 1993. Beegee is never far from a footy field, but that hip has given him a lot of gip over the years, and been surgically replaced a couple of times.

*

One of the real hard-luck stories of 'what might have been' centres on Jasin Goldsmith. The outside back had been a star for the New Zealand Secondary Schools team in 1987 and the New Zealand Under-19 side. His debut for Waikato came when he was aged only 17 and still attending Forest View High School. A year later he became the third-youngest All Black when, on the 1988 tour of Australia, he made his debut against Western Australia, scoring two tries. In all he played eight games on tour, playing at fullback, wing and centre. He was possessed of electrifying pace, with the ability to step off either foot and swerve effortlessly past defenders. Of solid build, he was also a fearless tackler.

After clocking up 24 games for Waikato, he moved north of the Bombays to join the Ponsonby club, and was immediately included in the Auckland squad. Then tragedy struck. On a sunny April afternoon at Eden Park, where Auckland were playing Canterbury in the South Pacific Championship, in a tackle that seemed no different from thousands of others, Goldsmith suffered a reported six fractures in one of his legs. The crowd at the ground (of which the author was one) didn't immediately realise the gravity of the injury, until play was held up for some time as the young man was stretchered from the field. It was just his second game for Auckland.

Goldsmith did return to rugby the following year, making the New Zealand Colts, but the injury had affected his speed, and to a lesser extent his agility when running. He dropped out of the game in 1991 then made a brief comeback for Bay of Plenty in 1993.

Given that while Goldsmith was recuperating, two All Black fullbacks (John Gallagher and Matthew Ridge) fell to the lure of huge cheques waved by league scouts, he would surely have cemented his place in the 15 jersey for the men in black. Still, what we did see of his natural talent remains vivid in the memory.

*

With nearly an hour gone in the second test against Argentina at Athletic Park in 1989, All Black team doctor John 'Doc' Mayhew heard a loud crack from the field and saw star flanker, 23-year-old Michael Jones, fall to the ground. Jones had attempted to toe the ball on just as an Argentine player dropped down on it. His left leg trapped, Jones's body turned one way while his lower leg stayed where it was. Everybody who saw him fall to the ground felt his pain. The gravity of the situation increased when he tried to stand and couldn't. It looked like a very serious knee injury.

Jones recalled:

> I thought I could click it into place, but then the deep pain came. Like my whole body aching. The nerves were all broken in that part of my leg ... this was dull, excruciating pain. This was quickly followed by thinking it would be all right and I could get moving again. But I couldn't move it.

Mayhew was quickly on the field, and many will recall the images of Jones being carried off Athletic Park. Remarkably, one might think, Jones wasn't taken immediately to hospital. He went back to the team hotel and returned to Auckland the following morning to be seen by world-class sports-injury orthopaedic surgeon Barry Tietjens. There had been a complete dislocation of the knee joint, with only one of four knee ligaments left working! Surgery had to be undertaken immediately.

Doc Mayhew had never seen a rugby injury so severe, nor had the team physiotherapist, David Abercrombie.

Quietly, there were fears Jones might never play the game again, or, if he did, only at the lower levels. In years gone by there would have been no doubt that it was a career-ending injury.

Making it back to play at international level would be something of a miracle. Well, Jones was a man of both prayer and great determination. Sports medicine had also advanced greatly.

Fourteen months later, after an injury akin to leg trauma associated with motor-vehicle accidents, Jones returned to the field for Auckland and made the All Blacks touring group for the end-of-year trip to France.

*

The late, great Jerry Collins — who tragically died in a car accident in France in 2015, aged just 34 — was as tough as they come. The Wallabies' nickname for him was 'Granite'. Legend has it he had the biggest biceps of any man to pull on the black jersey. But look at the list of injuries he had suffered while playing the game:

Both clavicles (collarbones) broken, with the left one being broken twice.

Ribs broken on both sides.

Broken finger and thumb on opposite hands.

AC joint (where collarbone meets shoulder bone) popped twice on both shoulders. Later, he had to have keyhole surgery on his right shoulder.

Multiple concussions.

The worst injury was the breaking of the fibula and tibia (the two long bones in the lower leg) in his right leg while playing just his sixth NPC game for Wellington. There is a story that as he was taken from the field, the Wellington physio, Glenn Muirhead, told Collins to squeeze his hand if the pain became too intense. Collins nearly crushed Muirhead's hand.

A year after making a full recovery and debuting for the All Blacks, he had to have further surgery to have the remedial metal rod removed from under his knee. Unfortunately, the bones had grown around the metal, making the surgery more involved than anticipated.

In 2007, he was carted off Jade Stadium while playing for the Hurricanes. With a neck brace on as he arrived back in Wellington, he looked to have suffered a serious, possibly career-ending injury. Not Jerry. He was back on the field in a couple of weeks.

*

In the lead-up to the Rugby World Cup in 2011, several of the more vocal rugby writers in New Zealand were proclaiming that the days of Richie McCaw as an All Black and captain should be over. It was considered that he was past his best, and that it was time for him to make way for somebody else, because we wouldn't be able to win the cup for the first time in 24 years if Richie was on the park.

How wrong the great flanker proved them. But what's more, in much the same spirit as Ron Elvidge back in 1950, McCaw led from the front while injured. Not that many people knew he was suffering from a fracture in a bone in his foot and deliberately delaying surgery so he could play in the tournament. The injury was so tender and would get so inflamed that he wouldn't take his boots off at half-time, for fear that the freed foot would suddenly swell and he wouldn't be able to get his boot on again.

Add in the fact that in the nerve-racking final against France it looked as though he had been eye-gouged at one point, the skipper (who was regularly a target for knees, elbows, foreheads and other niggles) put his body on the line for his team and country … and then played for another four years to lead the All Blacks to a back-to-back victory at the next Rugby World Cup. It makes you wonder just who really is 'past it' sometimes, the players or the media?

‘The whole of the stadium was *mal* [angry] with him. It’s just that I decided to do something about it. Referees around the world think they are bigger than the game and they’re not. Fans like me is what rugby is about.’

— an unrepentant Pieter van Zyl who ran on to the field during the All Blacks’ 2002 test against South Africa in Durban and attacked Irish referee Dave McHugh. Van Zyl was tackled by Richie McCaw and Springbok AJ Venter, but not before McHugh’s shoulder had been dislocated. The beer-bellied bozo left the field with a bloody nose and the infamy of possibly being the only person McCaw ever punched on a rugby field.

‘Blood on the ball, boys! I want blood on the ball.’

— debut halfback Mark Donaldson prior to the match against French Selection at Brive, 1977.

'THE HALF-BACK'S SWEETHEART'

Ernest L. Eyre was a journalist and poet, who in his younger years early in the 20th century moved around the lower North Island working for a number of newspapers. He later reviewed books, particularly collections of poems, in a regular newspaper column.

THE HALF-BACK'S SWEETHEART, 1920

There's a dainty little maiden, who is dressed in navy blue;
She is Rugby's chief supporter on the line;
If the forwards get a move on, or the backs come dashing through,
The way she yells encouragement is fine.
When the winter wind is blowing golden curls about her brow
She'll stand for hours and barrack till she's dumb;
She's the heroine of Rugby, and I'll introduce you now
To the sweetheart of the man behind the scrum.
She has always liked old Rugby, for her boy's a clever half,
And she follows up the game just like the men;
When her rivals barrack round her she can take her share of chaff,
But she mostly gets the last word back again!
She is generous when winning; as a loser she's a toff;
For when the beaten lads are looking glum,
You'll never hear excuses that the team's a trifle 'off,'

From the girl behind the man behind the scrum.
In her pretty sporting costume she is famous wide and far
What would Rugby be without the gentle sex?
For her sake the boys take chances, for a reckless crew
they are;
When they know she's on the line they'll risk their necks.
They will gather in the leather with will, and fairly blaze
With brilliance, as along the field they come;
They will rush opponents gamely just to earn a word of praise,
From the sweetheart of the man behind the scrum.
When she's settled down and married to her lover, will she
dream
And remind him of the days when he was proud
To win the captain's compliments, the goodwill of the team
And the confidence and cheering of the crowd?
But, where'er she is, I'm certain, she will nobly play the part
As wife and mother, loyal to her chum,
For the Queen of Rugby football, with a jewel for a heart
Is the girl behind the man behind the scrum.

'Looking at it now, I'd have to say New Zealand rugby was far more robust and physical in 1956. Maybe that was because there was a stronger farmer element in your provincial rugby teams then, where today [1981] there are probably more professional men playing the game. I guess the men playing rugby here today could be described as being more sophisticated.'

— Dr Johan Claassen, manager of the 1981 Springboks, who played on the 1956 tour of New Zealand.

RUGBY SONGS

There has never been a great tradition of singing at rugby games in this country. The closest we seem to come to rivalling choruses of the stirring Welsh anthem 'Hen Wlad Fy Nhadau' ('Land of My Fathers') or Ireland's passionate lament 'The Fields of Athenry' are drunken late-night hakas by Kiwis on their OE in London. At least we haven't appropriated an African-American spiritual to sing at our 'home of rugby' …

We did have something of an enduring rugby anthem, though, in 'On the Ball'. It was written by Edward Secker, an accountant from Palmerston North. Secker was captain of the 1885 Manawatu rugby side, which had a shocker of a year. Not only did they not win an inter-union game all season, they didn't even score a point. Still, this didn't dull Secker's enthusiasm for the game, and two years later he wrote the song, based on the tune of an old English fox-hunt chorus. The first rendition was sung as Secker and teammates travelled to Wanganui for a match. After finalising the music, and with interest from a publishing house, the song, describing the play of the time and themes of Victorian Christianity, became a 'hit'.

A year later, the New Zealand 'Native' rugby tourists were singing the song after their matches in Australia and England, which lead to it spreading, in several versions, around the United Kingdom. In New Zealand, up until World War II, the song was very popular with supporters travelling to games or celebrating wins in pubs after matches.

As late as the turn of this century, the author heard a regular elderly caller to a sports talkback programme sing part of the song.

ON THE BALL

Oh, some talk of Cricket and some of Lacrosse,
Some long for the Huntsman's loud call.
But where can be found such a musical sound,
As the old Rugby cry 'On The Ball!'

Chorus:
'On the ball! On the ball! On the ball!'
Thro' scrummage, three quarters and all
Sticking together we keep on the leather,
And shout as we go 'On The Ball!'

On a cold wintry day, when the ball is away,
Let sluggards at home then remain
We'll kick and we'll follow, we'll run pass and collar
As we shout the same merry refrain:
(Chorus)

This life's but a scrummage we cannot get through,
But with many a kick and a blow
And then in the end, tho' we dodge and we fend,
Still that sure collar 'Death' takes us low:
(Chorus)

But although brought down, there remains still a chance,
To pass, if we play the right game,

And the poor weary soul may at last win that Goal,
Which is ev'ry true footballer's aim:
(Chorus)

Remember then boys, as we journey through life,
There's a Goal to be reached bye and bye
And he who runs true why he's bound to get through,
And perhaps kick a Goal from his try:
(Chorus)

As the game with the oval ball became *the* winter game, and New Zealand's rugby footballers developed a winning reputation, amateur and professional musicians and composers celebrated the game in song.

When Dave Gallaher's 'Original All Blacks' team arrived back from their triumphant 1905–06 tour 'Home', songsmiths wrote rousing tunes to salute them. These were often sung as part of club 'smoker' nights, when a programme of recitals, both sung and spoken by club members or invited local performers, were the entertainment for the evening.

*

From the 1920s to until shortly after World War II, the number of published rugby songs declined. Perhaps they were seen as a bit quaint or old-fashioned when compared with exciting new international musical styles such as jazz and swing.

Then rugby songs changed in nature, from being rousing, patriotic and very serious in their praise of our footballing heroes to being much more light-hearted, tongue-in-cheek, satirical and even political.

In 1960, the Howard Morrison Quartet's reworking of the famous English skiffle song by Lonnie Donegan 'My Old Man's a Dustman' to 'My Old Man's an All Black' comically addressed the very serious issue of players of Maori descent not being allowed to tour South Africa. There had been widespread protest, with the catch-cry 'No Maoris — No Tour' being the dominant slogan. (That the NZRFU capitulated to the wishes of their South African counterparts remained a blot on the union and its attitudes, until an apology was extended to affected players by the South African government and the South African and New Zealand rugby unions in 2010.)

Quartet member Gerry Merito (whom the author had the pleasure to meet not long before his passing in 2008) was a small man with a big smile and a natural cheekiness. Hence some of his lyrics:

> Oh, my old man's an All Black,
> He wears the silver fern,
> But his mates just couldn't take him
> So he's out now for a turn.
> (Fi Fi Fo Fum, there's no Horis in this scrum.)
> Well the All Black team is leaving
> And the best of luck to them
> And if they find things tricky
> They'll have to play like men
> Cos the Springboks will be watching from Transvaal to
> Cape Town
> That team that ain't got Horis
> To score their last touch-down.

The most prolific musical satirist of New Zealand sport and culture during the 1950s and 1960s was Rod Derrett. Best known for 'Rugby, Racing and Beer' (with its catchy chorus of 'Down under they're mad over / their rugby, racing and beer'), many of the Christchurch schoolteacher's songs were parodies of popular songs, given a New Zealand setting. This was in the same vein as the hugely popular American parodist Allan Sherman, whose 'party record' sold by the truckload around the world.

One of Derrett's best rugby spoofs, lyrically, was 'The Local Football Ground', sung to the tune of 'Quartermaster's Stores'.

THE LOCAL FOOTBALL GROUND

My view is blocked, I cannot see
I'm wedged in tight and can't get free
Some great ox is standing in front of me.

There were cars, cars
stacked with food and jars
at the park, at the park.
There were jams, jams
with buses, bikes and prams
at the local football park.
There were scores more
queued up the night before
at the park, at the park.
And they froze, froze
in cold and icy clothes
at the local football park.

Some with sense, sense
climbed across the fence
at the park, at the park.
We were deaf, deaf

screaming, 'Lynch the ref!'
at the local football park.
There was smog, smog
lots of kiwi grog
at the park, at the park.
Oh, the grief, grief
dying for relief!
At the local football park.

Our view is blocked we curse and cuss
we're wedged in tight but do we fuss
when big blokes are standing in front of us?

There were tries, tries,
stale pies and flies
at the park, at the park.
There were fists, knees
lots of penalties
at the local football park.
What a roar, roar,
it ended up a draw
at the park, at the park.
What a brawl, brawl
But really worth it all
at the local football park.

Into the 1970s, rugby anthems again became more earnest, and proved that songs written by people who haven't played top-level sport attempting to sound as though they *have* played top-level sport, or are chest-poundingly proud in their lyrics, usually come off sounding too 'try-hard'.

Exempt from that, however, would be Murray Grindlay's 'Give 'Em a Taste of Kiwi', which had been inspired by the very successful Australian crowd-rouser 'C'mon, Aussie, c'mon'.

*

'The Rugby Deck of Cards' was a wonderful spoof of 'The Deck of Cards', a song that American country singer T. Texas Tyler wrote and recorded in 1949. This spoken-word song backed by violins (covered on numerous occasions by country artists such as Tex Ritter) told the story of a group of American soldiers who went to church during the North African campaign in World War II. All the soldiers took out their prayer books, except one. This young man had only a deck of cards. When charged with playing cards in church, and questioned by the provost marshal, the soldier explained how the different cards reminded him of aspects of faith and the contents of the Bible. Legend has it, Tyler based the song on a true story.

The New Zealand version, spoken by entertainer Laurie Dee (who at the time was a television sidekick of Billy T. James), was written by Christchurch satirists A. K. Grant and Chris McVeigh. In the tradition of some great song writers, says McVeigh, they were never paid for their lyrics.

THE RUGBY DECK OF CARDS

During the latter part of last season, a representative rugby team from a small provincial centre had been on an arduous tour of the South Island, when they arrived in a little town called Kaikoura.

The next day, being a Friday, the team went out training under the watchful eye of their coach, a retired All Black. After outlining to the team the best way to have a quick ruck, he told them to take out their New Zealand Rugby Football Union coaching manuals, and to pay attention to what was being said.

Those of the team who had their New Zealand Rugby Football Union coaching manuals did as they were told. But one player only had a deck of cards, so he spread them out on the bench in front of him. The coach saw the player and said, 'Boy,' for he imagined he was back in South Africa again, 'boy, put away those cards.' And after the coaching session was over, the player was taken away and brought in front of the New Zealand Rugby Football Union. And Russell Thomas said, 'Why have you brought this player here?'

'For playing cards during a training session, sir.'

'And what have you got to say for yourself, son?'

'Much, sir,' replied player said.

And Russell Thomas said, 'I hope so. For if you have not, I will punish you more severely than any player was ever punished. And that includes Keith Murdoch!'

The player said, 'Sir, I've been on an arduous tour of the South Island for some months now and I've had with me neither my New Zealand Rugby Football Union handbook, nor my Alex Wyllie Teach Yourself Stoush coaching manual. But I hope to satisfy you, sir, with the purity of my intentions.'

With that, the player began his story.

'Sir,' the player said, 'when I see the Ace, I think of the one great rugby leader Ces Blazey, who welcomed the Springboks with open arms and promptly got a kick in his principles.

'When I see the Two, I think of the two words which describe the single most important wooden object in New Zealand rugby. No, not Ron Don. The Ranfurly Shield.

'When I see the Three, I think of the three penalty points that New Zealand gets at Cardiff Arms Park whenever Andy Haden falls out of a lineout.

'When I see the Four, I think of the four points that Bob Deans wouldn't have been awarded by a Welsh referee if he had scored his try today.

'When I see the Five, I think of the Five Nations Championship. England, Ireland, Wales, Scotland and France. Put them all together and they still couldn't beat the All Blacks.

'When I see the Six, I think of the six penalties Don Clarke kicked at Carisbrook in 1959 against the Lions, teaching the poofy Poms not to try and win tests by scoring tries.

'When I see the Seven, I think of the number seven jersey worn by the great Graham Mourie and of the seven tries scored by his record-breaking All Blacks when they beat Scotland at Eden Park. The one time when Scotsmen should have worn their kilts on the field to cover up their mistakes.

'When I see the Eight, I think of the number of tests New Zealand have won against Wales.

'When I see the Nine, I think of the number of tests New Zealand will have won against Wales next time they play.

'When I see the Ten, I think of the tens of thousands of dollars the rugby union makes each year by managing to keep the game amateur.

'When I see the Jack or the Knave or the Devil's card, I think of the biggest single threat to the popularity of rugby, John Adshead, coach of the New Zealand soccer team.

'When I see the Queen, I think of Auckland, known as the Queen City. And if you've seen the way their forwards go into a ruck, you'll know why.

'When I see the King, I think of Colin Meads, the king of New Zealand rugby, a man who was obviously concerned about who was going to take over his mantle, because in every test match he played he went around crowning somebody.

'When I see the Joker, I think of Keith Quinn because his commentaries are always good for laughs.

'Sir,' the player went on, 'in my deck of cards there are 12 picture cards, the number of people who turned up to watch Canterbury on Saturday.

'There are 365 spots, the same number of penalties awarded against the All Blacks by South African referees in the last test series.

'There are 52 cards, the number of fullbacks the All Black selectors have chosen in the last two seasons.

'There are 13 tricks, the number of players left in the All Blacks' side at Brigend after John Ashworth and Graeme Higginson had been sent off [sic] for being the first to get their feet to the loose ball, not to mention the loose arm, the loose leg and the loose rib.

'There are four suits, which of course reminds me of the four great Ella brothers. Glen Ella and Mark Ella who played rugby. Their brothers Rube — who's a doctor — and Quin — who's a jockey.

'Sir, my deck of cards serves me not only as a New Zealand Rugby Football Union coaching manual but also as a New Zealand Rugby Football Union handbook.'

Friends, this story is true. I know, because Ron Don told me so.

*

Musicians banding together to sing in support or opposition to major events was very much part of the global pop music world in the 1980s. Band Aid's 'Do They Know It's Christmas?' and USA for Africa's 'We are the World' raised awareness and money for those suffering from famine in Ethiopia. Artists United

Against Apartheid's 'Sun City' featured a who's-who of early rap stars (for example, Run-D.M.C. and Afrika Bambaataa), rock legends (Lou Reed and Bob Dylan), contemporary rock stars (the ubiquitous Bono) and even Australia's rock music conscience (Peter Garrett).

With the All Blacks due to tour South Africa in 1985, the New Zealand population was plunged back into being 'for' or 'against', as they had been four years earlier. Don McGlashan, one half of the inventive and very funny cultural satirists Front Lawn, joined with former DIY punk Chris Knox and blues singer Rick Bryant to front an anti-tour song as Right, Left and Centre.

The song 'Don't Go' (written by McGlashan, Geoff Chapple and Frank Stark) had its most telling line aimed at the NZRFU: 'this bridge you are building brings apartheid here / do you really want to bleed this country white?'

Released as a 12-inch single, the song went as high as number two in the local charts.

It drew a response from a collective calling themselves The Silent Majority, who released a song called 'Let Them Go'. That single did not go to number two in the charts.

*

In 1987, with the Auckland rugby team very much on the ascendant as they entered their second full season defending the Ranfurly Shield, the 'official DB Auckland rugby song' was recorded. Released on the maxi-single-sized vinyl, it featured something of a Kiwi MOR (middle of the road) super-group: Bunny Walters, Hammond Gamble, Billy Kristian, Carl Doy, Peter Whitcome and Alan Galbraith.

The highly repetitive chorus, occasionally played over the public-address system at Eden Park during games, was:

We're Auckland.
Rugby,
We know how to win.
We're Auckland,
Rugby.
We know how to win.
We're Auckland,
Rugby.
And we're going to play to win.

The B-side, 'The Great Kiwi Game', was an eight-verse story of a boy growing up wanting to play 'The Great Kiwi Game / Of Rugby, Rugby's the game' for Auckland. Judging by the large box of copies of this record that the author saw in an Eden Park storeroom several years ago, demand for the record didn't threaten the chart-toppers of the time.

*

Rugby World Cups have seen songs released as part of the hooplah, much as they had for England's soccer World Cup campaigns. Few of those have been memorable, and only one — New Order's 1986 song 'World in Motion', for England's World Cup soccer campaign — stands alone as both a pop song and a celebration of sport.

Neil Finn recorded 'Can You Hear Us?' for the 1999 campaign, and we all know how that ended up!

Featuring nearly every professional singer working in New Zealand in 2015, the charity supergroup #KiwisCureBatten was a fundraiser for cancer research and a supporters' song for the Rugby World Cup 2015 campaign. Many of the lyrics came from children's ideas on how the All Blacks could win the tournament. The extended video skit, featuring Taika Waititi, was a bit self-indulgent, but did have All Black midfielder Ryan Crotty on a unicorn spreading rainbows.

*

A trio of All Blacks have released records, too. The first to do so was George Nepia, whose delightful version of 'Beneath the Maori Moon' was recorded at London's famous Decca Studios in 1935. Pat Vincent, who captained the All Blacks in 1956 before moving to California in the late 1960s, released a jazz EP, *Four of the Best*, in 1960. When the Maori All Blacks toured Spain and Wales in 1982, Waka Nathan invoked the spirit of 1960s Maori showbands with a supporters' songbook from a group called Waka Nathan's Quin Tikis.

*

Below is a list of 50 New Zealand rugby songs (most of which are not on Spotify).

1. 'Zealandia's Victory': words W. R. Wills; music J. H. Phillpot; 1888
2. 'Brace Ye Up Your Muscles, Boys': words Dr Millen Coughtrey; music Joseph Moss; 1888
3. 'The Grand Old English Game': words D. W. M. Burn; music A. J. Barth; 1889
4. 'Goal!': waltz by W. M. Newbould; 1890
5. 'The Song of the Footballer': words and music by D. A. De Maus; 1892
6. 'Forwards, On!': words 'J.B.W.'; music Reg. Hodder; 1892
7. 'The Boys of Crom-a-Boo': words E. D. Hoben; music S. Hoben; 1895

8. 'The Song of Football': words E. M. Dell; music George Garry; 1899
9. 'Bring Out Dat Team': words and music by Leon L. Smith; 1904
10. 'Welcome, All Blacks': words W. W. Boyes; music H. E. Light; 1906
11. 'Haere Mai Welcome, to the All Black Team': words and music by Bert Rache, Sydney; 1907
12. 'On! New Zealand': words and music by Walter Smith; 1924 (actually copied from 'On Wisconsin')
13. 'All Blacks': words R. R. Woodcock; music Roy Spackman; 1924
14. 'The All Blacks (Rugby Football Boys)': words Elizabeth Chandler; music Harry Hiscocks; c.1925
15. 'Football Greetings': words and music by Walter Burns and Dorothy Spinks, c.1938
16. 'The All Blacks' Marching Song': words 'Johnnie' Farrell; music Howard Moody; c.1942
17. 'All Blacks' Football Song': words and music by P. W. Gregory; c.1950
18. 'When the Scrum is on the Ball': words and music by Ken Avery; c.1956
19. 'My Old Man's an All Black': words Howard Morrison Quartet to the tune of 'My Old Man's a Dustman'; 1960
20. 'On the Rugby Playing Trail' (backed with 'What is a Rugby Supporter?'): words and music by The Rugbymen with the Halftimers / Alwyn 'Hop' Owen and John Pike; 1960
21. 'Rugby Rock': words and music by Alwyn 'Hop' Owen and John Pike, Radio 3YZ Westport; 1960
22. 'The Game is Football': words and music by Ken Avery, Christopher Jarman and Perce Barlow; c.1960

23. 'Big Bad Don' (parody of 'Big, Bad John'): words and music by Doug Catley; 1964
24. 'Rugby, Racing and Beer': Rod Derrett; 1964
25. 'The All Blacks are Reading' (backed with 'When the All Blacks Go Marching In'): words and music by Ernie Rouse, performed by Paul Walden with the Garth Young group; 1965
26. 'The Springboks and the All Blacks': words and music by Rod Derrett and The Cambridge Trio; 1965
27. 'The Local Football Ground': words Rod Derrett to the tune of 'Quartermaster's Stores'; 1966
28. 'The Feat of Fantastic Fergie' (parody of 'Sink the Bismarck'): words and music by Lew Pryme; 1969
29. 'All Black Hall of Fame': words and music by Garner Wayne; 1970
30. 'The Name of the Game': words and music by Canterbury Rugby team, Peter Dawkins and Garth Young; 1970
31. 'March of the All Blacks': words and music by 'Ngaire Kinder' i.e. Henry Shirley; 1972
32. 'Pine Tree': words and music by Des Gay and his Foolish Fags; 1974
33. 'All Blacks Song': words and music by Gray Bartlett and Brendan Dugan; 1976
34. 'Give 'Em a Taste of Kiwi': words and music by Black Bolt and the Silver Ferns (Murray Grindlay); 1980
35. 'Up and Under (The Song of the Waikato Front Row)': words and music by B. Ayson; 1980
36. 'Rugby Deck of Cards' (backed with Laurie Dee): words and music by A. K. Grant and Chris McVeigh; 1981
37. 'Don't Go': words and music by Right, Left and Centre; 1985
38. 'Let Them Go': words and music by The Silent Majority; 1985

39. 'Celebration': words and music by Rob Guest; 1987
40. 'We Know How To Win' (backed with 'The Great Kiwi Game'): words and music by Alan Galbraith and The Breakaways; 1987
41. 'Rugby is the Greatest': words and music by Buddy Oath and mates, Colin Parris; 1987
42. 'Black, Black, All Black': words and music by Howard Morrison; 1988
43. 'Can You Hear Us?': words and music by Neil Finn; Rugby World Cup 1999
44. 'My Black Jersey': words and music by Andrew Sadler and Ian Morris; 2005
45. 'Rugby World Cup': words and music by Dean Waretini; 2007
46. 'Men in Black': words and music by Bryce Taylor; 2011
47. 'Game of Our Lives': words and music by John Rowles; 2011
48. '24 Years' (parody of 'Living Next Door to Alice'): words and music by Miles Davis, Heimlich Manoeuvres in the Park; 2011
49. 'I'll Never be an All Black': words and music by Murray Costello, Miramar Chess Club; 2011
50. 'Team Ball Player Thing': words and music by #KiwisCureBatten; 2015

‘The car park will be about as big as Petone.’

— unknown All Black on the size of San Diego Stadium, the venue for the All Blacks’ 1980 win against the American Eagles, 53-6. In the days before the match, the All Blacks joined 58,000 spectators at the stadium to watch the San Diego Chargers play the Buffalo Bills. On the way there, the team bus broke an axle and the All Blacks were helpfully ferried to the game in private cars.

‘If I had been a man from Mars and dropped down into your main street, I would have said without hesitation that it was the dumping ground for the lunatics of the world. If this is rugby madness, give us more of it.’

— 1956 Springbok manager Danie Craven (a star of the 1937 series in New Zealand), arriving in Hamilton for the first tour match.

BOXING ON

For a number of decades before and after World War II, boxing was a staple of physical exercise instruction in New Zealand schools, particularly in all-boys schools. An annual boxing tournament, under the auspices of the local boxing association, would be held in a public hall or similar venue.

Bouts for junior and senior boys would be held across the weights: shadow, midget, paper, fly, bantam, feather, light, middle, light-heavy and heavy. There would be a prize for most technical boxer, but the biggest interest came when the big boys boxed, to find the heavyweight or school champion.

No surprise then that most rugby players were adept when using their fists on the footy field, or that a number of men who made the ranks of the All Blacks had well-publicised amateur careers with the gloves on.

If ever there were a couple of fellows who could instil a little bit of nervousness in the 'huge' South African forwards that toured the country in 1921, it was the combined Hawke's Bay–Poverty Bay team. Packing down for the East Coast selection were Maurice Brownlie — a farmer, war veteran and boxer with a rising reputation as a footballer — and Tom Heeney — a Gisborne plumber popular for his ring work.

Brownlie, weighing in at 12 stone, 8 pounds, had fought for the New Zealand amateur heavyweight boxing championship in

Napier the year before. His opponent was another rugby player — Brian McCleary from Ashburton, who that year had made his debut at hooker for Canterbury.

Brownlie was several inches taller than McCleary and a stone heavier, but McCleary was an accurate puncher with both hands and quick of foot. A newspaper report of the bout described it as:

> … the greatest bout of the evening. McCleary, with a knowledge of his opponent's disastrous punch, presented an elusive front, his foot-work being splendid. Brownlie was plainly seeking a knock-out. He delivered swings which beat the air or were half spent before they met their objective. The Ashburton man's condition began to tell at the end of the second round, and though he got some ugly-looking hits, he took them smiling, and sent back rattling connections which counted. In the final round McCleary made the pace. The Hastings man's punch was palpably weak and McCleary held command, winning the championship amid loud applause. McCleary was carried shoulder-high from the ring.

McCleary was then chosen as part of a four-man New Zealand team to compete at the Australian amateur championships.

Brownlie's days in the ring began to play second fiddle to farming and football commitments, but he had been proficient enough to spar against boxers visiting New Zealand of such calibre as Jimmy Clabby (an American world title contender) and Tommy Uren (an Australian middle-weight champion).

McCleary claimed the New Zealand amateur heavyweight belt again in 1922. With a record of 32 unbeaten bouts, he turned professional and won the national light-heavyweight and heavyweight titles. The following year he lost the light-heavy title to a boxer called Eddie Parker, and then came up against Heeney in defence of the heavyweight belt.

Heeney had just fought Cyril Whittaker over 15 feisty rounds, at which point the referee stopped the fight and awarded it to Heeney. Immediately afterwards, Whittaker collapsed in his seat. He was rushed to hospital and operated on in the early hours of the morning. After spending a day in a coma, he died. Devastated by the death of Whittaker, Heeney had some hesitation getting back into the ring, despite the fact that Whittaker should not perhaps have even had the fight after suffering bad headaches, which had resulted from copping a boot to the head in a football game.

Heeney's management lined him up against McCleary two months later in Christchurch, in a fight for the New Zealand title and a purse of £200. Heeney was a stone and a half heavier than McCleary, taller and with a longer reach.

The stirring bout had gone 14 rounds when, with a left and two rights, Heeney sent McCleary to the canvas for a nine-count. On regaining his feet, McCleary was knocked down again, and on rising for the third time, very groggily, he was floored again. Heeney won by knock-out. It was later revealed that he was ahead on points anyway, with the judges having scored him the winner of nine of the 14 rounds.

McCleary had been 'knocked out cold'. Unable to be revived, he was taken to a private hospital. Heeney feared the worst after the Whittaker affair. It was three o'clock the following morning before McCleary regained consciousness.

The *Truth*'s report of the bout described it as 'one of the most hard-fought and interesting battles seen in Christchurch', but expressed concern about the way the fight ended.

> There is considerable comment in Christchurch concerning it having been necessary for Heeney to administer the final

> punishment after McCleary was obviously in no fit state to continue, or even to defend himself. The popular opinion is that hostilities should have been stopped when Heeney had his man on the ropes after the latter had been down for nine.

There was some argument that, like Whittaker, McCleary should not have been in the ring thanks to football. A week before his fight with Heeney, he had played in a very physical North versus South football match.

McCleary retired from the ring after the fight with Heeney, with a record of 5–5 and 2 no contests. He then played a handful more games of rugby for Canterbury. As boxers do, he ruminated on the loss to Heeney, and at the start of February 1924 *The Sun* newspaper in Christchurch reported:

> Both in the boxing and football field [McCleary] is an exponent of the 'do or die' spirit. His fight with Tom Heeney, in which he was robbed of the heavy-weight crown, was to have been his last. But he received a fearful mauling, and he thinks this would be a poor ending to his boxing career. So he contemplates fighting again, and the opponent he most desires to meet is Heeney! Some may call his courage by another name. They still have the vision fresh of McCleary staggering around the ring under a fearful pounding from Heeney, and they have the memory of the weeks he spent in hospital thereafter. They heard no explanation at the time of McCleary's failure, because he is not the sort to put forward explanations. His friends, however, declare that he entered the ring in no condition to fight. The gruelling struggle of the inter-island Rugby match the week before had sapped deeply of his energy, and tiredness weighted his arms from the first round. There were no reserves of motive power to draw upon.

> Impossible was it for him to succeed against the powerful Gisbornite. In between whiles he keeps himself fit with swimming and shooting excursions, and it is his intention to fix up a ring and throw the gloves about. Should he be selected for the New Zealand Rugby team for England, he shall pack his travelling trunk.

McCleary did return to the ring, and had a title fight for the national light-heavyweight championship in April 1924, before being chosen to tour Australia, Britain, Ireland, France and Canada with the All Blacks, who became known as 'The Invincibles'. He only played in a dozen of the 30 matches, failing to make selection for the first seven games. The reason for this was revealed in a letter home to family, when McCleary wrote that he had been boxing with Maurice Brownlie and his (bigger) brother Cyril, and at some stage had received a strong blow to the head that caused him to feel ill, as he had when recovering from the fight with Heeney.

Of his 23 first-class games, 12 were on the Invincibles tour, where he was very much the epitome of the backup, midweek player who was never seriously considered for a test team while other players were fit.

A waterside worker, McCleary dropped out of rugby after the tour, but continued to box for several more years. The physical effects of his days in the ring were apparent when he tried to sign up for the Home Guard during World War II. He was found to be suffering from a nasal obstruction and osteoarthritis of both elbows and a knee.

Maurice Brownlie went on to become the greatest New Zealand forward between the wars, holding the record for most All Black appearances (61) for nearly 30 years after his retirement in 1928. A formidable opponent — even Colin Meads has said

Brownlie was probably a better player than he, from what he had heard from his father — Brownlie captained the 1928 All Blacks in South Africa. The 2–2 test series result was the best by an All Black team until Sean Fitzpatrick's side finally won a series in the Republic in 1996.

Tom Heeney left behind locking provincial scrums and fought around the world before working his way through the ranks of the contenders in the United States. On 26 July 1928, he went up against heavyweight Gene Tunney for the world title at Yankee Stadium. In a brutal contest that had American boxing fans admiring Heeney's courage, the referee stopped the fight in the 11th round while Heeney was being pounded by Brownlie. (Unbeknown to even Heeney's closest confidants, he had broken a thumb during his build-up to the fight.) Among Heeney's celebrity friends was writer Ernest Hemingway.

*

Another hooker from Ashburton with a Scottish surname who boxed in the heavyweight division was Allan 'Arch' McCormick.

His son, Fergie, played softball for the South Island before becoming an All Black. Fergie played 310 first-class games, and, besides his goal-kicking and punting, was known for the physicality of his tackles.

*

In 1938, the national amateur heavyweight title was won by Aucklander Morrie McHugh. During World War II, while stationed in Egypt, he was the New Zealand Forces champion and flew the flag for the New Zealand Army in inter-camp competitions.

McHugh made the All Blacks in 1946, and went on to play 14 games, including three tests for the All Blacks.

*

The 1947 national heavyweight champion was Kevin Skinner, having won the Otago title the year before. His All Black debut, as a prop, came in the disastrous 1949 test series in South Africa which the visitors lost 0–4. Despite this, the 'Boks acknowledged their respect for Skinner and fellow front-rankers Has Catley and Johnny Simpson by tour's end.

Skinner continued on as a mainstay of the All Black front row, captaining the side in two tests against Australia in 1952, until stepping back from international rugby at the end of 1954. His tally of 61 appearances in the black jersey equalled that of Maurice Brownlie, also a forward with a boxing background, who had proven, like Skinner, to be the most resilient of All Black performers.

When the Springboks took on the All Blacks in the 1956 test series, where the winner could claim bragging rights to being the best team in the world, their front row used every trick in the book to defuse the All Blacks' efficiency at that set-piece. Film footage from the time shows how their props — Chris Koch and Jaap Bekker — were boring in, pulling back and pinning their opponents. Such was the concern about how the All Black front row was being manipulated by the visitors that Skinner was recalled.

This is where the legend, and myth, grows. It was celebrated at the time, and for many years after, that Skinner simply pulled the black jersey on again, took to the field and, under instruction, gave his opposing prop a whack across the chops at the first scrum, changed sides, dished out a dose to the other prop, and the All Blacks were on top again.

That is only partially right. Without question, the return to the All Blacks front row by a man whose reputation as a heavyweight boxing champion and previously immovable scrummaging object raised concerns for the 'Boks. No doubt, there was the odd uppercut in the dark shadows of the scrummage — and in the line-out where Koch was proving himself a real nuisance — with Skinner making it known he was back in the game. But that all would have been pointless if the person dishing it out had not been a more than competent scrummager. It would also have lessened a great All Black to nothing more than a thug.

In his later years, Skinner was certainly embarrassed by the stories that had grown up around his return to test footy. He had, he said, swapped sides in the scrum (no easy feat) after asking teammate Ian Clarke how he was coping. Clarke said Bekker was giving him a torrid time and he needed a rest from his tactics. Bekker tried it on with Skinner, and quickly learned his nonsense wouldn't be tolerated anymore.

Skinner's appearances in the third and fourth tests gave him the record for the most All Black games, but it remained something of a shame that these were the games that defined him, not the 61 games that preceded them.

*

Besides McCleary, only one other All Black has had a stint as a professional boxer: Sonny Bill Williams (SBW). The youngest player ever to represent the Kiwis' national league side, he then code-hopped effortlessly into the All Blacks.

SBW's maternal grandfather, Bill Woolsey, was one of the real hard nuts of Auckland club league, and also boxed as an amateur in the light-heavyweight and heavyweight divisions.

That Williams is a superb athlete is without doubt, though he has been plagued by injuries and had long absences from Super Rugby. He has certainly matured as he has grown older and some of this he has put down to his time in the ring, where, under the mentorship of former Australian league player Anthony Mundine and the management of the enigmatic Khoder Nasser, Williams had seven professional bouts.

All of them were won, and Williams claimed the belts as New Zealand Professional Boxing Association Heavyweight Champion and World Boxing Association Heavyweight Champion. The value of both titles was questioned by many when Williams had to forfeit the belts given his failure to accept challenges for them, including one from the rising star Joseph Parker.

*

A number of All Blacks have held university boxing titles.

William Fea was well-known as a boxer while he was studying medicine at Otago University in the early 1920s. Although he didn't claim a title, he did appear in exhibition bouts. Boxing was something he had practised for some time, given that on a troopship to England with the 40th Reinforcements, towards the end of World War I, Fea had had a bout with a fellow soldier by the name of Tom Heeney. A future Otago footballer and one-test All Black (1921), Fea played at five-eighth. With Heeney a good number of centimetres taller and pounds heavier than his opponent, it must have been an interesting contest, to say the least.

Cantabrian Jim Burrows, a 1928 All Black, held the New Zealand Universities' middleweight and heavyweight titles. He had eight games as hooker for the All Blacks, and later, in 1937, became coach of the team. Burrows was also well-regarded as a medium-pace bowler, representing Canterbury.

Then there was Wilson Whineray (later the first former All Black to receive a knighthood) who was a keen and proficient junior boxer while at Auckland Grammar School in the early 1950s. He won the School Cup in the heavyweight division when still only in Form 5 (Year 11) and won the cup again in his final year at school.

During compulsory military training at Linton Army camp, Whineray won the camp title, and when at university represented Massey and then Lincoln universities at the annual Easter tournament, claiming the heavyweight titles in 1954 and 1955. His attempt at a hat-trick of titles was stopped by a big Fijian medical student from Otago by the name of Jim Samisone.

Two years on, Whineray was still annoyed about having lost his title and wanted the chance to reclaim it. The problem was that the Easter tournament bouts in Dunedin were on the same day as the South Island rugby trials in Christchurch, and Whineray was close to All Black selection.

With some arm-twisting of his coach Neil McPhail (also coach of Canterbury and later the All Blacks), Whineray was allowed to play half the trial game then have a mate drive him south to box.

Whineray, aged 21, had hoped to face off against Samisone, but the big man had decided not to get in the ring that year. Instead, Whineray faced an unknown boxer, but duly put him away and claimed the title for the third time in four years.

The good fortune for Whineray continued. He was chosen to play in the annual All Black trials at Athletic Park, and then named in the All Black side to tour Australia. Regarded as one of the greatest All Black captains, he played 77 matches, including 32 tests, from 1957 to 1965. He didn't need to use his boxing skills very often, as there were more grizzled, nuggety blokes in his teams who were only too happy to announce that Whineray's men wouldn't be putting up with any nonsense.

'You couldn't ask for 15 guys to give more than those All Blacks out there today. They were pumping on adrenalin for the last 15 minutes but they held on.'

— Coach Brian Lochore after his 'Baby Blacks' team with 11 new caps defeated France, 18–9, at Lancaster Park, June 1986.

MEX SAID

Murray 'Mex' Mexted could not be supplanted at the back of the All Black scrum for seven seasons, 1979–85. The Wellingtonian played 34 consecutive tests, which is a measure not only of his fitness but also the consistency of his form. The man in the All Black coaching job changed several times during that period, but Mex was always one of the first names down on the team sheet. He covered a lot of ground on the field, both on attack as a support player and in defence, was a rangy runner from the back of the scrum, a solid tackler, and one of the best tails of the line-out jumpers we've had.

A product of Tawa College, he captained Wellington from 1983 to 1985, and played club rugby in France in the late 1970s, where, he often says, he 'learned how to drink red wine, eat cheese and speak to beautiful women'.

For a time he was married to Miss Universe 1983, Lorraine Downes, their nuptials being front-page news and great fodder for the glossy women's magazines.

In all, he played 72 matches for the All Blacks, his top-level rugby ending with the rebel Cavaliers tour to South Africa in 1986.

Mex was a founder of the International Rugby Academy of New Zealand in Palmerston North. Now the managing director, his school of rugby has an international reputation for the way it prepares and enhances the skills of players, coaches and referees.

From 1991 to 2011, Mex had a much more public role: as a comments man for SKY's domestic rugby coverage. He has said that he thought of his role as like sitting on the couch watching games with a group of mates. As such, that relaxed attitude led to Mex's comments being renowned and remembered for double-entendres, rather than the level of insight he has into the game.

The famous English satirical magazine *Private Eye* has for many years had a regular column called 'Commentator Balls', where the best of unintentionally funny comments from sports commentators are reproduced. It highlights how sometimes sports commentators can try to say too much. The late John Clarke, aka Fred Dagg, was also very good at highlighting how ridiculously serious the language of sporting commentary can be.

Here are some classic quotable 'Mex-said's:

- Both sides are here to play rugby.
- Paul Tito looked like a blind man in a brothel, just left groping.
- Well, either side could win it, or it could be a draw.
- Rico Gear. What a great-sounding name. He sounds like a drug dealer from Brazil.
- It's all tied up at 14–13.
- Andy Ellis, the 21-year-old, who turned 22 a few weeks ago.
- Strangely, in slow-motion replay, the ball seemed to hang in the air for even longer.
- And he kicks it with his left-handed foot.
- I don't like this new law, because your first instinct when you see a man on the ground is to go down on him.
- I'm not sure if those people in the crowd are Russians or just Taranaki people with their fists clenched.
- The line-outs of course are a great artform; I've always fantasised about line-outs, even in my sleep sometimes.

- As you know, I've been pumping Marty Leslie for a couple of years now.
- He scored that try after only 22 seconds — totally against the run of play.
- There's nothing that a tight forward likes more than a loosie right up his backside.

'BATTLES' ON THE FIELD

HAWKE'S BAY v WAIRARAPA 1927

RAILWAYS. RANFURLY SHIELD FOOTBALL MATCH (HAWKES BAY r. WAI RARAPA), AT SOLWAY, 9th JULY.
Special excursion tickets to Masterton and Solway, available for return until 11th July, 1927, will be obtainable by morning trains on 9th July from Napier, Wellington (Lambton), and intermediate stations and branches, and from Woodville, Palmerston North, and intermediate stations. These tickets are available for break of journey only at Solway and Masterton.

Train Arrangements, 9th July. WELLINGTON–SOLWAY–MASTERTON. Train leaving Wellington 7.50 a.m. stops at Solway to set down passengers.

Train leaving Waterloo 7.54 a.m. connects at Petone with 7.50 a.m. Wellington–Woodville train.

Return train, stopping where required for passengers, leaves Masterton 6.10 p.m., Upper Hutt 9.30, Lower Hutt 10.19, Petone 10.23 (connects at Petone with 10.15 p.m. Wellington–Waterloo train), Wellington arr. 10.41 p.m.

WOODVILLE–MASTERTON. Special passenger train leaves Woodville 9.58 a.m., arr. Masterton 11.45 a.m. Return train leaves Masterton 5.15 p.m., arr. Woodville 7.43 p.m. These trains stop where required for passengers.

Usual 12.15 p.m. Cross Creek-Woodville train will be accelerated to leave Featherston 12.37 p.m., Masterton arr. 1.44 p.m.: thence on usual times.

Usual 4.16 p.m. Wellington–Masterton train will be delayed to leave Wellington 5.08 p.m, Lower Hutt 5.27, arr. Masterton 9.1 p.m.

Train leaving Woodville 12.13 p.m. stops at Solway to set down passengers.

NAPIER–MASTERTON. Special train, stopping only at all stations between Napier and Dannevirke inclusive, leaves Napier 6.25 a.m., arr. Masterton 12.10 p.m.

Return train, stopping only at all stations between Woodville and Napier, leaves Masterton. 6.30 p.m. Seats to and from Masterton may be reserved from any station between Napier and Dannevirke, both stations inclusive. Fee 1s.

PALMERSTON NORTH–MASTERTON. Train leaving Palmerston North 11.3 a.m., Masterton 2.09 p.m., stops at Solway to set down passengers. Return train leaves Masterton 6.30 p.m., Woodville arr. 8.00 (change), dep 8.28, Palmerston North arr. 9.25 p.m.

MASTERTON–SOLWAY. Special trains leave Masterton for Solway 1.05, 1.50 p.m. Return train leaves Solway 4.40 p.m., and connects with 5.15 p.m. train for Woodville at Masterton.

The above was a newspaper advertisement ahead of the most anticipated rugby game of 1927. Hawke's Bay and neighbours Wairarapa clashed in a rematch on 9 July, five weeks after the latter had ended the Bay's five-season grip on the Ranfurly Shield with a 15–11 win in Napier.

The Solway Showgrounds in Masterton had a capacity of about 5000 spectators, but twice that number ended up crowding the sidelines and the small grandstand. Two motor stands collapsed under the weight of people standing on them.

Trains carried hundreds to the game, and nearly 1000 private motor vehicles crossed from the Bay to the Wairarapa. So many cars were expected to drive north from Wellington that the District Engineer of the Public Works Department warned drivers of the 140 men undertaking roadworks on the Rimutaka Hill.

There were many little subplots to this game, beyond it just being a clash between neighbours, one of whom was still disgruntled at having lost the Shield.

Leading players for Wairarapa were Bert Cooke and Bill Irvine, two men who had been at the heart of the Hawke's Bay team but had crossed the provincial border in the off-season. The well-known and influential Wairarapa rugby brothers the McKenzies had feet in three camps. Ted was the sole Wairarapa selector and secretary of the union. Norman was the sole selector for Hawke's Bay. Bert was the referee.

Did Bert get caught up in the atmosphere of the day? He was highly regarded as an officiator, but the match started off in a very spirited fashion, and with every attacking surge by one team, their supporters inched nearer and then over the sideline, encroaching onto the field of play. The pitch grew narrower and narrower as the game went on, with police hopelessly trying to hold the sea of people back.

Skirmishes between players had spectators urging them on, although when on one occasion someone yelled that a Bay player was being choked, a dozen or more from the crowd ran in to assist the chokee.

Then in the middle of the field, two big All Black teammates began to wrestle: Maurice Brownlie and Quentin Donald. Whether it was just Donald holding Brownlie back or the trading of punches over some unknown comment or earlier niggle, the thousands of witnesses later seemed unable to agree. Referee McKenzie had apparently warned both players (and teams) early in the game to settle down, but that was as futile as asking a sheep to bark.

The crowd saw the tussle first, their noise alerting McKenzie, who promptly sent both men off.

All that action, and half-time hadn't even arrived. In fact, there were so many stoppages that the first 40 minutes took an hour.

At the final whistle, it was Hawke's Bay who had scored the most points, winning 21–10. Immediately after the game, Wairarapa began an appeal to the NZRFU about the eligibility of Hawke's Bay's Wattie Barclay (see page 62).

Although Masterton was, by legislation, a 'dry area', it was apparently awash with grog that night. Maybe there had been some generosity from the people of the Bay after all.

It remains a matter of dispute as to just how rough and dirty the play was in this game, or whether it was just a very chaotic and frenzied atmosphere. Nonetheless, it quickly became known as 'The Battle of Solway', with the *Wairarapa Daily Times* saying of it:

> If Ranfurly Shield matches are to produce football of the 'slaughterhouse' type, as seen at Solway on Saturday, the sooner the N.Z. Rugby Union burns the Shield in the interests of clean Rugby the better.

AUCKLAND v SPRINGBOKS 1956

Touring international teams were always given great welcomes as they travelled through the provinces. There were main-street parades pre-match, dinners post-match, and the reception desk at the hotel where the players were staying would be flooded with invitations to visit households, schools, churches or marae, or be taken on excursions on the players' days off.

That was off the field.

On the field, it was no holds barred.

Provincial players, many of whom would have been playing their only game against international sides, wanted to prove themselves against the best from another country. This was the biggest game for an amateur player.

For the tourists, such games were their chance to enhance selection for the test matches.

Prior to the 1956 Springboks' game against Auckland at Eden Park, there were *four* junior boys' curtain-raiser games, the first of which — Papatoetoe versus Eastern Suburbs — began at 10 am.

At 1 pm was the senior secondary schools match between Mount Albert Grammar (MAGS) and Auckland Grammar (AGS). Turning out for MAGS was a rising athletics star by the name of Peter Snell, who would go on to become one of the greatest middle-distance runners the world has ever seen. He later recalled: 'I played three seasons for the First XV — halfback in 1955, second-five-eighth in 1956 and first-five and wing in 1957. This was a fairly natural promotion away from the pack where I think I was fouling the team up a bit too much.'

Captaining AGS was Keith Nelson, a future All Black, but also a man whose name would become synonymous with a later bad-tempered game between Auckland and another touring side, the Lions, in 1966. (One of the jokes after the game was that Nelson's team were trying to drum up business for their skipper, who was a dentist!)

Also played before the game was the (then) Auckland Supporter's Club song, 'Victory'. Set to the tune of 'Stein Song' and played by the Northern Military District Artillery Band, the lyrics were:

VICTORY

Drink to all our victories,
Drink to our lasting fame,
We have conquered all along
Whenever we have played the game.
Drink to our fallen foes
Drink deep to Auckland's name,
Supreme in rain or cloud or sunshine,
Our colours blue and white shall reign.
From the pack,
To the Backs,
The ball goes on in an endless chain;
Up and down,
In and out,
The team has gone over the line again;
From the half,
To the wing,
The flight of the ball is hard to see;
In the rush,
In the crush,
The forwards are battling free;
Drink to all our victories,
Drink to our lasting fame,
Drink to those who've gone before us,
The masters of the grand old game.

The president of the Auckland union, Mr S. A. Cleal, wrote in his welcome to the Springboks, in what was something of a template for match-day programme welcomes, that he hoped the match 'and your tour throughout New Zealand [will] be most enjoyable and continue to strengthen that bond of friendship and comradeship which exists between two Rugby-minded countries'.

The public had the same expectation, with thousands queueing from the early hours of the morning to get seats on the terraces. By kick-off, 51,586 were in attendance. This was a real 'outing', with men and women in their best clothes, replete with hats, coats, gloves, handbags, and so on. Boys wore their 'Sunday best', too, which for many was actually their school uniform, as several changes of clothes were a luxury many families did not have.

For all the finery and expectation, the match did not meet any of it. Both teams seemed intent on scoring points over their opponents, in the manner of punches, kicks and scragging. Every now and then they remembered they were supposed to be playing rugby. If Auckland had put their minds to it, they should have emulated Waikato's effort against the tourists on their first stop of the tour and won the game, rather than surrender 3–6. Even more so, considering Auckland had a two-man advantage with two of the 'Boks having to leave the field injured.

The man with the whistle for the match was former All Black Eric Tindall of Wellington, who happened to also play cricket for New Zealand. At centre for Auckland was Frank McMullen, who after retiring from play in 1960 also took up the whistle, becoming only the second former All Black to referee an international.

Post-match, there was widespread condemnation of both teams, and criticism of Tindall's handling of the game.

Dunedin's *Evening Star* newspaper published a souvenir of the tour. Their description of the match, accompanied by a photo of an injured player leaving the field, included this:

> With both teams content to play hard, rugged forward Rugby and to neglect back play, this match was a bitter disappointment to the huge crowd ... most patrons were left with worthless impressions of the only definite features of the

> game — line-outs, fists and penalties … a bad game played in bad spirit.

In their history of international teams who toured New Zealand, *The Visitors*, Rod Chester and Neville McMillan described the game as 'among the worst big games seen on Eden Park … It was a wretched exhibition of rugby.'

CANTERBURY v BRITISH LIONS 1971

Lions Tour '71, a 'complete pictorial souvenir' published by Wilson and Horton and costing 50 cents, carried nine pages of photographs from the Canterbury game. They ranged from a panorama of the crowd on the western embankment to Lions' wing John Bevan carrying a stray fox terrier from the ground.

Under the headline 'The name of the game is?', there were five photos and a cartoon depicting fighting during the match.

> The conditions were perfect — a firm ground, blazing sunlight, a light, drifting breeze. But the play was far from perfect: it was a torrid match marred by flailing boots and punch-ups … it was a match that took the sport out of Rugby — and put the spite in.

Canterbury were the Ranfurly Shield holders, while the Lions had been unbeaten in the first seven games of their tour, dazzling with their inventive back play and the robustness of their forward packs, led by the magnificent Irish lock Willie John McBride.

The All Blacks selectors — Ivan Vodanovich, Pat Walsh and Bob Duff — were rightly worried by the Lions' form, and used the media to raise concerns about the legality of some of their forward play. Vodanovich went so far as to make the absurd comment that if the Lions tried underhand tactics there would be such a response from the Canterbury players it would 'be another Passchendaele'.

Fighting from both sides began with the opening play and the Lions' prop Sandy Carmichael had his tour ended. The day after the match, a picture of his face was in all the country's newspapers, sporting two big 'shiners', the result of six fractures in his face. It also appeared in papers overseas, casting New Zealand rugby and Canterbury in a very bad light. Not wanting to let the facts get in the way of a very emotive story, it was only later in the year that Carmichael revealed in an interview that one of the shiners had actually happened in training.

Post-match, there was much comment about the violence, and the finger was pointed at the referee, Wellingtonian Dr Humphrey Rainey. Several journalists claimed that he had either lost control of the game or had surrendered his responsibilities to police foul play. Reporter John Reason, a man whose writings about the All Blacks in the *Daily Telegraph* could be anywhere between deliberately mischievous and downright malicious, had match reports titled 'You're Just Animals Canterbury' and 'Carmichael KO'D for Two Tests'. Reason made the claim that Rainey had told the players: 'From now on I'm going to follow the ball and if anything else goes on it's up to you two to sort it out.' The comment became a 'fact', and part of historical reviews of the game whenever the Lions later toured.

Rainey later refuted he had said such a thing. First, he only spoke to the two captains, Canterbury's Ian Penrose and the Lions' John Dawes. And, second, what he actually said was: 'It is hard enough trying to follow the ball and at the same time control the players in the mood they're in.' Quite a different statement.

Penrose didn't speak to Reason after the game — in fact, at the after-match the atmosphere was so frosty between the sides that there was little fraternising — so the 'Chinese whispers' must have been between Dawes and Reason.

For the record, the Lions had won, 14–3.

Once the Lions had returned home, normal service resumed in the national provincial game. Auckland challenged Canterbury for the Ranfurly Shield. Ash Edwards, a loose-forward who had been in and out of the Auckland team since 1966, suffered horrific rucking to his neck. It was too much for the zambucks to staunch, so Edwards was taken to hospital. Thirty stitches were needed to close the wound, which may not have felt so painful afterwards given that Auckland won, 20–16.

LIONS TOUR 1983

If ever there was a rugby tour of New Zealand that deserved the label 'spiteful', the 18-match visit by the British and Irish Lions in 1983 was it.

Match after match featured fisticuffs and foul play. From head-butts and blatant punches after the whistle by Lions forwards (seen by spectators and viewers on television, but not, it seemed, by Lions managers or some of the trailing Northern Hemisphere media) to rucking by New Zealand provincial teams that earned the very public wrath of the tour managers, Willie John McBride and Jim Telfer, along with skipper Ciaran Fitzgerald (an Irish army captain).

Telfer, who had been a player on the ill-fated and bad-tempered 1966 Lions tour, commented that he had experienced similar foul play before in this country. McBride pointed the finger at local referees who tolerated degrees of rucking that, in his opinion, would see players sent from the field in the Northern Hemisphere.

Fitzgerald was quoted as saying: 'If a forward stamps an opponent off the ball while that player is pinned defencelessly at the bottom of a ruck, then he is a coward in my book.'

Former All Black lock Frank Oliver, who opposed the tourists for Manawatu, scoffed at the verbals, rebutting that: 'They just lie there in the middle of the ruck, the ball tucked under the arm, and expect that we won't do anything about it. They must be naïve.'

One New Zealand newspaper cartoon was of the All Blacks coach, Bryce Rope, at a team meeting pointing out to a set of his forwards the difference between two oval shapes drawn on a blackboard. One was a ball, the other was a head.

Fortunately, rugby internationally has been free of the hooliganism, sometimes deadly, that had been a blight on the game of soccer. However, the whirl of on-field punches and constant scragging proved infectious when the Lions played Counties at Pukekohe on 9 July 1983.

After the Lions defeated the home side 25–16, three of the non-playing reserves — Irish Gerry McLoughlin, Scotland halfback Colin Deans and Welsh captain Eddie Butler — went for a run around the ground as most spectators trudged away. A few dozen remained by the grandstand observing post-match interviews for television and radio. As the Lions trio stretched out after 'riding the pine' for the afternoon, several local boof-heads thought it funny to disrupt and annoy the visitors. McLoughlin fumed to the point where he was about to clock one of the irritating idiots, but a quick retreat to the dressing rooms under the stands was decided upon instead.

The Counties fans gave chase, with one of them bringing Deans to the ground in an ugly tackle.

Eventually, the trio escaped the commotion, and the incident was laughed off by the tour party. Eddie Butler went on to be a well-recognised voice commentating on Welsh rugby internationals, while the bloke who tackled Deans probably still dines out on the tale of the great tackle he made on a Lions player at Pukekohe stadium.

ALL BLACKS v FRANCE 1986

When the All Blacks toured France, they knew what their opponents' tactics would be, particularly in the matches against provincial selections: rough up the All Blacks any way you can, and think about doing things with the ball later.

The worst examples of this came on the 1986 tour. It was brutal. There is a story that, during the four-week tour, Sean Fitzpatrick had nearly 200 stitches applied to cuts on his head. The All Blacks won their first seven games, including taking the first test 19–7. In only three games did their opponents get into double figures, but what a physically demanding trip it was.

For the final match of the tour, the second test at Nantes at Stade de la Beaujoire, France were determined to win — having lost the first test 7–14 — and the passing of time has revealed they were prepared to do anything to get that result. According to investigative journalist Pierre Ballester in his book *Rugby à Charges, l'enquête choc* (*The Case Against Rugby*), that included the taking of amphetamines by a number of their players.

Buck Shelford knew things weren't normal before taking the field.

> When I came out of the tunnel and I saw them, I looked into the eyes of many of the players as I walked past them, and their eyes did not say that they were going into a game against the All Blacks. Their eyes just looked like they were on something.

The French eight played attacking rugby, literally. They had turned their back on the All Blacks' haka the weekend before. For this one, they stood and steamed like bulls ready to be released to rampage across the field.

Their sustained ferocity from the kick-off was extraordinary and brutal.

Twenty minutes into the game, Shelford was pinned at the bottom of a ruck. A French boot went to work on him, knocking out four teeth and tearing his scrotum so badly he almost lost a testicle. With needle and thread, the injury was repaired on the sideline and Shelford returned to the boiling pot of play.

When Shelford finally left the field early in the second half due to a concussion from a blow to his head, prop Kevin Boroevich replaced him. But he moved to lock, with Andy Earl (who had been in the second row replacing Gary Whetton, who was another match casualty) moving to number 8. The All Blacks physiotherapist, Neil Familton, was run ragged patching and wrapping players as they came and went from the sideline. At one point, flanker and captain Jock Hobbs (playing his last All Black game) was on the wing! Shelford apparently had very little recall of the match.

John Kirwan described the 3–16 loss as 'a s*** fight', while David Kirk described it as 'the most physical and physically aggressive off-the-ball, or in circumstances where players have an opportunity to physically attack another player, game I've ever played in'.

It makes you wonder just what the South African referee Steve Strydom was watching in the game. Mind you, those who had been on the rebel Cavaliers tour earlier in the year had experienced similar unbridled aggression in the Republic.

It was a bad end to a tricky year, where one of the most inexperienced All Black test teams — 11 new caps — had taken the field and defeated France in Christchurch. This plethora of new caps was due to the Cavaliers tour of South Africa. When those players and their bulging wallets had returned from the Republic, they were suspended from selection for the two-test French series and the first test against the touring Wallabies in Wellington.

The Wallabies inflicted defeats at Athletic Park and the third test at Eden Park (22–9), which at the time of writing was the last time the All Blacks lost there.

Coach Brian Lochore used the end-of-year France tour to meld the two groups back into one cohesive, united All Black team. Proof that he had done this, despite the loss at Nantes, came with the All Blacks dominating and winning the inaugural Rugby World Cup the following year. And who did they beat in the final? France.

NORTH HARBOUR v AUCKLAND 1994

The National Provincial Championship (NPC) final between Auckland and neighbours North Harbour, on 15 October 1994, has become known as 'The Battle of Onewa Domain'. The *New Zealand Rugby Almanack* of that year described it as being a game containing 'many shameful acts by well-known players'.

Games between the two sides have been colloquially known as 'The Battle of the Bridge' from the time the North Harbour union was formed, taking a northern slice of Auckland's clubs. At North Harbour were a number of players who had been infrequent members of the Auckland team (such as Buck Shelford and Frank Bunce) who now could command positions in a first-class team, and show Auckland's players, spectators and administrators what they had lost.

Losing to North Harbour was non-negotiable for the Auckland team. Beating big brother Auckland would mean more to Harbour players than just about anything (the Ranfurly Shield excluded).

North Harbour were having a superb year in 1994. They beat the visiting French side (who defeated the All Blacks in both tests) and conquered Auckland at Eden Park for the first time, coming back from 17 points down to win 34–31. In their NPC home semi-final they absolutely outplayed Canterbury, 59–27. Had Canterbury not crossed the line four times in the later stages of a game Harbour had well and truly won, the end result would have been even more humiliating for the red-and-blacks.

Auckland had travelled to Dunedin for their semi-final and had eventually overcome Otago, 33–16.

Due to the vagaries of the NPC rules, as Auckland had hosted the round-robin game against Harbour, the team on the north side of the bridge would host the final. Onewa Domain's capacity was only about 10,000 spectators, but North Harbour administrators refused to shift the game to a larger venue. Better that Harbour have their supporters close to the field, they thought.

Auckland, coached by Graham Henry, wanted revenge for their loss earlier in the season, and the fire in their bellies was fuelled by word that Harbour were already planning a victory parade. There had also been provocative billboards by Nike, who happened to sponsor both teams. Just before taking the field, Auckland captain Zinzan Brooke had told his players to 'go out there and kill them'.

From the get-go, both sets of forwards were at each other. Harbour's Blair Larsen and Eric Rush were swinging punches at all and sundry. Zinzan Brooke and Robin Brooke were loving it — even though Zinzan was at one point flattened by a Rush punch — and offering their own back. Both Rush and Robin Brooke were sent off.

Match referee Colin Hawke (whose yellow card barely spent any time in his pocket) later said he had been caught by surprise by all the foul play — but it was really the NZRFU judiciary who were caught by surprise, as a total of seven players had to appear before them. There were so many, the judiciary assembled in a hotel in Auckland rather than at NZRFU headquarters in Wellington. The naughty boys all sat together in a corridor waiting their turn in the hearing room!

What about the score? 22–16 to Auckland. But no one seems to remember that.

SCHOOLBOY RUGBY AND ARMY CUPS

> You could say that my football career began when I was a boy kicking an empty jam tin about Manners Street in the late 1880s but my ambition to play the game properly dates from watching Stoddart's [Great Britain] team versus Wellington at the Basin Reserve in May 1888. By 1892 I was picked for the first Wellington primary schools representative team to be selected and we beat the Wairarapa primary schools at Masterton ...

So wrote Billy 'Carbine' Wallace for Gordon Slatter's 1970 jubilee history of New Zealand rugby, *On the Ball.*

Wallace, who played for the All Blacks from 1903 to 1908, remains one of the greatest players the game has seen. He was this country's first points-scoring machine, his accurate place-kicking and frequent try-scoring accruing 379 points for the All Blacks. Of those, 230 were collected on the 1905–06 tour of Britain, Ireland and France. It was a tally that was never threatened by later tourists and, with the days of the long tour now a thing of memory, it will never be beaten. The first man in New Zealand first-class rugby to pass the 500-points mark, he was later made a life member of the Poneke club, managed All Black and Maori teams on overseas tours, and was involved in administration at the highest levels of the NZRFU. No other All Black fullback has scored a try while wearing a sunhat, as he did against Cornwall in 1905! And it all began with kicking a tin around on the street.

Nearly every man and woman who has worn the black jersey will have taken their first steps towards becoming international players in the likes of primary-school lunchtime 'stadia', the games of tackle, touch or force-back, the summer beach games where the more who played the merrier, and where rugby heroes were imitated.

Thousands of us have stood around shivering at suburban and school sports grounds on Saturday mornings prior to kick-offs, having sprigs checked by the referee, waiting for pungent liniment to warm up cold muscles, while parents sit in warm cars or hop from foot to foot in jackets and raincoats. (These days, of course, those on the sideline clutch disposable coffee cups ...)

This is where the lifelong love of the game begins, and future All Blacks and Black Ferns begin their rise on footy fields where high-pitched voices call for the pass, where a bang to the shin can feel excruciating, and where oranges (depending on affordability) are still gnawed on at half-time.

Junior rugby has been the very broad and solid foundation stone of New Zealand rugby. And during World War I, it was schoolboy rugby that kept the game alive in this country while our men were serving overseas.

*

El Moascar (which means 'camp' in Arabic) is a place in Egypt that was used as a large tent city by the horsemen of the New Zealand Mounted Rifles (NZMR) and their Australian counterparts during

World War I. It was the base for campaigns in the deserts of the Sinai Peninsula and Palestine.

Rugby was an important recreational sport for New Zealand soldiers in the theatres of war, as well as in training and recuperation camps. A number of men who had been All Blacks before the war, or would wear the silver fern post-war, played in desert rugby matches for the Mounted Rifles. Most notable among them were the legendary Brownlie brothers, Maurice and Cyril.

While players for New Zealand Divisional teams in England and France played their inter-services games on muddy, wet fields, the Mounted Rifles matches were always on the hot, sandy desert in an area notable for its strong winds.

At the conclusion of the war, it took months and months to return all of the Kiwi soldiers to New Zealand by ship. Many grew very frustrated with the lengthy wait, and so to help alleviate the boredom, rugby competitions between nations were organised.

In England, the New Zealand Divisional team played sides representing the armies of Australia, Mother Country (England), Canada and South Africa, and reigned supreme in a tournament for the King's Cup, which was presented by King George V. That trophy is still proudly in the possession of the New Zealand Defence Force, and annually Army, Navy and Air Force teams play each other with the cup at stake.

The troops in the desert played their own tournament in January 1919. It was organised by the grandly named Ismailia Rugby Union. (Ismailia being a city to the east of Moascar.) Five Australian, four British and one New Zealand team — the NZMR Unit and Depot — competed in the tournament. At stake was the Moascar 'Camp' Cup, an Irish silver cup reportedly bought in Cairo.

The Kiwis won the tournament with a record of nine wins and one draw, scoring 147 points and only conceding three. Further matches were played against South African and Welsh teams. (One story has it that the written match reports were lost somewhere on the return to New Zealand, but fortunately the cup was not.)

Sometime between the end of the tournament and embarking for New Zealand, part of the propeller of an enemy plane that had been shot down in Palestine was attached to the cup. It does not appear in photos of the cup when it was first won.

Wondering what to do with the trophy once they were home, members of the NZMR team unanimously voted that it would be presented to the NZRFU for it to be used in a secondary schools competition. Thus, once back in New Zealand, the commanding officer of the NZMR, Lieutenant-Colonel E. J. Hunter, gifted the trophy to the NZRFU.

Elimination tournaments in the North and South islands were held to find the first finalists to play for the cup. Christchurch Boys' High School (CBHS) and Palmerston North Boys' High School (PNBHS) squared off at Athletic Park, Wellington, in September 1920. The weather was so dire that many thought the match should have been postponed.

In the mud and rain, no points had been scored by the end of regulation time, so the referee called for 15 minutes of extra time. He told both captains that if no points were scored, a force-down (having to defensively force the ball in goal) would count as a point for the other side. When a PNBHS player ran the ball dead in goal, the referee awarded the match to the Cantabrians. There were protestations from the PNBHS supporters, and the principal of CBHS generously offered to replay the match within a week. However, he was told by the NZRFU that the referee's decision was final and they were to be the cup holders.

The prime minister, William Massey (who had adjourned parliament to be there), presented the cup to the winners, but was quick to say he wished there were two cups to present to acknowledge the spirit in which the game was played. That evening, the NZRFU hosted the players at a special dinner.

In 1923, the Moascar Cup became a challenge cup.

In 2019, the centenary year of the creation of the cup, the Moascar Cup remains a nationally important relic, a reminder of New Zealand's World War I desert soldiers and the game that was an important distraction from the horrors of conflict. It also acknowledges the place schoolboy rugby has had in New Zealand.

At the beginning of the 2019 schools rugby season, St Peter's College in Auckland held the Moascar Cup. They had won it (for the third time) by beating Napier Boys' High School in the New Zealand Barbarians National First XV Top Four final. Their win was extraordinary, because they came back from 5–21 down to win 31–28. Captain of the St Peter's team was Niko Jones, son of All Black legend Michael.

*

Only one player who has taken the field for the All Blacks had their occupation listed as 'secondary school pupil'.

When the All Blacks played Fiji at Eden Park on 13 September 1980, selecting players who had not been on the recent tour to Australia saw Craig Wickes go on as a replacement for the final 15 minutes of the 33–0 non-test win.

A pupil at Palmerston North Boys' High School, Wickes was into his second season as a Manawatu rep, and earlier in the year had played for the New Zealand Colts in Australia. (Other future All Blacks in that group were captain of the team Albert Anderson, brothers Gary and Alan Whetton, Warwick Taylor, Kieran Crowley, Robbie Deans, Ian Dunn and Victor Simpson.) Wicke's twin sister, Collette, played in a curtain-raiser to one of his Manawatu matches in 1980.

A noted sprinter and powerful runner, the future looked very bright for Wickes, but sadly he was plagued by knee injuries that saw him drop out of rugby at the end of the 1981 season. In 1986 he made a short comeback, running out four times for Manawatu.

Although still at school and aged 18 years and 200 days, Wickes was not the youngest player to have appeared for the All Blacks. Many might say, no, of course, that was Jonah Lomu. Incorrect. Jonah remains the youngest All Black *test* player, at 19 years and 45 days, but the youngest to play in an All Blacks game was Lui Paewai in 1923.

Having finished his time being educated at the Mormon Maori Agricultural College, Lui was just 17 years and 36 days when he played for the All Blacks against New South Wales in 1923. The Hawke's Bay youngster had made his provincial debut the year before. He was not a one-match wonder, going on to be part of the 'Invincibles' tour in 1924–25. Unfortunately, the tour was a frustrating one for him, with illness restricting his appearances to just seven of the 30 tour games.

There is more to the Paewai name in New Zealand rugby folklore than what occurred on the field, though. Paewai's mother once famously cured George Nepia of a bad thigh haematoma, which may have led to severe blood poisoning if the clot wasn't broken. After two weeks of massage treatment from a well-regarded local physiotherapist without improvement, Nepia went to the Paewai farm at Tahoraiti, outside of Dannevirke. There, Nepia and Mrs Paewai collected strips of bark from the north-facing sides of kowhai trees, hammered each piece until it was bruised, then boiled them for a couple of hours in a big copper. This liquid was then put into a bath, in which Nepia lay for an hour or more. Mrs Paewai then made little incisions in his thigh with a piece of glass, and Nepia spent more time in the bath. By this time, the coagulation of the bruise had been broken and the blood started to ooze from the cuts in Nepia's leg. A week later he was back on the field.

Not long after Paewai arrived home from the 'Invincibles' tour he had a court appearance for assault, after roughing up a local mechanic who would not attend to his car as urgently as he desired. There was further car trouble later that year, when a vehicle he was driving hit a bank and rolled in Norsewood. Fortunately, neither he nor his three passengers was seriously injured.

Paewai moved, with some haste it seemed, to Auckland to play footy, despite being named in a Hawke's Bay team to defend the Ranfurly Shield. News of the move was the subject of a poem in *The Auckland Star* by a writer using the pen-name 'Sinbad'.

Says Lui Paewai, Rugby crack, in recent seasons known to fame,
a wearer of the jersey black and expert of the five-eighths game,
'I have devised an enterprise on Auckland's Rugby fields to play.
It's now not pleasant in my eyes to be the mainstay of Hawke's Bay.
That province long has held the shield, though others sought it earnestly.
Now we to Wairarapa yield, and that is no surprise to me.
We were a very happy crew, with wondrous teamwork did we play,
but now I see a doleful view as all my cobbers drift away.
George Nepia is married now, and Jimmy Mill with all his tricks,
apparently has made a vow that games and marriage do not mix.
With Cooke and Irvine likewise gone, where are my friends of former time?
This scene I shall not linger on, I'll seek a friendly warmer clime.'

The move north may have been because of offers to play rugby league, which complicated his initial eligibility for Auckland, but eventually he turned out for the blue-and-whites and the New Zealand Maori in 1927–28. A dislocated shoulder while playing for the latter against New South Wales brought an end to his rep career. He was then only 22!

In his later years Paewai returned to the Dannevirke area to farm, and in 1950 he was convicted and fined £300 for failing to file tax returns. His lawyer, a Mr Poole, claimed in his defence that 'it was the first prosecution of its kind against a Maori in this district and he understood that one of the reasons it had been brought by the Tax Department had been to bring to the notice of Maoris the fact that they were not exempt from taxation'.

Paewai's high standing in the local community was acknowledged by the judge.

When Maori players were banned from the 1960 All Black tour to South Africa, Paewai joined Nepia and several high-profile Maori leaders in speaking out against the trip on behalf of the Citizens All Black Tour Association at a public meeting in the Wellington Town Hall.

Lui Paewai passed away in January 1970. Two nephews and grand-nephews have played provincial rugby and for the New Zealand Maori, making a proud legacy of the Paewai name.

*

As mentioned earlier in this chapter, at the end of World War II, as soldiers waited impatiently to sail home, the War Office mooted the idea of an 'Army Football Competition (Rugby)' and representatives of the various national forces met in London to plan a tournament of fixtures to be played around Britain. It would be a celebration for players and spectators of unity, mateship, sport and the end of hostilities. The British Army side (made up of English, Welsh and Scottish soldiers) played under the moniker of 'Mother Country', while the Royal Air Force was just that. The Royal Navy couldn't muster a team of sufficient quality to be included.

King George V, a rugby fan, offered to donate an eponymous cup, thus elevating the competition to something more than a mere festival of matches. National pride was now at stake back on the sporting field, and, although the NZRFU had no involvement, the reputation of the game they governed was under threat.

The New Zealand Services team had already begun playing matches in and around England against both services and club teams. In fact, two teams were being fielded, and on more than one occasion the 'All Blacks', as newspapermen called them, played at the same time but on different grounds.

One of their games was the first time a New Zealand team had played at Twickenham, and the only loss for the New Zealanders came against the Australians, a team that was captained by Nelson-born Bill Watson, who had represented Australia from 1912 to 1914.

With the cup competition complete, the New Zealanders, as winners, returned to Twickenham to play the French Army side. Before the game, King George V presented captain James Ryan with the Inter-Services and Dominion Forces Championship Rugby Football Challenge Cup.

Following the King's Cup success, New Zealand Army Headquarters in London accepted an invitation from their South African counterparts, at the urging of the Transvaal Rugby Union, for the Services side to play in the Republic on their way back to New Zealand.

However, two players originally selected did not take part on account of not being granted the necessary documentation to visit

South Africa: Ranji Wilson and Parekura Tureia. One excuse for Tureia not being part of the side was that he 'missed the boat'.

The name of the captain of the side that went to South Africa, Charles Brown, has been engraved on the cup, rather than the winning captain in England, James Ryan.

The King's Cup, after some years out of sight gathering dust, was renamed the King George V Cup and put up for contest in 1947 between New Zealand Army, Navy and Air Force sides. It is still highly prized at the annual Defence Force rugby tournament, and celebrating the possession of it can go long into the night (something the author well knows, having had the privilege of drinking from it at a post-competition celebration).

LEAVE MR BROWNLIE ALONE

In a 1925 provincial game between Southland and Hawke's Bay, Bill Hazlett, a young 19-year-old stag, clashed horns with Maurice Brownlie. Apparently, the referee then told Hazlett to 'leave Mr. Brownlie alone'. The formality in referring to Brownlie, albeit somewhat facetiously, was the subject of much mirth around the country. The *NZ Truth* newspaper printed a poem from a contributor using the pen-name 'Acey' spoofing the incident.

The southerners all stood a-trembling with fear
As the referee strode up the ground.
In Richardson's eye stood a glittering tear:
His emotion, though deep and profound
Could find no expression in gesture or word —
Could his team such an error atone?
And this was the sentence the Southlanders heard:
'You leave Mister Brownlie alone.'
As Maurice came down at the head of a rush
Young Hazlett dived in at his knees.
His skipper reproved him 'Young fellow, don't brush
'Into Maurie, I beg of you, please!
'You may tackle Falwasser, or Grenside, or Mill;
'But surely you ought to have known
'You may jump on Bill Irvine, or Nepia kill

'But — you leave Mister Brownlie alone.'
The crowd on the bank were quite merry and gay;
And they cheered themselves hoarse with delight,
As they gladly predicted a win for the Bay
And a filling of tankards at night.
But look! He is down! Who has rashly presumed!
From the 'fans' comes a sorrowful moan,
When up swaggered Bill, and then angrily fumed,
'You leave Mister Brownlie alone!'
But Maurice just grins and caresses his shins
Then jumps for the ball on the line.
Down the field like a flash, in a rattling good clash
With his team mates all backing up fine.
But he suddenly gasps, as he lands on his head,
And says in a comical tone,
'Now, didn't you hear what the referee said?
'Just buzz off, and leave me alone.'
So all other forwards take warning from me:
When you meet the Bay team at its best,
In the heat of the fray, should you mix it that day
Don't put your own prowess to test.
Be gentle; don't tackle your foeman too hard,
Lest the side line unto you be shown.
The goal-line your full-back can easily guard;
And you — leave Mister Brownlie alone.

OVERSEAS SELECTIONS AND TWO GAMES IN ONE DAY

En route to South Africa in 1960 and 1970, with the All Blacks by then travelling by air rather than the previous passenger liners, the touring party stopped off in Australia to play a few matches.

In 1960, they played five games, beginning with a double-header at the Sydney Sports Ground. The first game was against Queensland, who travelled south across the state border to oppose the men in black, in what was an away game for them, too.

The All Black management had to spread their players across two XVs, but, with injury and illness ruling out two New Zealanders, local players were enlisted to make up the numbers. (An early example of overseas-based players being selected for the team?)

The Australians called up to play were Maurie Graham and Eddie Stapleton.

Graham had played against the All Blacks thrice before, and had probably been very close to selection for the Wallabies during his playing career. On the first occasion, in 1951, he was not yet 20 years old when he captained the New England side from fullback against the visiting All Blacks in Armidale. The second time was six years later when he played for the Australian Barbarians against the All Blacks in Sydney. A mere 48 hours later he was pulling on the kit of the Riverina combined side to run out against the All Blacks in Wagga Wagga.

Stapleton was not an unknown, either, as he had toured New Zealand three times with the Wallabies (1952, 1955 and 1958).

Thus both players joined the very small club of non-New Zealanders who have played both for and against the All Blacks. The list of local players who have achieved that feat is surprisingly long, given that in the early half of last century the All Blacks would play one or more warm-up games against New Zealand provincial sides prior to travelling overseas.

Stapleton moved into an even more rarefied club when he scored the first try of the game, the touch-down allowing him to boast of having *scored* for and against the All Blacks.

Three days later, the All Blacks played another afternoon double-header, this time in the country town of Orange. There, two different XVs met Victoria–South Australia and New South Wales County. No ring-ins were required.

Come 1970 and the All Blacks played a couple of games (President's XV and Western Australia) on the same day in Perth to stretch the legs. This time the vacancy in their line-up was caused by Sid Going's 'no playing on Sunday' stance, and saw a local club player drafted in. In this instance, it was a Singaporean-born Scot, Jamie Hendrie, who was studying medicine at university in Perth. Two days earlier he had turned 19.

That's not where the trivia of the All Blacks playing two games in one day ends. Those matches in Perth saw Otago wing Bruce Hunter not only play in both games for the All Blacks, but score tries in both games. Two other All Blacks, Bevan Holmes and Bill Davis, came on as replacements.

Only a small amount of catering would have been required for a reunion of players who have played two games for the All Blacks in one day!

'There were no true world champions in the 1987 and 1991 World Cups, because South Africa were not there. We have proved our point.'

— South Africa's Rugby President, Louis Luyt, at the post-Rugby World Cup final dinner, 1995. Sean Fitzpatrick walked out with his team. The England and France teams followed.

ADVERTISING

Even rugby players succumb to coughs and colds, and in the 1920s associating one's products with football and the All Blacks was commonplace and didn't seem to require any permission or licensing from the NZRFU.

The following are two examples of newspaper ads from the time; Hean's was a cough and cold syrup available in Australia and New Zealand from around the time of World War I, while Pulmonas were throat pastilles or lozenges sold in small tins.

> **THE ALL BLACKS TOOK 'HEENZO' WITH THEM**
>
> One item of the All Blacks' baggage was a case containing enough 'Heenzo' (Hean's Essence) to last the team for the entire trip. They realised how handy it was in case of sudden chills. A little taken in hot water wards off risk of coughs and colds. Try 'Heenzo'. See how simply the half-crown bottle makes a pint of the most efficient cough-cure you ever used — see how it saves you money and does you good; and then, send in your entry for the Heenzo Experience Letter Competition. Please keep it under 200 words. £100 in prizes, £50 first prize — 71 other cash prizes. Send along your entry now. Heenzo experience letter competition, P.O. box 1490, Wellington. Closing date. 30th September. N.B.; Try a packet of Heenzo cough diamonds. Quick relief for any cold. [1924]

FOOTBALL TEAM'S MOTOR TRIP

Driving a monster char-a-banc [an open topped motor-coach] from Auckland to New Plymouth in the heart of winter, and with a football team as passengers is no joke. As a precaution the driver bought a big tin of Pulmonas — driver and players shared the Pulmonas — all arrived happy and well. Pulmonas for coughs, colds, bronchitis, asthma, influenza, etc. All chemists and stores 1s 6d and 2s 6d. [1927]

The following 1901 poem was used in advertising by Woods, makers of a peppermint cure-all.

It's football that works up the muscle,
And gives a man plenty of dash,
Its kick, and its scrum, and its bustle,
And a general looking for lash.
In the good old hunt for the leather,
If a cold you should have to endure,
You will soon pull yourself altogether,
With Woods' Great Peppermint Cure.

Companies producing household products such as detergents often advertised poetry writing competitions in newspapers, offering the cash prize of a guinea for a short poem that mentioned their brand. Here are two winning entries that mentioned rugby.

CHEQUE for £1 1s has been sent to the writer of this verse, Master R.F., The Manse, Waikouaiti, Otago:

We sang the 'All Blacks' praises
When they won their honour bright
But now we sing of SAPON
Which makes the all-black white. [1907]

CHEQUE for £1 1s has been sent to the writer of this verse, Miss R.E.F., Hampden, Otago:

New Zealand wins at football,
Australia wins at cricket,
SAPON wins at washing clothes:
There's nothing else can lick it!

WIN A GUINEA! Prize Poem published every Saturday. Best short four-line advt verse about SAPON wins each week. SAPON wrapper must be enclosed. Address, 'SAPON' (Oatmeal Washing Powder), P.O. Box 635 Wellington.

'In the school holidays I went home to Nuhaka and one night got into a party which developed, after we had played games, into a session of fortune-telling from cards by a man called Ropitini. I was just looking on when he suddenly said to me, "Let me tell your fortune, George."

He gave me the cards to shuffle. I did what I was told and handed them back to him. He began to lay the cards face upward on the table. As he did so, he began to speak (and I must tell you that he had a reputation among us Maoris as a seer).

"George," he said, "in the near future you are going overseas. You are going to be famous. You are going to be successful. Your name will become a household word, not only in New Zealand but all over the world. This is what the cards tell me — and they never lie."'

— George Nepia recalling a prediction made a couple of years before he was chosen for the 1924–25 'Invincibles' All Blacks' tour of Great Britain, Ireland, France and Canada, on which he was widely regarded as the greatest fullback the game had seen.

DONNYBROOKS

There is a word, now seldom heard, that was often used to describe action on the rugby field: **Donnybrook**. It had nothing to do with rugby originally, as it was actually the name of an Irish fair held annually for 600 years in Donnybrook, Dublin. Notoriously, in the 1800s, as the fair became more and more a day for workers to have a day off indulging in stout and whiskey, it would often descend into chaos.

Those who did not like the game of rugby after its introduction and establishment in New Zealand in the late 1800s would disparagingly view it as nothing more than an organised 'Donnybrook'. By 1904, the word was being widely used to describe games that had descended into brawling and foul play.

A Wanganui club game in June 1904 was reported in a newspaper as being 'Very like Donnybrook Fair':

> The senior football match Kaierau v. Pirates, played on Saturday, was extremely rough and a number of the players were injured. A player named Quarterman was kicked in the stomach, and was removed to the hospital in a bad way. Another, named Loveridge, was kicked in the head, and had to be carried off the field in a dazed state. Holland received a cut over his right eye, necessitating several stitches being put in. Mitchell had his hand broken, and Harris his knee

injured. Thomson was stunned by a blow on the bead, while Guscott sustained a broken collarbone. There were other minor accidents as well. Six of the injured were Pirates, but most of their injuries were due to the vigor [sic] of their own players.

In May 1926, the usually impeccably behaved George Nepia was sent off in a Wairoa club game between Nuhaka and Pirates. The match was a tempestuous one, with a number of players injured on both sides. Newspaper headlines referred to it as a 'Football Donnybrook'.

Two months later, newspapers reported another Donnybrook, this time on the West Coast.

TROUBLE AT RUGBY GAME. MATCH ENDS IN DISORDER

The nearest approach to a public melee that has occurred at Hokitika for many years took place on Saturday at a football match, in which Hokitika won the senior cup by defeating Star (Greymouth) by eleven points to nil. The referee's rulings dissatisfied the Star players, and a large proportion of the spectators. The position was so tense that it appeared as if proceedings would finish up in a 'Donnybrook'. The game was punctuated by blasts from the referee's whistle, the visitors being penalised no fewer than eleven times in ten minutes. Hokitika were penalised twice during the afternoon. The last stages of the match were featured by Star players repeatedly walking off the ground, and the final whistle blew amidst general disorder. Pring (Star) and Carter (Hokitika) were ordered off the field by the referee.

*

The word **slipper** used to be in common rugby usage, as in 'giving it a bit of slipper' or 'using the slipper'. A polite way of referring to someone putting the boot in.

With long tours not part of the professional era, the term **dirt-tracker** isn't used very often anymore. It was used to describe the midweek players. A variant of that, the **dirty-dirties**, is still used to refer to players in a squad who are neither in the run-on XV nor the reserves.

The kick that is today known as the 'bomb' (or the halfback's variant, the 'box-kick') was for many years known as the 'up-and-under'. In both hemispheres, but more so in Great Britain and Ireland, it was also known as the **Garryowen** after it was repeatedly and successfully used as a tactic by the champion Garryowen Football Club (Limerick) in the 1920s.

Next, the origin of word **strip**, as in 'playing strip'. The word 'strip' in terms of a sporting uniform was used as far back as the 1890s in this country. That may have been before it was used in Britain. Match participants would wear their match clothes to the ground under their normal clothes, then strip to their playing gear. Thus we get the phrase 'playing strip'. Newspapers described players 'stripping in the pink of condition', 'being prepared to strip' to take the field, or 'will strip on Saturday'. Supporters of the club would be in charge of collecting all the discarded 'civvy' clothes.

The last time an All Black kicked a **goal from a mark** in a test was Don Clarke in the 9–6 win against England at Lancaster Park in 1963. For some years a player could catch a kicked ball anywhere on the field and, driving a heel into the ground to mark the spot as their arms collected the ball, call 'mark'. They then had a free kick, and could attempt to score points with a shot at goal. The last goal from a mark in a first-class match in New Zealand was 14 years after Clarke's effort. It was kicked by Kit Fawcett (an All Black in South Africa the year before) for Waikato against

Wairarapa in September 1977. 'Free kick' rule changes that year saw the 'mark' only claimable in a defender's 22, and thus by virtue of distance it became a non-scoring free kick.

As the Garryowen or up-and-under became more of an attacking tactic, especially with big, fearsome wingers charging towards the nervy fullback as he waited to claim the ball, the need for the catcher to mark the spot on the ground with his heel was removed, as some argued it left the catcher off-balance and susceptible to injury when tackled in the act of catching the ball. The player simply had to be stationary. (But some rulings on this by referees have proven either very strict or very lax ... like most rules of this complicated game.)

Crowds would hold their breath as high kicks sailed towards the 22, not so much in the hope the ball would be caught, but in anticipation of what sort of dangerous collision would take place. For a time in the 1980s and early 1990s, fullbacks were being mown down and it is remarkable no very serious injuries occurred.

Something else we don't see anymore: All Black forwards kicking goals. In the early part of last century, it was often forwards who would kick off or take shots at goal, particularly in bad weather, as the leather balls became very heavy when muddy and wet. Maurice Brownlie at one point jointly held the record of 19 for most points in a Ranfurly Shield game after scoring three tries and kicking five conversions in the 77–14 win over Wairarapa in 1926. For many years that was the highest score in a first-class game in New Zealand.

When was the last time an All Black forward kicked a penalty in a test match? Well, if you are under 40 it didn't happen in your lifetime. In 1977, big Otago loose-forward and lock Gary Seear kicked a booming 45-metre penalty against France in Paris. Those weren't the only points he scored from the boot in his 34 games for the All Blacks. Two conversions and another penalty were also chalked up by him.

'There are only two excuses you can use for missing rugby training — death and docking!'

— attributed to Grizz Wyllie when coaching Canterbury.

'There's no doubt about it, he's a big bastard.'

— Scotland captain at the 1995 Rugby World Cup, Gavin Hastings, talking about Jonah Lomu after Scotland's 30–48 quarterfinal loss to the All Blacks at Pretoria.

'Wassup, Mike?'

— debutant Wellington rugby loose-forward Jerry Collins introduces himself at a line-out to the man he considered a real legend: Michael Jones.

'There was so much chatting going on, I almost picked up a British accent.'

— Paul Henderson, Southland captain, in 1993 after losing to the Lions, 16–34.

'I've pulled a hamstring.'

— All Blacks 1987 Rugby World Cup captain Andy Dalton, prior to the first game, against Italy.

DID HE SCORE?

For more than a century, one disputed score has remained at the very core of New Zealand rugby folklore: the try that Canterbury midfield back Bob Deans (great-uncle of 1980s All Blacks Robbie and Bruce) did or did not score against Wales on 16 December 1905 at Cardiff Arms Park. History records that he did not score it, as it was not awarded by the referee. But should it have been? Its contention is often brought up in conversations between Welsh and New Zealand supporters, and is something of commonality in a rivalry between the two small rugby-mad nations. (That relationship seems to have soured somewhat in the professional era.)

All Blacks playing at the Arms Park for the first time would be taken to the spot where Deans crashed into the turf. On one occasion, the great Welsh player and commentator Cliff Morgan was in the ground's broadcasting box. As a group of All Blacks stood about the historic try line, Morgan yelled out a window: 'He didn't score!'

All Blacks fans made visits to Cardiff to be shown the almost scared site where Deans did(n't) score. Like religious pilgrims who brought home bottles of holy water from Lourdes, they tried to smuggle out clumps of turf dug from that hallowed spot.

Back in 1905, the All Blacks had gone to Cardiff feeling fatigued. They had played 28 games in 88 days. Although unbeaten, there were injuries and illness. Painful boils were the most common ailment.

The Welsh team had developed a formidable reputation. They had won the 1905 International Championship played between the Home Unions. In doing so, they had claimed the Triple Crown by defeating England, Ireland and Scotland. In fact, they had been undefeated on Welsh soil since 1899. The unofficial title of 'Best in the World' was at stake. In preparation for their meeting with the All Blacks at Cardiff Arms Park, the Welsh players and management had attended several of the New Zealanders' tour matches. They had also assembled for a number of practices, focusing on executing special backline moves they hoped would lead to victory.

When the All Blacks arrived in Cardiff, every person they spoke to told them they were about to lose their unbeaten record.

Dave Gallaher had long been worried about the scheduling of the Welsh test, and his players' health by then. After a practice run the day before the game, the All Black selection committee struggled for *seven* hours to select 15 fit players to take the field.

The All Blacks stayed in The Queen's Hotel, a short distance from the park — roughly one minute's walk. All morning the players had been able to hear the gathering Welsh masses in full, expectant voice. Welsh representative (and visitor to New Zealand in 1904) Rhys Gabe stopped in at the hotel to see the All Blacks. Afterwards, he told his teammates that Gallaher's men looked 'keyed-up and ill at ease, with the thought of a possible defeat'.

The confident, carefree All Black players seen at the start of the tour in Devon were now weighed down by their own achievements and the expectations of the footballing public at home. Looking out their hotel windows, they could see the human tide swelling, slowly moving through the streets towards the gates of Cardiff Arms Park. At half-past one, the ground was at its capacity and the gates were shut. From then until the players took to the field an hour later, the excitement built.

When both sides came out onto the field, the crowd erupted. Match time at last! The All Blacks grouped together for their haka, and the crowd fell respectfully silent. Following the 'war cry', the masses roared their appreciation, clapping and cheering. Then they suddenly fell silent again as the Welsh team clustered together in the middle of the field. The players in red began to sing their national anthem. Their voices were joined by 40,000 more, and a thunderous, rousing rendition of 'Hen Wlad Fy Nhadau' ('Land of My Fathers') reverberated around the stadium and its neighbourhood. These were special moments in football history, and unlike anything the All Blacks had experienced before.

The home side had the better of the first 30 minutes of the match, while the All Blacks' play was muddled and error-ridden, and then Welsh winger Teddy Morgan scored as the result of a planned move from a scrum. The crowd was ecstatic.

At half-time it was Wales 3, All Blacks 0.

The All Blacks were dominant throughout the second half. Winger Simon Mynott was held up over the line, and a try by Duncan McGregor was ruled out after referee John Dallas (a former Scottish international) and the line umpire deemed the final pass as forward.

Then, out of nothing, came another opportunity. After the ball had been hacked through by the Welsh forwards from a line-out, the covering Billy Wallace scooped up the ball. On the left-hand side of the field, and just inside his own half, he saw more space than defenders ahead of him. Off he went, building a scything run, typical of the wonderful pace and vision he possessed. The crowd was yelling for their boyos to stop him. Several defenders were unable to even land a hand on him. He continued on to inside the Welsh 25. The tryline loomed. There was still one red-jerseyed man who could save the day: Welsh fullback Bert Winfield. Then, at his shoulder, Wallace heard Bob Deans calling for a pass.

Drawing Winfield, Wallace sent the ball to the young Cantabrian, who charged on. There were no red jerseys in front of him, just a white line. Changing direction slightly, he headed towards the posts, mindful of the team needing a try and a goal to win. This change of angle was a blessing to a chasing, desperate Welsh defender, Morgan. Deans was now within reach. As the solid centre made his dive for the line, Morgan's arms wrapped around his legs and the players fell to ground. What happened over the next few seconds has been a matter of conjecture ever since.

The New Zealand players' view, best recounted by Wallace as he had been right up with the play, was that Deans grounded the ball over the line and then was pulled back into the field of play by the arriving Welsh players. The ball, he said, was moved similarly.

George Gillett, for one, had no doubt that Deans scored. 'Deans went over the line by about nine inches and grounded the ball,' he said later. 'A man from behind him pulled him back, and another who was on the line pushed him. I was close up to Deans at the time.'

Another All Black, George Nicholson, who was also a touch judge, was sure of what he saw. 'It was a try, true enough,' he later said.

The Welsh opinion was that Deans was brought down about six inches short of the line. Rhys Gabe is said to have asked Deans after the game: 'Why did you try and wriggle onward?'

Referee Dallas was some way behind the play, and when he arrived (with the crowd in stunned silence according to some reports) he saw the position of the ball and whistled 'no try'. The silence was broken by the relieved crowd and the protestations of the All Blacks.

Did Deans score? Rugby historians have playfully argued over that question for a century. No examination here will change the result of the game. Wales 3, All Blacks 0.

Gallaher knew his side had not played well. Ultimately they were responsible for their loss, not the referee. When a reporter asked him what he thought of the match, Gallaher said, 'It was a rattling good game played out to the bitter end with the result that the best team won.'

'Is there any point about the defeat which you regard as unsatisfactory?' the reporter probed.

'No. As I said before, the better team won and I am content.'

'Did your team play up to its best form?'

'On that point I have nothing to say.'

'What of the refereeing? Have you an opinion favourable or otherwise to express?'

Apparently, this question brought a wry smile to Gallaher's face, and he replied: 'I have always made it a point never to express a view regarding the referee in any match in which I have played, so you must excuse me.'

Manager George Dixon wrote in his diary post-match:

> Right on the line [Wallace] passed to Deans who dived over and grounded the ball well over the chalk mark. He was at once dragged back and out into the field of play, and when the referee who was fully 40 yards away at the time caught up, he gave a scrum five yards out. That this was an absolutely fair try there is overwhelming evidence, including Gabe [sic] who tackled Deans as he was fading and pulled him back into play and Llewellyn the Welsh line umpire.

While Dixon had no beef with the Welsh players, he was highly critical of referee Dallas:

> The refereeing was not what would be called first class according to my standards. What would be thought of

> a referee in NZ who went out to control a first class game on a greasy surface in ordinary walking boots, no buttons on them and clad in heavy ordinary clothing including orthodox stiff high collar?

However, Dixon did concede that: 'I am of the opinion that on the day the NZ team did not deserve to win but they actually made a draw of it I am assured. Draw fair reflection of play.'

As word spread that the win for Wales may have been controversial, *The Daily Mail* sent a return cable to the All Blacks' hotel asking who claimed to have scored. Deans sent a famous reply: 'Grounded ball 6 inches over line. Some of Welsh players admit try. Hunter and Glasgow can confirm was pulled back by Welshmen before Referee arrived. Deans.'

Perhaps the answer to the controversy lies in that very answer by the young man who had the ball at the crucial moment. Aged just 21, Bob Deans was a man whose sincerity, maturity and unquestioning generosity were remarkable for someone his age. He was as honest as the day is long. Never was his integrity questioned in any capacity by those who knew him personally or played alongside him. There is no reason to think that his character would change to the extent that he would lie in the aftermath of a match.

Back in New Zealand the result did not come through until Sunday morning. In Christchurch, *The Lyttelton Times* reported that 'for an hour after the announcement Cathedral Square was dotted with groups of talkers, nervous, dejected-looking critics who spoke calmly enough, but very sadly, of the national calamity'.

As time passed and the full report of the match was published in New Zealand newspapers, so incensed were the rugby public by the 'stolen' result that schoolchildren began to sing a jingle which began 'Taffy was a Welshman, Taffy was a thief'.

It was a controversy that remained alive. In 1924, Teddy Morgan signed a dinner programme for Billy Wallace, writing the words: *Deans did score.*

Bob Deans died suddenly. After going into hospital for a routine appendix operation, complications set in and he passed away on 30 September 1908. He was only 24.

*

In 1978, Graham Mourie's All Blacks were hoping to become the first New Zealand team to complete the Grand Slam — tour wins over England, Ireland, Scotland and Wales.

First up: Ireland. A try to Andy Dalton minutes before the end of the game saw the All Blacks break a 6–6 deadlock to lead 10–6. Ireland attacked passionately in the time remaining, but the All Blacks held on to win.

A week later they were at Cardiff Arms Park and behind the Welsh, 10–12, with three minutes to play. A line-out 10 metres or so from the Welsh 22 saw big All Black lock Andy Haden suddenly tumble from the line of black jumpers. Arms in the air, he fell to the ground trying to milk a penalty.

Referee Roger Quittenden of England, whistling his first test match, blew the whistle. Arm aloft, he awarded the All Blacks a penalty. How the Arms Park crowd howled. They had all seen Haden's Hollywood performance. 'Bloody cheating!' cried some.

But Quittendon had seen something else awry in the line-out.

'Bobby Windsor threw in and in that split second the Welshman's [Wheel] hand went over on to the shoulder of the All Black [Oliver]. The other man [Haden] who took a dive was never seen by me to be pushed. It was a piece of play-acting. He was pretending he had been barged. His action was totally irrelevant,' he later said.

So, the All Blacks had their chance to win the match. But the penalty had to be kicked. First-choice fullback and kicker Clive Currie had left the field only minutes after the start with a fractured jaw, with Southland's Brian McKechnie taking his place. McKechnie had already kicked two valuable penalties, but had also missed a couple of kicks.

Up he stepped and started to hack his heel into the turf to place the ball for the kick.

'It briefly went through my mind that during the game against Cardiff [in October 1938], the ball fell over as Clive Currie was about to kick at goal and the crowd made a racket that might have helped him miss the attempt,' said McKechnie later. 'I thought I'd better not let that happen to me, so I just dug the hole, placed the ball and shot. It was a great feeling to see it go over, and it was really only then that I realised the sound from the crowd — it was deafening.'

The All Blacks won, 13–12. The television replay of Haden's dive was replayed over and over again in the valleys, as Welsh fans continued to cry foul, ignoring Wheel's play.

The All Blacks went on to complete the Grand Slam with victories over England (16–6) and Scotland (18–9).

Just over two years later, double-international McKechnie found himself in the spotlight again, this time facing Trevor Chappell's underarm delivery at the Melbourne Cricket Ground. What were the chances of two of New Zealand's most notorious moments, in different codes, seasons and decades, featuring the same Kiwi sportsman?

*

The original Cardiff Arms Park is no more. After many developments over the last century, it morphed into the Millennium

Stadium in 1999. It was there in 2006 that Welsh Rugby Union (WRU) officials told the All Blacks they were to do their haka before the Welsh national anthem instead of after so as not to gain an 'unfair advantage'. It is worth noting that the previous year, when the All Blacks were playing in Cardiff, the haka was done before the home anthem, as the occasion marked the centenary of matches between the two countries. In reluctantly agreeing to do it in that way, then, the All Blacks had been assured it would be a one-off.

When it became apparent the WRU were trying it on again the next year, the All Blacks team and management said they would not be 'bullied' by the WRU, and instead opted to perform the haka in their changing room before running onto the field.

All Blacks assistant coach Steve Hansen said: 'Doing it between two national anthems is a cop-out. It's trying to interfere with tradition and the culture of the team and we weren't prepared to put up with it.'

WRU group chief executive Roger Lewis said: 'The WRU were only officially informed by New Zealand on the morning of the match that the haka was not going to be performed. This kind of brinkmanship is not good for rugby; it's not fair on the fans.'

The All Blacks did feel for the crowd, and so a television camera was allowed into the changing room so the foundation-shaking haka could be broadcast on the ground's big screen and on networks around the world.

An hour and a half later the Welsh players were probably wishing their union hadn't been so stubborn. The fired-up All Blacks won, 45–10.

'To anyone, young Māori/Pasifika people especially, who may be struggling with their identity — please know that it is ok to be you. You are perfect as you are. Do not let these comments keep you from being yourself. Polynesia has been sexually diverse since forever.'

— All Black halfback TJ Perenara's Twitter response to the first of Israel Folau's controversial tweets, April 2018.

JOKES, PRANKS AND TALL TALES

The All Blacks were playing England at Twickenham, and the home team were still in shock after Jonah Lomu had demolished them in the Rugby World Cup semi-final. At half-time the score was 50–0 to the All Blacks, so coach John Hart sent Jonah out to play the second half by himself. The rest of the team went and enjoyed a long soak in the famous Twickenham baths from where they could hear occasional loud cheers.

When they came out again, Jonah was sitting in the dressing room. They asked him what the final score was. He told them: 55–21.

'What happened?' asked one of the All Blacks.

'Bloody ref sent me off after two minutes, and every time England got into our 22, Jonny Wilkinson kicked a dropped goal.'

*

Which was the best football team to leave New Zealand?

The 1937 Springboks.

*

At a football match an old gentleman was watching from the grandstand. At half-time he pulled a bulky cigar case from his

1970 South African tour souvenir. So much has changed since then. (MATT ELLIOTT COLLECTION)

Cartoon ad from the 1972 All Blacks v Australia test programme.
(MATT ELLIOTT COLLECTION)

1974 advertisement for the biography of Colin Meads, which sold over 60,000 copies! (MATT ELLIOTT COLLECTION)

Wessel Oosthuizen's famous photo of a bloodied Kevin Eveleigh, South Africa, 1976.
(MATT ELLIOTT COLLECTION)

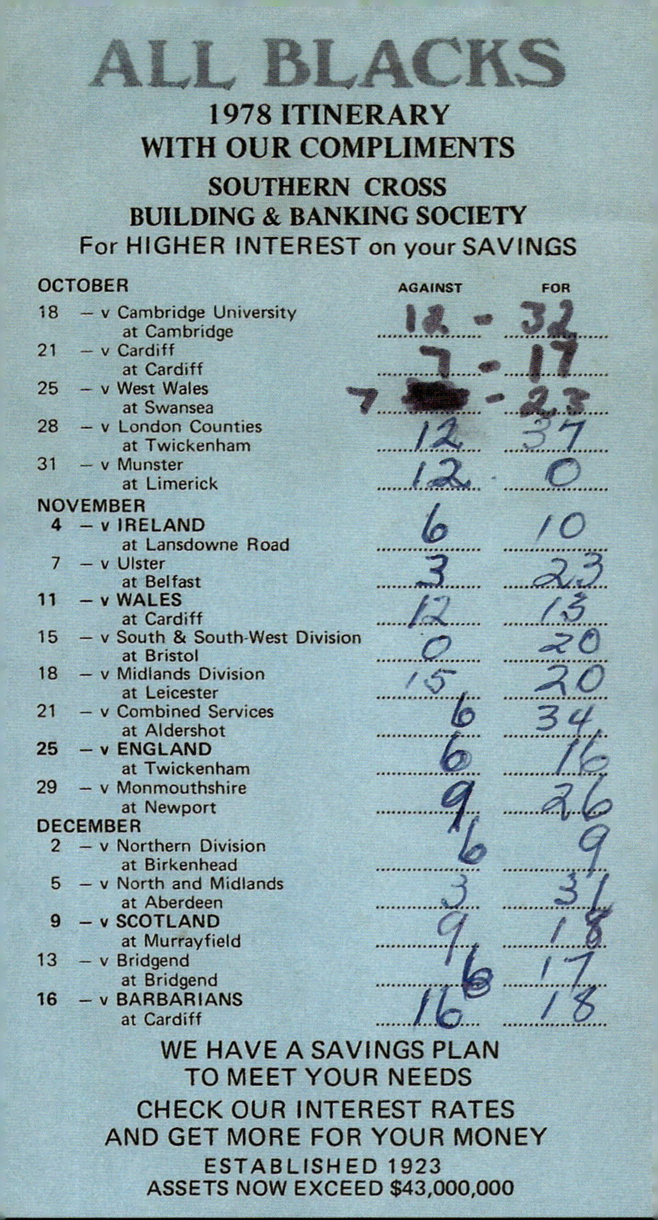
ALL BLACKS
1978 ITINERARY
WITH OUR COMPLIMENTS
SOUTHERN CROSS BUILDING & BANKING SOCIETY
For HIGHER INTEREST on your SAVINGS

	AGAINST	FOR
OCTOBER		
18 — v Cambridge University at Cambridge	12	32
21 — v Cardiff at Cardiff	7	17
25 — v West Wales at Swansea	7	23
28 — v London Counties at Twickenham	12	37
31 — v Munster at Limerick	12	0
NOVEMBER		
4 — v IRELAND at Lansdowne Road	6	10
7 — v Ulster at Belfast	3	23
11 — v WALES at Cardiff	12	13
15 — v South & South-West Division at Bristol	0	20
18 — v Midlands Division at Leicester	15	20
21 — v Combined Services at Aldershot	6	34
25 — v ENGLAND at Twickenham	6	16
29 — v Monmouthshire at Newport	9	26
DECEMBER		
2 — v Northern Division at Birkenhead	6	9
5 — v North and Midlands at Aberdeen	3	31
9 — v SCOTLAND at Murrayfield	9	18
13 — v Bridgend at Bridgend	6	17
16 — v BARBARIANS at Cardiff	16	18

WE HAVE A SAVINGS PLAN
TO MEET YOUR NEEDS
CHECK OUR INTEREST RATES
AND GET MORE FOR YOUR MONEY
ESTABLISHED 1923
ASSETS NOW EXCEED $43,000,000

Itinerary cards were given to customers by all sorts of businesses and avidly filled in as tours progressed. (M. J. FORD/MATT ELLIOTT COLLECTION)

All Black lock Graeme Higginson. Sent off but not sent off against Llanelli in 1980. (PHOTO BY BOB THOMAS SPORTS PHOTOGRAPHY VIA GETTY IMAGES)

Hika 'the happy hooker' Reid dots down in the centennial test against Wales, Cardiff Arms Park, 1980. (PHOTOSPORT/PETER BUSH)

A poster advertising Waikato Rugby Union's celebration of their 1980 season, in which Arthur Stone's famous intercept helped win the Shield. (MATT ELLIOTT COLLECTION)

TWO flour bombs drop from the light aircraft as it makes another bombing run over Eden Park. The plane dropped pamphlets, flares and flour bombs on spectators and players during 69 "bombing runs" over the ground. Picture, BARRY DURRANT.

Dramatic images from Eden Park's 'Flour bomb' test, 1981, captured by John Selkirk for *The New Zealand Times*. (MATT ELLIOTT COLLECTION)

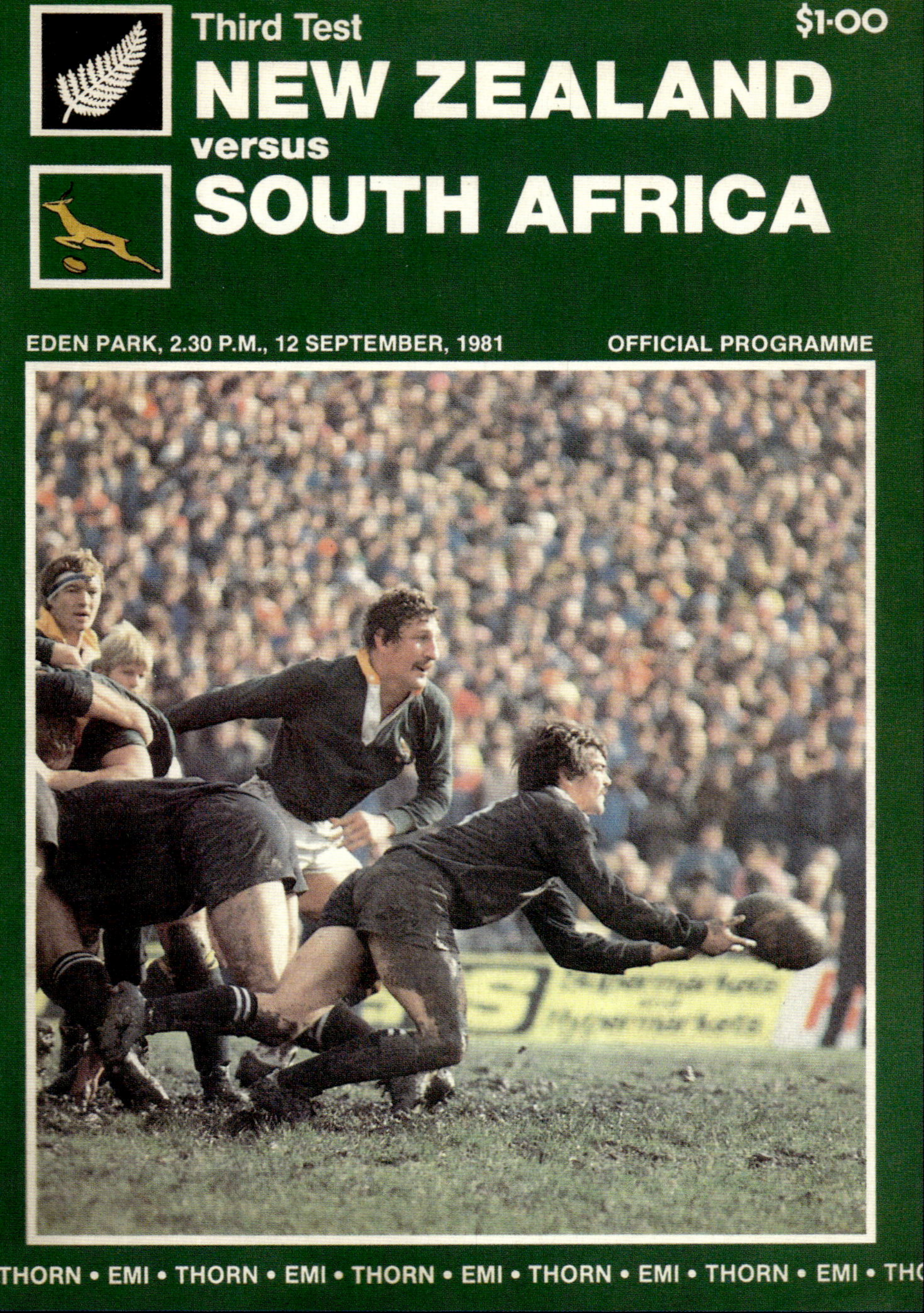

Programme from the most dramatic match played in New Zealand. (MATT ELLIOTT COLLECTION)

New Zealarders get to know their rugby heroes from a young age.
(MATT ELLIOTT COLLECTION)

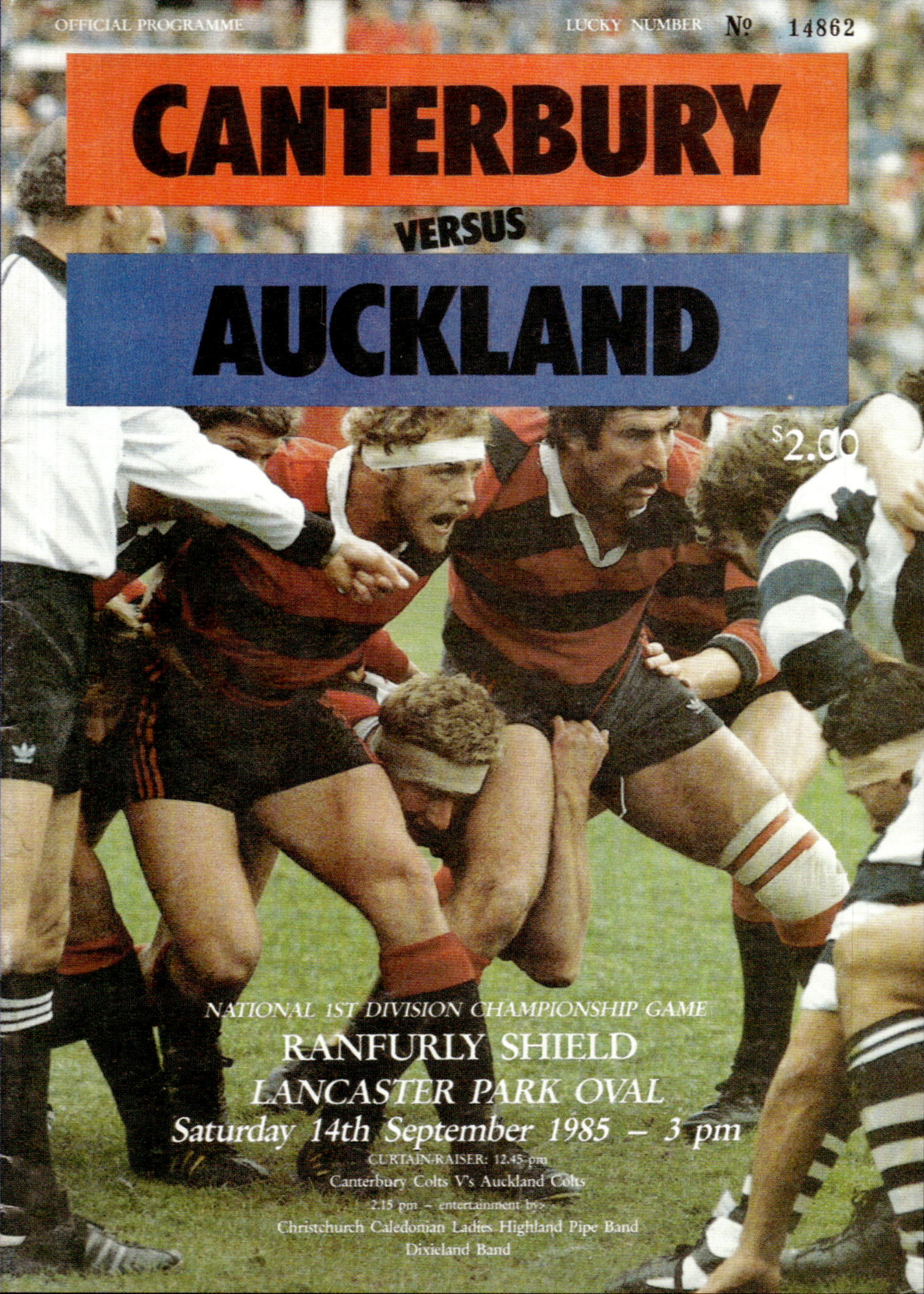

Programme from the epic 'Game of the Century', when Auckland claimed the Shield from Canterbury, 28–23.
(MATT ELLIOTT COLLECTION)

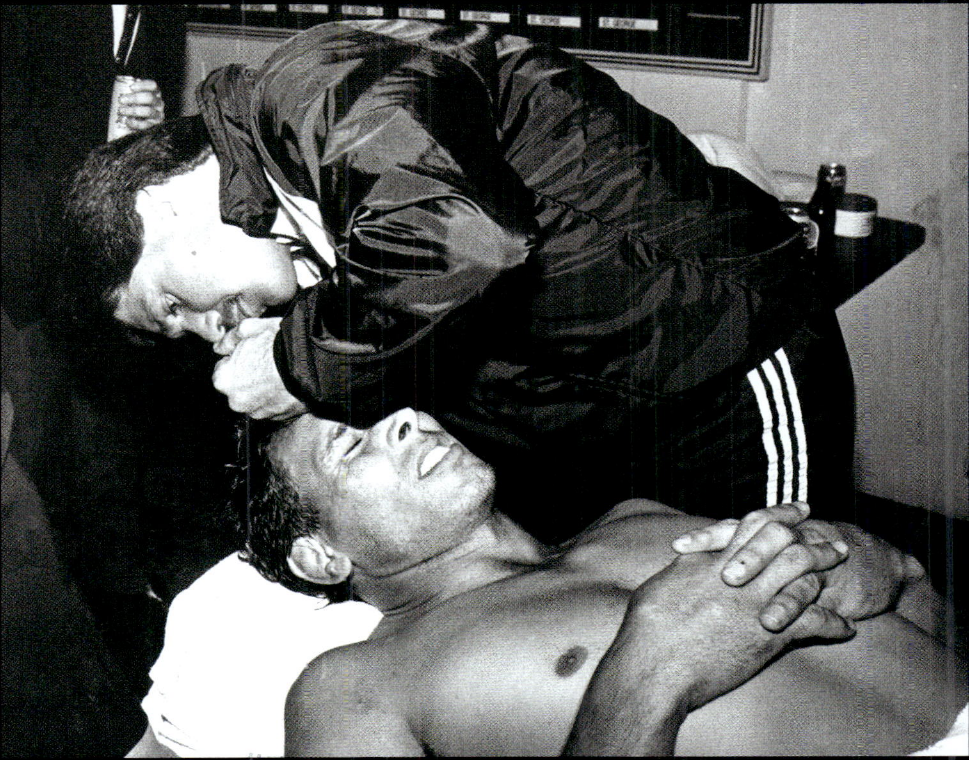

No anaesthetic, thanks Doc. John Mayhew stitches up Buck Shelford after one of the 1988 tests v Australia.
(PHOTOSPORT/PETER BUSH)

Chalk, cheese. Oil, water. All Blacks coaching pair John Hart and Grizz Wyllie. (PHOTOSPORT)

Otago hooker David Latta (centre), whose anguish at conceding a last-minute penalty in the 1994 Ranfurly Shield challenge against Canterbury embodied just what the trophy meant to those who played for it. (PHOTOSPORT)

North Harbour wing Eric Rush (centre, holding ball) was one of the stand-out players for all the wrong reasons in the ill-tempered 1994 NPC final v Auckland at Onewa Domain. (PHOTOSPORT)

Crazed South African pitch invader Pieter van Zyl is dealt with by Richie McCaw in the 2002 Durban test. (PHOTOSPORT)

Going underground. The All Blacks perform their haka under the stands before taking the field for the 2006 test v Wales at Millennium Stadium after the Welsh Rugby Union insisted it be performed before the home side's anthem. (AFP PHOTO ROSS LAND/POOL)

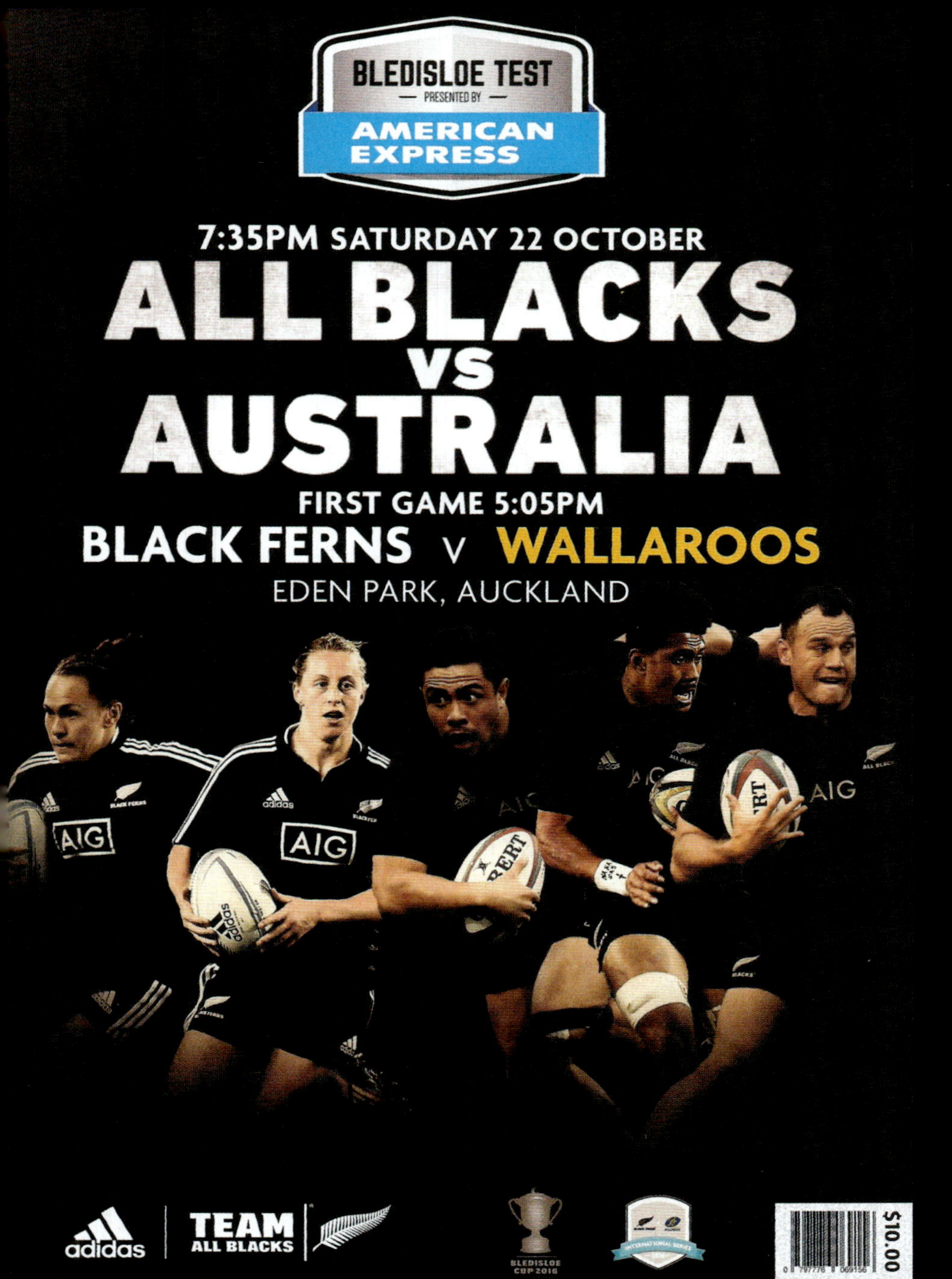

The Black Ferns playing the curtain-raiser to All Blacks' tests is becoming a more frequent occurrence. This 2016 Bledisloe test was the third time in five seasons, and the cover of the match programme perfectly demonstrates the growing prominence of women's rugby on the international stage.

(MATT ELLIOTT COLLECTION)

Sonny Bill Williams became just the third All Black, and the first back, sent off during an international when French referee Jérôme Garcès showed him a red card in the 2017 test against the Lions, Wellington. (PHOTO BY PHIL WALTER/GETTY IMAGES)

The Log o' Wood has had its fair share of scrapes since first being played for in 1904. (BRUCE LIM/WWW.PHOTOSPORT.NZ)

Rugby could rightly call itself 'the game for all New Zealand' in 2018 when Black Fern Kendra Cocksedge was awarded the highest accolade for a player, the Kelvin R. Tremain Memorial Trophy.
(PHOTO BY HANNAH PETERS/GETTY IMAGES FOR NZRU)

pocket and, turning to an enthusiast who was sitting beside him, asked, ‘Do you smoke?’

The enthusiast, expecting a nice cigar, promptly replied ‘Yes.’

‘Ah, then, you won’t mind me smoking,’ replied the canny old gentleman. [1904]

*

A joke that was popular in the 1920s and early 1930s involved a wager: ‘I will bet you half a crown that I can tell you the test score before the match.’

Many produced their 2s 6d waiting to hear a predicted score. Instead, they lost their money when they were told that the score *before* the match was nil-nil. There could be no score until play had begun.

*

A young American guy was in Te Aroha as part of a working holiday, and after his first day at his new job his workmates took him to the Princes Hotel for a pint. When he was buying a round, the barman said to him, ‘You’re a good-sized bloke. Our club is looking for a lock.’

‘I don’t know the first thing about rugby,’ said the American.

‘That’s okay,’ said the barman, ‘we’re short of refs here, too.’

*

A nice old story carried in several newspapers in the 1940s involved a play on the brands of cigarette companies.

Mr Charlie H. McIntyre, the manager of the Waikato Rugby team, which challenged Otago for the Ranfurly Shield in 1949, wandered through Dunedin town on the morning of the match, looking for a shave. After several visits to barbers' shops, he found none were giving shaves as they were preparing to go out to see the match.

At the last shop Charlie said, in facetious exasperation: 'Oh, well. Give me a packet of those Capstan cigarettes you have under the counter before you go to Carisbrook.'

The tobacconist replied that they did not do such things as that in Dunedin. So Charlie thought it might help if he said he was manager of the Waikato team.

'Oh, are you?' replied the shop-man. 'Then it's Players you require, not Capstan.'

*

At Carisbrook, an old man was asking one of the white-coated gate attendants what the prices were.

The attendant said, 'Four dollars for a seat in the grandstand, two dollars to sit in the Southern Stand, one dollar to sit on the Embankment, and programmes are twenty cents.'

'Alright then,' said the old man, 'I'll sit on a programme.'

*

A couple of Canterbury supporters got on a bus at Karori, heading to Athletic Park for a Ranfurly Shield challenge. One of them had a lamb under his arm.

As he walked down the aisle of the bus, an old bloke with a black-and-yellow rosette on his jacket said loudly, 'They won't let you take a pig into the park.'

'It's not a pig,' snapped the Canterbury supporter.

The old man turned around and said, 'I was talking to the lamb.'

*

On the day before the All Blacks played France at Eden Park in 1961, two 'officials' from the Mount Albert Borough Council inspected the park's facilities. They returned again on the morning of the match, and a couple of hours before kick-off were causing a bit of a stir among the busy Auckland Rugby Football Union (ARFU) staff with their demands to inspect the public lavatories to see if they were up to standard.

Having carried out their inspection, they asked where their seats were for the big game. They were told the match was a sell-out and there were no spares.

One of the men apparently said, 'But we must have seats. As you can see by our cards of identity, we are on official business.'

'In that case,' said a frustrated ARFU staffer, 'I shall be very happy, gentlemen, to see that you are accommodated on the seats which are of such concern to you. Anywhere about the ground, I shall make sure that there are two toilet seats for you!'

*

Two blokes were at the All Blacks test against Ireland in Wellington in 2008. It was a freezing cold June night, with sleety rain falling throughout the first half of the game. At half-time, the men's jeans were soaked through, and they were shivering like nothing else. The score was only 8–8. One man turned to the other and said, 'Tell me how much fun we're having. I keep forgetting.'

*

A Blues fan was in the pub at Wellsford with his dog watching a Super Rugby game. Every time points were scored against the Blues, the dog would run around the pub pushing chairs over and biting people's ankles.

'What's up with your dog?' asked a couple of out-of-towners who had stopped in for a drink.

'He hates it when the Blues lose,' said the man.

'What does he do when they win, then?'

'Dunno,' said the man. 'I've only had him two years.'

*

The South African Super Rugby team the Cheetahs were so bad and had so little success that by the end of their last season they were doing a lap of honour whenever they were awarded a penalty.

*

Many years ago, Snow White arrived home one evening to find her house had been destroyed by fire. She started panicking because she knew the seven dwarfs had been asleep inside. As the firemen were dousing the fire and checking through the remains of the house, they heard a voice saying, 'Otago to take the Shield, Otago to take the Shield.'

The firemen looked at Snow White.

'Thank goodness,' she cried. 'Dopey's still alive!'

*

Two rugby fans were standing outside Cooks Gardens in Whanganui.

'I wish I'd brought the piano along,' said one.

'Why would you want to bring a piano to a footy game?' asked the other.

'Because I left the tickets on it.'

*

Two Australian rugby fans were caught climbing over the fence at the Olympic Stadium in Sydney.

When they were hauled down by security, one guard said to them, 'I'm getting sick of this. Get back in there and watch the game until it's finished.'

*

At the Blaketown rugby club in Greymouth, a former long-serving player who had taken a few too many knocks to the head arrived at the game with about 20 minutes to go. Standing in the mud next to an old mate, he asked, 'What's the score?'

'Nil-nil,' said his mate.

'Oh,' said the man, 'and what was it at half-time?'

*

A staunch Waikato fan was on an All Blacks supporters' tour to the 1991 World Cup. Every night when the group would get together to have a few drinks before or after dinner, he would go on and on about Waikato flanker Duane Monkley not being in the World Cup squad while Auckland's Mark Carter was.

When the All Blacks played Canada in the quarter-finals in Lille, France, the Waikato man had had a few too many red wines with lunch and was rather vocal during the game.

'Oh, can't you tackle, Carter?'

'Jeez, catch the ball, Carter!'

'Try something new, Carter. Win the ball at a ruck.'

Eventually, one of the exasperated supporters sitting near him said, 'Carter's not even playing.'

The Waikato man replied, 'That proves my point. He's not good enough to be out there.'

*

Many years ago, Wellington had a tiny halfback who, as they say, barely weighed 8 stone soaking wet. He made his debut against Otago at Carisbrook. The southerners had a fearsome forward pack at a time when rucking was very much part of their game.

A couple of minutes into the game, the little halfback had hung back near the sideline in the 25 to take a mark. As soon as the ball touched his arms, the rampaging Otago forwards knocked him to the ground and rucked over the top of him. As play moved on, the little halfback was very slow to get to his feet. While he was standing there dazed, a zambuck ran over to him and asked him if he was okay.

The halfback looked around the stands and said, 'How did they all get back into their seats so quickly?'

*

After a provincial game a well-known winger was being ticked off by his coach for all the mistakes he had made. The put-upon player finally had enough and loudly asked the coach, 'Okay, how should I have played the game?'

One of the nearby props said, 'Under an assumed name.'

*

How did Jonah Lomu change a lightbulb?

He held it in the air and the world revolved around him.

*

Not long after World War II, Wellington University were playing Hutt Old Boys. The referee made the toss under the grandstand and the two captains shook hands.

'May the best team win,' said the Hutt captain.

The University captain replied, 'You mean, may the better team win.'

*

Against the 1977 Lions, new All Black fullback Colin Farrell had a debut to forget, dropping the high ball and throwing a few wayward passes. At the after-match, he was approached by a man who said to him, 'You had a bit of a tough game. I think I might be able to help you.'

'Oh, really,' said the young All Black. 'Do you do a bit of coaching?'

'No,' replied the man. 'I'm an optician.'

*

There is an old story that after one of the New Zealand Army team matches in Paris in 1918, 'an older All Black' woke early in the morning to find himself lying next to what felt to be a beautiful but stone-cold woman. He got the fright of his life. Was she dead? More light revealed that it was a large statue of Venus that his teammates had seconded from the hotel foyer and put in bed with him when they had tucked their mate into bed after a late night.

*

In 1946, newspapers reported the (very harsh) 10-year ban on two players who had played a 'joke' on a referee:

> Two players, T. Bartosh and D. Udy have been debarred by the management committee of the Bush Districts' Rugby Union from playing for 10 years. This was decided at a meeting of the union, which heard a report from a referee, Mr. R. Brown, that after a match between Hukanui and Konini, he was rolled in the mud and generally roughly handled by the two players, reports the *Dominion*.
>
> To questions, the referee said that he had been attacked from behind and there was, in his opinion, no explanation or justification for what occurred. Neither player apologised, but the team captain did. The two players, who appeared before the committee, said that the whole incident was a joke. The game was played in bad weather and as they were leaving the field it was remarked that the referee was the only person not covered with mud. They then tackled him as a bit of horseplay.
>
> After questioning and discussion, the management committee reached the decision stated.

*

Many who have played the game over the years will know about having to return jerseys at the end of the game (or season), or having turns to take them home to have the team kit washed. In 1932, *The Waikato Independent* reported that the local union was 'annoyed' and threatening 'drastic action' if some new jerseys were not returned.

Considerable concern was expressed at last night's meeting of the Waikato Rugby Union when the manager of the recent 'A' team to Te Awamutu (Mr W. Webber) reported the loss of seven new rep. jerseys, this making the season's losses up to sixteen.

Mr Webber said the jerseys had all been handed in and checked, but had been taken from the bag on the way home after the match. The president, Mr Cubiis, said that the union could not, and would not, put up with this practice and the opinion was freely expressed that disciplinary measures must be taken.

Mr Boulton was of opinion that probably the jerseys had been removed as a practical joke by some of the boys at the expense of the manager. This view was supported by Mr Sefton, who said that he felt sure the jerseys would all be returned this week. If, however, this surmise proved incorrect, then the affair became serious, and was a matter for keen investigation. He moved that the matter be left in abeyance until next meeting. After further discussion this course of action was agreed to.

*

In 1931, the *Otaki Mail* reported that players in a Taranaki club game at Pukekura Park, New Plymouth, tried to pull a swiftie on the referee:

An Old Boys player had left the field on account of an injury and been replaced by another man. Some little while after there was a little 'incident' which resulted in another player of the same team being ordered off by the referee. The first player, who was still near the side line, crept back to the field of play and resumed his place in the team unnoticed by the

> referee. Some of the spectators observed the move and enjoyed the joke, and wondered how long the trick would go undetected. It was not long, however, before the referee either spotted the player or had his attention called to what had happened. The whistle was blown and there was a kind of general muster of players and a counting of heads, with the result that the 'injured' player again left the field. Matters were equalised for the teams a few minutes later when an Inglewood player was injured and had to retire, and the visitors had no emergency to fill the gap. It was near the end of the game, however, and for the remaining few minutes the game was played with teams of fourteen-a-side.

*

According to an item in the *Otago Daily Times* in 1939, during a Technical versus Havelock North senior club match in Napier, a second ball found its way onto the field of play. It was 'seized on enthusiastically by the Technical forwards as the correct article. Unfortunately, the Havelock backs had already got going with the rightful ball, and for a few seconds two distinct games were going forward on the same ground.'

*

Famous is the story of Billy Wallace wearing a sunhat while playing for the All Blacks in England in 1905. Teammate George Gillett wore the same in another match, too.

In a club game between Kia Toa and Fielding in Manawatu in 1921, a player wore a much more distinctive piece of head-gear: a Stetson hat. What's more, he spent time during the game smoking a cigarette.

At a meeting of the Manawatu Rugby Union management committee, a Mr Thompson expressed the opinion that after the performances of the Seniors team on Saturday they ought to discontinue playing the games for the Abraham Cup. He stated that the game in which the player wore the Stetson was 'a farce ... After discussion, it was decided, with regret, that the matches must be continued.'

*

The following is a newspaper headline about the identity fraud of a well-known All Black ... in 1897!

> 'SKINNY'S DOUBLE' CURIOUS INCIDENT ON FOOTBALL TOUR
>
> NEW ZEALAND PLAYER IMPERSONATED

Arthur 'Skinny' Humphries, the great Taranaki and New Zealand Rugby half of long ago, had a curious experience during his first visit to Australia with the 1897 New Zealand team. At the dinner following the team's first game in Sydney, Skinny received a message that he was wanted at the chairman's table.

Wondering somewhat at the request, Humphries made his way to the 'king' table, where he was greeted with the question: 'Are you Humphries?'

Arthur blushingly pleaded guilty.

'Quite sure?' was the next question.

Arthur now began to have doubts about it, but stuck to his previous assertion.

'Well, then,' came the next question, 'how do you account for this?'

'This' was a wire from someone in Bathurst, New South Wales, asking: 'Is Humphries in Sydney?'

A reply was dispatched stating that Humphries was undoubtedly in Sydney.

When the team reached Bathurst a few days later, the mystery was explained.

A few days before the arrival of the team in Sydney, a stranger bearing some superficial resemblance to the redoubtable Skinny had appeared in Bathurst. He sought out a leading hotel-keeper and told him a wondrous tale, in which he claimed that he was the only and original Humphries; that he had arrived in Sydney before the other members of the team; and that he had gone on a bender there. Then, having run out of cash, he had set out to walk to Bathurst to obtain some much-needed rest before the arrival of his mates and the start of their campaign.

It seemed a tall tale, but the stranger told it convincingly, and furnished what appeared to be adequate proof of identity. He convinced the Bathurst folk, and on the strength of his football reputation was most hospitably treated. The hotel-keeper put him up, and he was called upon to take in hand the coaching of the Bathurst football team. The first suspicion as to his bona-fides arose when Skinny's name appeared among the team for the first match in Sydney. Hence the wire.

When the answer arrived from Sydney that the real 'Skinny' had played that day, the large hotel-keeper arose, took the impostor gently but firmly by the scruff of the neck, and led him forth.

'Now, then, me lad,' he said. 'You took the name of Humphries when you came; you take the name of Walker now, son, and git!'

And he got!

*

When the 1924–25 All Blacks were at the end of their tour, their final game was against France at Toulouse. Alf West, a World War I veteran, Taranaki loose-forward and general hard-case, was asked by officials from Toulouse to allow three of the New Zealanders to pose as Frenchmen in a game that had been arranged between Toulouse and a Pyrenean side.

The trio agreed, just for a laugh. Near the end of the first half, West actually scored a try. The player who had tried to tackle him immediately gave him a bit of a spray in French. West had no real command of French, so quickly answered 'Oui, oui.'

The Pyrenean became very suspicious, realised he was not a Frenchman and nor was another of his teammates. He insisted they leave the game. (The third 'French' All Black escaped detection.)

As West left the field, with a nod and a wink he had another All Black replace him. The fourth Kiwi knew a bit of French and introduced himself among the Toulouse players, and then played undetected for the remainder of the game.

*

In 1930, representative players were feeling that the seasons were too long. The Auckland Rugby Union staged a final game between the union representatives who had been away on a tour of the provinces and those who had stayed in Auckland, for one reason or another. But nobody was that interested in playing.

According to a report in *The New Zealand Herald*, the match was:

> ... [a] farce rather than a game of football. It is hard to understand why the match was staged, as many of the players would sooner have stood down after a very strenuous season. As it was, the teams did not take the field as originally chosen, and at three o'clock Rugby Union officials were looking for players to fill vacancies in each side. The majority of the

players treated the match as a joke, and nearly half the four hundred odd spectators showed their opinion of the game by leaving the ground at half-time. Complaints were heard about the Rugby Union charging for admission to the ground and staging such farcical football as a reward. Even the referee joined in the farce by converting one try in front of the posts, and, to end it all, the timekeeper rang the bell when Corner was running over to score, the ball boy attempting to convert the try.

WILLIAM WEBB ELLIS AND THE EVOLUTION OF THE GAME

Elizabeth 1st — Good Queen Bess — has a closer connection with rugby than has William Webb Ellis, says Max Cryer, renowned historian of words, myths and their origins.

When still a princess, Elizabeth was presented with sweetmeats with a flavour new to her: ginger. Still relatively unknown in England, ginger was being imported by Lawrence Sherriffe, an enterprising London grocer.

Such was the success of his gift to Elizabeth, that she placed frequent lavish orders with him, and even more when she became queen. She often gave numerous ambassadors, official visitors and senior staff many, many gifts of gingerbread figures. Sometimes they were life-size!

The Queen's generous and consistent custom helped make Lawrence Sherriffe very wealthy. In his will, he left a considerable amount of money for establishing a boys' school in the small market town where he had grown up. That small town had been named in the Domesday Book of 1086 as Rocheberie. Its name later modified into Rokeby. But by the time Mr Sherriffe died in 1567, the name had morphed again, from Rokeby into Rugby.

For the next 300 years, there was very little awareness of the town or the boys' school that Sherriffe had endowed.

But in 1876, a mysterious — and totally false — legend arose.

A man called Matthew Bloxam wrote that he had met an 'anonymous informant' who said that he (the informant) remembered someone called William Webb Ellis at Rugby School. Fact, Webb Ellis had attended the school. But, the story continued, the informant said that Webb Ellis had been seen, over 50 years earlier in 1824, 'to pick up the ball and run with it' during a game of football.

Four years after publishing this, Bloxam unexpectedly changed tack, and wrote about the 'legend' again (still not naming his source) but now re-remembering the date not as 1824 but 1823.

Then, unbelievably, Bloxam came up with yet another date, moving the date to 1825, disregarding the fact that Webb Ellis is known to have left the school before 1825.

The supposed incident, and the three differing dates offered for it, have never been validated. Because of some caution about Bloxham, his dodgy dating, and his unnamed 'informer', the Old Boys society of Rugby School felt impelled to check on the veracity of this so-called incident of a Webb Ellis 'clutch and run'. Sure, 50 years had passed but they could find not one single witness, not a solitary written word, not even a syllable of hearsay evidence to support the William Webb Ellis story.

By the time of the 'revelation', William Webb Ellis was dead. After school he had gone to Oxford University, showed no interest in rugby, and played as a representative cricketer for Brasenose College, before becoming a clergyman. He died in France aged 66, in 1872.

Nobody had ever asked him about the 'newly remembered incident' and he died not knowing his name would go down in history associated with something for which there was absolutely no evidence.

Thomas Hughes, author of the 1857 novel *Tom Brown's School Days*, was at Rugby School seven years after Ellis left, and Hughes said he had never heard of Webb Ellis as a footballer, adding that 'any tradition including Webb Ellis had not survived to my day'.

By 1872, the Rugby Football Union had been formed. But no reliable evidence had ever been found from anybody who witnessed the so-called incident of Webb Ellis running with the ball and nobody had ever contacted the man himself.

Webb Ellis's so-called connection with rugby is now viewed as non-existent. World Rugby (a.k.a. International Rugby Board) words it carefully: 'The validity of the Webb Ellis story has been questioned.'

Rugby academic and historian Derek Robinson affirms that there is not a shred of evidence that the 'running incident' ever happened.

The curator of the World Rugby Museum admitted, 'There is no evidence to support the story.' A somewhat blunter critic decreed, 'The legend of the game's origin has more gaps than a disorganised rugby back line.'

Over the years, a fiction, a myth, had taken root as an oft-quoted 'truth'. But the public often prefers the legend to the truth. Salome is never mentioned in the Bible, nor does the Bible mention three wise kings visiting Jesus. Arthur Conan Doyle never wrote the words: 'Elementary, my dear Watson.'

At least one thing about young William is known as fact; if ever we had heard him speak he would have sounded familiar to thousands of British television viewers. Ellis was born in Salford, Manchester, the exact area in which *Coronation Street* is set!

But whatever the vagueness about its origins, the game took a firm hold as an exciting competitive sport. And it owes a gentle nod to Elizabeth I whose liking for crystallised ginger helped her grocer accumulate enough money to found a boys' school that, whether it invented a game or didn't, at least provided a now global game with a name.

Fortunately, at the time of the grocer's bequest in 1567 the town's name had changed. Any earlier and we might be celebrating a Rocheberie World Cup, which somehow doesn't sound quite right.

*

In 1888, *The Lyttelton Times* newspaper published the interesting reminiscences of an unknown correspondent about his school days, 40 years earlier, when he had played a game that was essentially 'football and handling the ball'.

This would have been at a time when early variations of rugby, Celtic football and Australian Rules football were in their genesis. Rugby evolved in a number of different English schools — such as Charterhouse, Westminster, Harrow, Shrewsbury and Rugby — but how it was played depended on the environment of each educational institution. Schools in rural settings played a more open game, with what we would call mauling, while those in urban settings, with walled play-yards of cobbles and brick, tended to favour dribbling the ball more, as this was less injurious.

FOOTBALL REMINISCENCES 1888

In my young days I was a great admirer of football, and at College did all I could to sustain and increase its popularity amongst my follow students. The football we played was not that of the Rugby Union, nor was it exactly the 'Association' [football or soccer] game, but as far as I can understand the reports I read in the newspapers, and the conversation of my young friends, it approached more nearly the Association than the Rugby. It was essentially football, and 'handling' the ball, except to catch and drop it, was strictly tabooed. Such a thing as 'passing' was never dreamt of, but the art and science of 'dribbling' was greatly cultivated. There was no limit to the number of players in a game, but only on rare occasions were there more than twenty on a side.

At my College, the rival game during winter was 'bandy', known elsewhere as 'hockey' or 'shinty', the glories of which game had been celebrated in verse by some admirer possessed of a poetic genius. His poem was frequently quoted amongst the students, and no doubt tended to keep alive an enthusiasm with which I felt no sympathy. My 'love' was football, and I felt aggrieved that her charms had been celebrated by no bard. Like many another love-sick swain, I sought in rhyme an outlet for my sentiments, and the following was the produce of my untrained muse:

'Tis Tuesday, and the day is fine.
No luckless urchin has a line
To learn by heart, or has to stay
And waste the moments of so grand a day,
Within the precincts of a corner vile,
With nought to amuse him in the while
But counting o'er and o'er the cricks,
Or play sundry awkward tricks
With half a dozen bits of sticks.
To football, then, with soul and heart,

We each and all straight way depart;
And after sides and goals are made
And coats for 'standing line' are laid,
With clamour dire, or dreadful din,
We onward rush through thick and thin,
Unmindful of a broken shin,
Or rubbing off a bit of skin
From where by rights it should have been.
'Midst cries of 'Gainst your Side' and 'standing!'
'Back!' 'That's not fair, you're always handling!'
'That's past for us!' 'Don't kick so high!'
'Confound the ball, it will not fly!'
Midst such-like clamour, then, I say
We onward force our reckless way,
Unheedful of the boots that flay
The tattering shin;
All careless of the storm of blows
Which falls on our unlucky nose
Or that the blood in to rents flows from ruptured skin
Unheeding aught is all this host
But that which forms our greatest boast,
The gaining of a jolly toast, so hot, so thin.
'Tis thus the football game proceeds.
Whilst coming darkness no one heeds,
Till halt the party's done up quite
The other halt, scarce fit to fight,
Agrees to leave. They seize the poles
Which form, you know, th' accustomed goals.
And homeward drag their wearied legs;
Whilst every brat a master begs
To give his toast,
Breathes there a lad with soul so dead.

Who, after this description's read,
And when ha's stretched upon his bed
And sleep his aching eyes hath fled,
Can think with scorn on what's here said
If such there be his brain is lead.

Ah me! How the perning of the above brings back to memory the days when I was young! That 'standing in a corner' — what an abominable punishment it was! How ashamed and how disgusted were the young fellows of fifteen or sixteen to be subjected to a penance from which they had deemed themselves to be emancipated when they doffed pinafores! No wonder I used the epithet 'vile'.

The 'standing line' was half-way between the goals. It was like the equator, in being what the geographies call 'imaginary' but at either end of this imaginary line was a heap of coats. No player was allowed to stand still on the adversaries' side of this line, unless the ball was between him and the adversaries' goal. Should he do so he must not kick the ball until he had got back into his own territory; and, in the event of his breaking this further regulation, the cry of 'Back!' was raised, and the ball became dead until it was brought back to the place from which he had kicked it.

'Past for us!' was a cry raised frequently just after a desperate struggle had taken place near the goal, when one of the players belonging to the jeopardised goal, in order to save his side, had kicked the ball — by the way, the ball was not oval in those days — past his own goal. When this occurred, one of the attacking side had the privilege of throwing the ball into play from the spot where it had crossed the goal line. Our goals had no top pole, so that a good 'dribbler' frequently scored without having to kick high.

The 'jolly toast', alluded to in the text, refers to the custom of giving each player on the winning side at cricket, and each scorer — only goals were scored — at bandy or football, a round of toast at tea the same evening. As the teachers, invariably called 'masters', frequently played with the students, and thus became entitled to a 'toast', the younger boys, in the text styled 'brats', obtained from the masters a reversion of their toast, the perfection of which was that it should not be thick and that it should be hot.

'If ever there was anybody built like a brick s*house, there it is.'**

— comment in the press-box when All Black prop Billy Bush ran out onto the field against Cambridge University, 1978.

LETTERS TO THE EDITOR II

A century, or even half a century ago, if you left a rugby ground feeling aggrieved by the refereeing or the play of the opposition or wanted to boast of your team's success, what were your outlets? First up was probably the pub, where, across bar leaners, glasses of beer would be quickly consumed before six o'clock closing while discussing the just-finished game. There may have been a long-suffering wife who had to hear her husband drone on and on about the game over dinner. After dinner, the disgruntled fan, his hackles still raised, could sit down and write a letter to the editor of the local newspaper.

Such a letter would often encourage other submissions from those both for and against the original opinion. The use of sporting nom-de-plumes aided anonymity.

The following letters were published in *The Otago Daily Times* in 1931, several days into published correspondence regarding a match between Kaikorai and Southern.

DOUBTFUL PLAY AT RUGBY FOOTBALL

Sir, — Surely. Mr T.M. Woodrow is exaggerating when he draws the conclusion that I endorse, in the main, 'Fair Plays' statements. The only point on which I agreed with 'Fair Play' was that dealing with offside play. With regard to my statement regarding the Kaikorai–Southern match, I still maintain, as anyone else will who witnessed the game, that there were two Kaikorai players who had more than a marked tendency to play offside. This is not denied by Mr Woodrow. As to the students during Capping Week, it must be remembered that the time is a privileged one, but why bring the students into the discussion at all?

Mr Woodrow accuses me of saying that the Kaikorai supporters do not like being told that their team is always offside. I would strongly advise him to read correspondence with more care, since his accusation is not founded on fact. If he watches football in the same slipshod method as he apparently reads letters in the newspaper it is not to be wondered at if he fails to perceive offside play. 'Lady Spectator' says that the insinuations which 'Fair Play' has levelled at the Kaikorai football team are unjust and untrue. Then, again, she makes reference to 'tactics of shinning, etc.' 'Fair Play' mentioned offside play in his letter, and surely the 'insinuations' and the 'etc.' in this include offside play. Mr Woodrow, being an old Kaikorai forward, is consequently broad-minded and endowed with a large share of common sense, and will, therefore, agree that 'offside play' was implied in the letter from 'Lady Spectator'. If it is to be taken that I am one of the non-players on the line I would like to say that I have played Rugby for several years. And now for the gem of the whole proceedings Mr Woodrow is pleased that I agree with him in stating that the referees are a band of good sportsmen, but that I contradict myself later on. I assure all readers that no contradiction was implied or intended. Referees cannot possibly see everything. Mr Woodrow is willing to hand in his name to the Referees' Association provided 'Fair Play' and I do likewise. Sad to relate for Mr Woodrow, 'Onside' was at one time a referee, but, owing to his calling, was compelled to retire from service. I hope sincerely, however, that this will not prevent Mr Woodrow from handing in his name, for men such as he can ill be spared from the game. I repeat that my letter was written against, the prevalence in senior football of offside play, and against that only. Hoping to see Mr Woodrow next season garbed in a white jersey, with a whistle in one hand and a telescope in the other. — I am, etc., Onside. July 23.

Sir, — There is something to be said in support of 'Fair Play's' letter in your journal of Saturday last, despite the protests from a referee and others, and the vilifying which a writer often gets when using a nom-de-plume. It is only natural, too, that supporters of a team that is being criticised should rally round and, lifting their hands to heaven, cry, 'We are not as other teams are; we wouldn't do that!' On innumerable occasions I have seen the Kaikorai and University play, and on very few occasions have I come away feeling that the fairest of tactics have been employed. Kaikorai play hard football, but no one but a one-eyed supporter would say that it is the cleanest team in the competition. We have seen in days gone by deliberate offside play, unnecessary tackling, and questionable tactics in the scrum, and the playing of the man instead of the ball. These irregularities are not peculiar to the Kaikorai team, we know, but they make up part of its game at times. We must make allowances in every game, and I feel sure these tactics are done largely in the heat of the moment through over-eagerness and keenness. Nevertheless, they should be sternly checked. The Kaikorai has a very fine team, with an exceptionally capable and clean leader, in [Charlie] Sonntag [1929 All Black], and it is to be hoped that its players can rise above the undue 'willingness' and illegal practices of the past games with University, and give us a game to be remembered next Saturday. I have no hesitation in saying that I am, and always have been, a University supporter, for one reason alone — its splendid style of open play has appealed to me and thousands of others for its cleanness and sportsmanship I would like to say that to brand a correspondent as one-eyed because he makes known absolute facts concerning a team's serious faults, which the football public at large knows to be correct, only goes to show that some people see through coloured spectacles, and allow their sense of partisanship to outrun their better judgment. All I am concerned about with those who do not care a brass farthing which team wins the flag, is that we get what we pay for — something in return for our entrance money, in the form of good, clean open football. — I am, etc., Clean Sport.

Sir, — It seems that most of your correspondents have overlooked the fact that the original letter was simply a little splash of class mud. Football has always been barnacled with a type of follower who imagines his side is of superior clay to the other clubs. It is purely psychological. — I am, etc., Bandy Harry.

Sir, — I would commend Ernest L. Eyre's poem, 'The Player in the Stand', to the notice of 'Fair Play'. I suggest to him that when he attends the match at Carisbrook next Saturday he should act up to the principles expressed in his own letter, and then he may realise that the thousands who support him are, after all, only delusions. — I am, etc., Outram, July 22. J.G. Wilson.

*

Here is the aforementioned Eyre poem. A humorous dig at those spectators who think they know it all. It was written in 1921 while Eyre was living in New Plymouth.

THE PLAYER IN THE STAND

You may be a football hero, quick to score and quick to pass;
You may gallop like a greyhound on the short crisp winter grass;
On defence you may be clever, bringing huge opponents down;
You may wriggle like an eel, and prove the smartest back in
town;
You may leap like 'Opai' Asher, in a way that beats the band,
But you'll ne'er play Rugby football like the player in the stand!
If you 'field' the ball, and kick it, lift a beauty down the line
You will hear remarks flung at you, and you'll take them as
a man
That same barracker's dissatisfied with you, or with your game;
If you shine at 'intercepting' you will hear them just the same,
If you work the 'blind side' quickly with a smart and clever hand,
You're bound to hear it better done by Percy, in the stand!
'Tis the same the wide world over — there's a chap who sneers
and rags
Because you do not please him as you play between the flags.
Take the champion 'All Black' players — even they could never
suit
The player on the benches who would greet them with a hoot.
Though they conquered all before them in the south, and
every land,
Most of them were 'mugs' and 'wasters' to the rotter in the
stand.
Give me men who'll don the jersey and who'll dash into the old
Gallant game of Rugby football, sturdy players, grim and bold.
It takes pluck to play at Rugby, there is danger in the ruck;

But the player in the grandstand has the voice, but not the
pluck!
He sits back in his ccsy seat, by gentle breezes fanned.
And smokes cigars, while 'screwing' countless scrums up in
the stand!
I wonder if our hero when the judgment trumpet's blown,
Will play the game in Heaven in a grandstand of his own!
I wonder if he'll teach the saints to pass the ball along.
And grumble when they make mistakes, and prove their play
so wrong!
I fancy I can see him now, with angel wings outspanned,
Give 'points' to angel players, from his throne upon the stand!

‘For an 18-month suspension, I feel I probably should have torn it off. Then at least I could say, “Look, I’ve returned to South Africa with the guy’s ear.”’

— Springbok prop Johan le Roux facing a long time on the sideline after being found guilty of biting Sean Fitzpatrick’s ear in the 1994 test at Athletic Park.

THE BOOK OF RUGBY

As befits the country with the proudest and most envied record in rugby history, national interest in the game and its players is reflected in something of a publishing phenomenon — the rugby book.

For over 140 years, fans of the game in New Zealand have shown a desire to read accounts of tours and the revelations of players (often after they have hung up their boots). That is not to say that other countries haven't published in this genre. In the early half of last century there were a number of notable rugby writers in the United Kingdom who, as ex-sportsmen turned broadsheet journalists, often wrote wide-ranging tomes on 'Rugger', discussing everything from the annual games between Oxford and Cambridge universities, to the best tries they had ever seen and the play of international visitors from the Southern Hemisphere.

New Zealanders have always loved reading match reports, and the newly released rugby biography or tour summary was a staple Father's Day or Christmas present in many households.

The man who can be credited with beginning this was Samuel Sleigh. He wrote a book — *Northern Tour of the Dunedin Football Club* — about a tour that took place in 1877, which he had participated in as a player. Within the match accounts were Sleigh's somewhat Presbyterian views on the value of sports.

> Whenever the sun shines and the free breezes of heaven blow, whether on the cricket field, the water, or the football ground, there is to be hoped the sons of this soil will always be found. Every manly virtue grows and flourishes where outdoor exercises are relished. Everything that is crawling and vile takes quick root, and grows like a weed, when these sports of the field fall into disrepute.

Four years after the publication of that book, as provincial unions became established, Sleigh was the first secretary-treasurer of the Otago Rugby Football Union.

In 1884, he was one of the two organisers (along with Cantabrian William Milton) of the first incarnation of our national rugby team. Sleigh managed their unbeaten eight-match tour of Australia.

The following year, he wrote *The New Zealand Rugby Football Annual*. Around this time there was a proliferation of provincial annuals. Their content was largely administrative, containing things such as rules, club delegates and other administrivia.

In 1896, eight years after the 'Native' rugby team's 107-match tour of Australia and Great Britain, the organiser of that private venture, a civil-servant and former Land Wars soldier, Thomas Eyton, compiled *Rugby Football (past and present) and the tour of the Native Team in Great Britain, Australia and New Zealand, in 1888–89, also, hints to club and young players, &c*. Also contributing to the content were well-known veteran players from the side, Joe Warbrick (who had four brothers in the touring side), Henry Wynyard (one of three brothers who toured) and George 'Bully' Williams (one of five non-Maori players in the team).

The captain of the 'Native' team had been Thomas Rangiwahia Ellison, who was hugely influential as a player, administrator and even a referee. When the NZRFU was established in 1892, white knickerbockers were part of the uniform. Ellison moved that the national 'strip' be a black jersey emblazoned with a silver fern, and white pants. This was based on earlier uniforms worn by teams such as the 1888–89 Maori team, which in turn was based on the dark blue jerseys and gold ferns of the 1884 uniform. But, in a time when the newly established provinces were highly competitive, the national team could not be seen to bear too close a resemblance to the colours of a province such as Otago, hence the switch to black and white.

(The author read a letter in *The New Zealand Herald* several years ago where a correspondent from Northland was claiming that Ellison's strip had the black originating from the nocturnal hokioi, once the world's largest eagle, the silver fern from scouts leading parties through forests, and that this meant the jersey represented strength and purpose. This is silly historical revisionism with no evidence to support it.)

In 1902, Ellison authored *The Art of Rugby Football*, which included sections on the history and development of the game in this country, as well as tactics and skills and 'General observations' such as those below:

> Kick to gain ground and run to score.
>
> A good start is a game half won.
>
> In or near in goal, kick the ball dead, rather than make it dead by falling on it.
>
> Kick rather than mark, and save forwards from rushing back, unless opponent's goal is within easy range.
>
> Mix your game. If one system of play is inefficient, play another.
>
> Never play the defensive game until you are compelled.
>
> Wear gloves in wet weather. Old worn-out white kids, not too bad.

Forwards, always wear shin guards! Small ones under the stockings are best. They need not be shown. They look a bit ferocious.

Examine your bars [forerunner to sprigs], before starting.

Bar across toe, put the wrong way, splendid for scrummers.

Here is a list of other rugby books, published between 1906 and 1960. The titles show how, ever so slowly, interest began to focus on individual All Blacks, not just the team, which has resulted in the regularly published player biographies we see today.

1906: *1905, The Triumphant Tour of the N.Z. Footballers*, George Dixon

The Complete Rugby Footballer on the New Zealand System, Dave Gallaher and W. J. (Billy) Stead

1907: *Modern Rugby Football: New Zealand Methods: Points for the Beginner, the Player, the Spectator*, Albert Baskerville

1908: *With the British Rugby Team in Maoriland: True Story of the Tour*, R. A. Barr

1910: *Players and Slayers*, Leo Fanning, with some remarks and reminiscences of Bernard Fanning

1911: *The History of Rugby Football in Wellington and the Wairarapa*, Dan McKenzie

1920–32: *New Zealand Rugby Annual*, Tom Jones (editor)

1925: *The Triumphant Tour of the All Blacks in England, Ireland and Wales, 1924–1925*, L. T. Watkins

1926: *Heroes of the Silver Fern: being a record of the 1924–25 tour of the All Black rugby football team, New Zealand*, published by Edward H. Marriner & Co.

1928: *With the All Blacks in Great Britain, France, Canada and Australia, 1924–25*, Read Masters

With the All Blacks in Springbokland 1928, Mark Nicholls
Heroes of the Silver Fern: being a souvenir programme of the 1928 tour and a record of previous tours and matches of the 'All Black' rugby football teams, published by Simpson and Williams Ltd., Printers

1929: *Canterbury Rugby Football Union Jubilee, 1879–1929*, W.G. Garrard
New Zealand Rugby Football: Some Hints and Criticism, Irwin Hunter

1930: *With the British Rugby Team in New Zealand, 1930*, G. Alley

1933: *1883–1933, Fifty Years' Record of Rugby in Auckland*, Arthur Billington

1935: *Rugby Almanack of New Zealand*, Arthur Carman, Arthur Swan and Read Masters

1936: *The Tour of the Third All Blacks, 1935*, Charles Oliver and Eric Tindall
The All Blacks of Jubilee Year, 1935: an interesting account of all matches played in the United Kingdom, with comments and criticism of the play and players, photographs of teams, records of players, matches, etc., L. T. Watkins

1938: *Rugby Players Who Have Made New Zealand Famous*, R. A. Stone

1948: *Five Seasons of Services Rugby: The History of the New Zealand Services Team in Great Britain, Ireland and France, 1941–1946*, Arthur Swan and Arthur Carman
The History of New Zealand Rugby Football, Volume 1, 1870–1945, Arthur Swan

1950: *The All Blacks on Trek Again: The Complete Story of the 1949 New Zealand Rugby Team in South Africa*, Winston McCarthy

1951: *Wellington's Rugby History, 1870–1950*, Arthur Swan and Gordon Jackson

1954: *Rugby Football in Canterbury, 1929–1954*, J. K. Maloney
Round the World with the All Blacks: The Story of the New Zealand Tour to the British Isles, France, Canada and America, 1953–54, Winston McCarthy
Bob Stuart's All Blacks, Terry McLean

1956: *The Bob Scott Story*, Bob Scott and Terry McLean

1957: *The History of New Zealand Rugby Football, Volume 2, 1946–1957*, Arthur Swan
Great Men of New Zealand Rugby, H. Tillman

1959: *Great Days in New Zealand Rugby*, Terry McLean
Kings of Rugby: The British Lions' 1959 Tour of New Zealand, Terry McLean
The ABC of Rugby, Charlie Saxton
I, George Nepia: The Golden Years of Rugby, George Nepia and Terry McLean

1960: *Springbok and Silverfern: The Great Tests Since 1921*, Reg Sweet
All Blacks in South Africa, F. W. Boshier
Beaten by the 'Boks: The 1960 All Blacks in South Africa, Terry McLean
Trek Out of Trouble, Noel Holmes, with a summary of the tour by Tom Pearce
All Blacks in Chains, J. M. McKenzie
On with the Game: The Rugby Reminscences of Norman McKenzie, Norman McKenzie
The Log o' Wood: Complete History of the Ranfurly Shield, Arthur Swan
The All Blacks' Book for Boys, Pat Booth

ADOPT A LION

When the 1966 British (and Irish) Lions toured New Zealand, each of the 30 players and the two managers accompanying the team were 'adopted' by a different boys' college. The students would cut out newspaper clippings and compile scrapbooks for their allocated player.

Older readers may well remember being part of this, following the tour progress of their appointed player, or even cutting out newspaper items to be sent overseas.

The players and their schools were:

M. J. Campbell-Lamerton (capt.): Marist Brothers High School (Invercargill)

D. I. B. Bebb: Southland Boys' High School (Invercargill)

C. N. H. Gibson: Gisborne Boys' High School

D. Grant: Timaru Boys' High School

A. J. W. Hinshelwood: King's High School (Dunedin)

D. K. Jones: Otago Boys' High School (Dunedin)

K. W. Kennedy: Christchurch Boys' High School

F. A. L. Laidlaw: Hastings Boys' High School (Hawke's Bay)

R. A. Lamont: Christ College (Christchurch)

A. R. Lewis: Hutt Valley High School (Lower Hutt)

W. J. McBride: Wellington College

C. W. McFadyean: Nelson College

R. J McLoughlin: Sacred Heart College (Auckland)

N. A. A. Murphy: Hamilton Boys' High School

C. H. Norris: New Plymouth Boys' High School

D. O'Brien: St Bede's College (Christchurch)

A. E. I. Pask: Rotorua Boys' High School

D. L Powell: Freyberg High School (Palmerston North)

B. E V. Price: Whangarei Boys' High School

G. Prothero: Westport Technical College

I. D. Rubins: Onslow College (Wellington)

D. Rutherford: Auckland Grammar School

K. F. Savage: Kelston Boys' High School (Auckland)

J. W. Telfer: Papakura High School

W. D. Thomas: Mt Albert Grammar School (Auckland)

J. C. Walsh: St Patrick's College (Wellington)

D. Watkins: Westlake Boys' High School (Auckland)

S. J. Watkins: Takapuna Grammar School (Auckland)

M. P. Weston: Napier Boys' High School

D. Williams: Wairarapa College (Masterton)

S. Wilson: Te Aute College (Hawke's Bay)

R. M. Young: Wanganui Boys' College

The majority of the players managed to pay a visit to the schools allotted them. The whole school would turn out for a welcoming assembly and the Lion would, in some cases, read a passage from the Bible, talk about rugby, New Zealand and the tour to that point, and answer a few questions, some of which were cheekier than others.

*

Three years later, when the visiting French team arrived in Blenheim to prepare for the first match of its 12-game tour, against

Marlborough, local schoolteacher Shelley Brown of Witherlea School sent the group a letter.

> Although you are too busy to see us in our new school we would like to do something for you to make you welcome. If you wish we will write to your team's children at home in France every week you are in New Zealand. We could send them newspaper clippings, too. You would need to send their names (printed), addresses and possibly the name of their schools. If this is not possible we still wish you a good safe trip home. Play good rugby and may the better team always win.

France lost to Marlborough, 19–24. They also lost the three tight tests to the All Blacks, but did win the other eight provincial games. Still, the New Zealand newspaper clippings wouldn't have made the best of reading once the Frenchmen returned home!

'If you believed everything that was published in the big city papers about all the wonder boys there, you wouldn't dare step foot on the same field.'

— Waikato coach George Simpkin prior to his side's successful challenge against Auckland for the Ranfurly Shield, 1980.

'That's from New Zealand!'

— All Black centre Frank Bunce to England captain Will Carling, as he rubbed his head in the turf at Newlands during the 1995 Rugby World Cup semi-final.

'Why not try and make a young fella's night? Hopefully, he'll remember it for a while. I know he will appreciate it, and when he gets older he will be telling his kids. That is more special than it just hanging on a wall.'

— Sonny Bill Williams after giving his 2015 Rugby World Cup winner's medal to schoolboy Charlie Line.

YOU'RE OFF!

The first time an All Black was sent from the field was way back in 1893 on the tour of Australia (which actually just meant the two state rugby strongholds: New South Wales and Queensland).

The New Zealand player given his marching orders was William 'Offside Mac' McKenzie. His nickname came from the fact he was an expert exponent of the controversial wing-forward position, a New Zealand variation of forward play that saw a loose-forward feed the ball to the scrum, and then, as long as he had his hand still on the scrum, he could hold his ground and prevent the opposing halfback from advancing beside the scrum.

Having this man feed the scrum also meant, with a quick heel from one of the two hookers in the front row, the halfback merely waited for the ball to come through his forwards' legs before quickly sending his backs away.

Anyway, on this tour of Australia, the All Blacks were playing the last of 11 unbeaten matches (having also had a farewell game against a Combined XV in Wellington before departing). Their opponent this particular afternoon was New South Wales, who they had played earlier in the tour as well. Halfway through the second half, referee James McCausland (a former New Zealander) sent McKenzie from the field for some act of foul play.

McKenzie, who had reportedly been having a splendid match, put on a fake limp as he left the field. The spectators, thinking he was leaving the field injured, gave him a great round of applause, making it one of the few occasions when a disgraced player has left the ground with the full support of the crowd!

*

Ten years later, in 1903, again in Sydney against New South Wales, the Merivale and Canterbury forward Reuben 'Ru' Cooke was sent off by another ex-New Zealander and former All Black Tom Pauling.

There had been some niggle in the game, the first of 10 tour games over the ditch, with a New South Welshman by the name of Harold Judd doing his best to get up the noses of both Cooke and his fellow forward Archie McMinn.

With only a few minutes to go in the game, Cooke was punched by Judd and fired a retaliatory shot at him. As one Australian reporter covering the tour wrote for New Zealand readers, 'While footballers are men and not angels, they will do as Cooke did. Cooke is not an angel.'

Pauling whistled for play to stop and, after speaking to Cooke, sent him from the field.

With news of the ordering-off reaching Wellington, a NZRFU committee convened to discuss whether Cooke should be recalled from Australia. He was informally 'suspended' while he waited for an Australian Rugby Union (ARU) meeting to discuss the matter. They didn't meet until the end of the week, which meant Cooke wasn't available for the next tour game.

The ARU decided that the charges against him weren't sustained, so he continued on with the team. He played eight further matches on tour, including New Zealand's first-ever test match — against Australia in Sydney — which the All Blacks won 22–3.

Cooke was in contention to play against the visiting Great Britain side in 1904, but had to withdraw due to injury, and was on the longlist of players initially considered for the 1905 tour 'Home', but was not one of the final selections. His representative career for Canterbury ended at the end of that season, but he remained active as a long-distance runner, competitive cyclist (he had come fourth in the New Zealand Wheels Race in 1899), amateur boxer, and boxing referee throughout the wider Canterbury province and for New Zealand championships. One story has him boxing the Australian heavyweight Bill Squires in a private bout, and proving a good match for the famous pugilist.

In about 1913, Cooke moved to Melbourne. There he continued his involvement with rugby, later becoming patron of the Kiwi Rugby Union Football Club.

A couple of years before his death in 1940, he visited New Zealand for the first time since his move to Melbourne. His arrival by ship in Auckland was the subject of a number of newspaper items in papers around the country. He spoke of wanting to visit tourist spots such as Rotorua and catching up with a 'host of friends ... We can spend many happy hours fighting old battles over again,' he said on his arrival.

Cooke's brother Alf was also an All Black, playing one match in 1894. Six years later he was tragically killed at Lake Ellesmere while shooting birds with a mate by the name of William Skelton. A target flew across the lake and it was Skelton's turn to shoot. As he did so, Alf Cooke stood up in the line of fire and suffered a fatal and gruesome head wound.

Skelton was charged by police with having 'slain' Cooke, and appeared in court two days after the accident. Following evidence from the coroner, the jury returned with the verdict of 'Accidental death'. The next day, Cooke was buried.

*

The second All Black tour party to Great Britain and Ireland, in 1924–25, had won 27 games in a row. Next up they faced England, who in the period 1921–24 had won 13 internationals, lost two and drawn one. They had won the Five Nations Championship, claiming Grand Slams and Triple Crowns, and were the undisputed champions of Northern Hemisphere rugby. But when a Rest (of England) beat the preferred England team in a trial match, the selectors suddenly got the jitters and made seven changes to their original England side.

The English captain, William Wavell Wakefield (easily identified by the cloth head-gear he wore), was an imposing loose-forward who helped mould the role of the modern English flanker as a terrier, ball-runner and general nuisance to opposing backs.

Much pre-match comment focused on the merits of the respective forward packs, with the home side's 3-4-1 scrum expected to easily dominate the All Blacks' 2-3-2 formation.

By mid-morning on the day of the match, traffic jams clogged the roads surrounding Twickenham. Half an hour before kick-off the ground's gates were closed, and a record attendance of 60,000 waited as HRH The Prince of Wales was introduced to the teams. (A little over a decade later, he would abdicate the throne.)

The All Blacks management had chosen Welsh referee Albert Freethy to whistle his sixth game of their tour. After just eight minutes he made a decision that gave the game an unparalleled infamy. For the first time, a player was sent from the field for foul play in an international match. That player was Hawke's Bay and All Black loose-forward Cyril Brownlie.

Although the biggest man in the All Black touring party at 6 foot, 3 inches and weighing 15 stone, Brownlie was a quiet giant. He had seen active service with the Mounted Rifles in Palestine during the Great War. He had the pace to match most of his backs, and strength that often saw him loaded down with tacklers as he made his way up-field.

There was much contention as to why Brownlie was sent from the field, in a match that had numerous incidents of rough-housing from both sides. Indiscretions named in newspapers included back-chat, stomping a player on the ground, and a variety of retaliatory punching scenarios.

The All Blacks expressed some frustration that the alleged initiator of the to-do, Reg Edwards, had no action taken against him. Edwards stood out thanks to his bald pate, and had stirred things up a bit during the All Blacks' feisty last-minute win over Newport in October. Interestingly, he never again played for England after this match.

Deathly silence descended over Twickenham as Brownlie left the field. Not even a reported half-time approach to Freethy on behalf of the Prince of Wales would see Brownlie return to play.

The legendary New Zealand fullback George Nepia later recounted in his autobiography seeing the despairing Brownlie sitting underneath the stands.

> He is sitting upon a bench, still in his togs. Brownlie has been a soldier and a farmer, as both he has become inured to the cycle of life and death that governs our lives. He is a big, powerful, mature man. Yet the tears are rolling down his cheeks. You carry the lump in your throat for the rest of your life when you think of him sitting there in his loneliness. Poor Cyril! We did our best to comfort him then, later and for the rest of the life that was cut off far short of his time.

England were the first on the board, 10 minutes after Brownlie's departure. Following a dominant England scrum, English player

Ronald Cove-Smith ended a dribbling rush by diving on the ball as it rolled across the in-goal.

Steeled by having to watch his brother walk off was Maurice Brownlie. He played like a man possessed, determined that the All Blacks would not lose a man *and* the game.

In one charge, Maurice was stopped just short of the try line. The ball was then swung to the other side of the field where Kenneth 'Snowy' Svenson scored for the All Blacks. Not to be denied a second time, Maurice later scooped up a loose ball inside the England 25-yard line and with 10 determined strides stormed towards the right-hand corner.

Jim Parker and Jack Steel also scored tries, to give the All Blacks a 17–3 lead.

Having to play the majority of the game on a heavy ground with only 14 men (and a gusty breeze in their faces during the second half), the All Blacks noticeably began to tire. Adding further to their struggles was the fact they only had six in the forward pack, when loose-forward Parker moved into the backs to cover for the hobbling Steel.

In the absence of Cyril Brownlie, the canny Wakefield called for scrums rather than line-outs to restart play when the ball went out. As a result, there were over 80 scrums in the match! They sapped the legs of the All Black forwards, and in the final quarter England's quest for points saw the backs running the ball from everywhere and easily making ground.

Leonard Corbett quickly scored a penalty for England by drop-kicking the ball between the uprights. Wing Harold Kittermaster then showed his electrifying pace with a try under the posts after a run that began around halfway. The Twickenham stands shook as the crowd's thunderous shouts of 'Go! Go!' urged him to the line.

Eight points in 10 minutes for England, but then they ran out of time. Freethy called 'No side'.

The crowd had witnessed what remains as one of the most dramatic matches in international rugby.

Read Masters, the Canterbury lock, later published an account of the tour and described that match as 'the hardest and most gruelling game I have ever played in'.

Stan Dean, the All Black manager, commented after the game: 'We beat England with a man short and I suppose we should feel triumphant. Instead, we feel sick about the whole show.'

Referee Freethy was asked to submit a report to the RFU the day after the game. He wrote that he had seen Brownlie kick the leg of an English player who was lying on the ground, something Brownlie firmly denied.

In later years Freethy was often asked about that infamous moment. He was once quoted as saying: 'Cyril Brownlie was no better and no worse than any of the others. He was unfortunate that he was the player in my line of vision when I made my decision.'

On another occasion Freethy was heard to say: 'At no point did I see Cyril Brownlie kick an English player.'

*

The first tour to the Republic of South Africa by the All Blacks came in 1928. Led by Maurice Brownlie, their test record of a drawn series (2–2) wasn't bettered until Sean Fitzpatrick's 1996 side won a series over there.

Brownlie's team had a long and arduous tour, sailing for South Africa, then playing the first match at the end of May. They left there four months later, having played 22 games. Outside of the test matches, they lost three games (Cape Town Club 3–7, Transvaal 0–4, Western Province 3–10) and drew 18–18 with Northern Province.

The match against Transvaal, in front of nearly 30,000 spectators at the recently opened Ellis Park in Johannesburg, was a particularly spiteful game. At half-time the home side led 3–0. Shortly after play resumed, Innes 'Bunny' Finlayson, the Maungaturoto-born loose-forward with a solid reputation as a 'good sport', was sent from the field by the referee, former Scottish international Mr G. Finlay, for punching an opponent on the ground. The reason Finlayson punched the player, a big forward by the name of Geere, was because he was being held in a headlock.

With head bowed, the 6-foot, 2-inch Northlander — who had begun his senior club football days playing at centre for Kamo — walked towards the stand, with booing and jeering rising in volume as he approached the touchline. It began to get so vociferous that several policemen accompanied him the last few metres to the entrance to the rooms beneath the stand. This police presence only added to the impression of Finlayson's 'criminality'.

Finlayson was quick to apologise to Geere and the Transvaal Union after the game, and in their report to the South African union Transvaal recommended that no further action be taken against Finlayson.

The manager of the All Blacks, Bill Hornig, remained hot under the collar about the treatment of Finlayson on the field. His mood was not improved by his side losing, too.

'There was no question that Geere was trying to screw Finlayson's head off,' Hornig said. 'If the referee had seen that part of the incident, both players would have been sent off.'

The following year, Finlayson again fell foul of a referee, this time in a Whangarei club game. Finlayson's side were on attack, and quick passing made it look as though a try was about to be scored. That was until the referee got in the way of the ball. Finlayson, by his own admission, told the man with the whistle to 'get out of the [bleeping] way', and was given his marching orders.

The North Auckland Rugby Union's management committee held a hearing several days later, at which the referee, still unnamed, presented his evidence that Finlayson 'used two adjectives ... one being obscene'. The committee decided no further action would be taken against Finlayson, and expressed some dissatisfaction at the evidence of the referee.

Finlayson's All Black career ended in 1930, due to injury, by which time he had played 36 games, including six tests. He was later a North Auckland selector and a popular participant at country sports days around the Kaipara, collecting a few wood-chopping titles along the way.

*

> He had only 25yd to go to the grandstand entrance but it must have felt like a mile with a large section of the 60,000 crowd standing up to boo.

So said the *Auckland Star* newspaper caption under a photo of Colin Meads walking off Murrayfield, having been banished by Irish referee Kevin Kelleher during the international against Scotland on 2 December 1967. Meads was wearing head-gear to hold in place a bandage covering a wound that had required 17 stitches (sewn into the back of his skull without anaesthetic), resulting from being kicked in the head by a French player in the Paris test two weeks earlier.

The Scotland match had only five minutes to play when Meads, flung from a maul by Scottish lock Mike Hall, set off towards the loose ball a few metres away. He flung his big boot at the ball just as Scottish halfback David Chisholm grabbed hold of it. In the words of the great Scottish commentator Bill McLaren, Meads was 'trying to loosen the ball with his foot'.

Chisholm was tripped up, but still managed to get a pass away as he lay on the ground. The referee blew his whistle as the jeers of the crowd grew thunderous. As referee Kelleher spoke to Meads, Chisholm walked up and tapped Meads on the arm, then walked off. No harm done. (There is a very famous rugby photo of Kel Tremain doing exactly the same thing as Meads, without punishment. The speculating kick at the ball just as a player grabbed at it was a common occurrence, and had been since the game's earliest days in which forwards would have a 'dribbling rush', toeing the ball forward at speed.)

Kelleher briefly spoke to Meads, telling him he was to leave the field, all before captain Brian Lochore and others could protest.

Meads later told biographer, former national hockey representative and highly respected poet Brian Turner:

> I was trying to get back on our side. One fellow was belting me. Their hooker Frank Laidlaw was trying to pull me out. I could see the ball clear and I flew through. I could also see their fly-half Chisholm rushing across to clear the ball. I thought I could get a foot to the ball before he got to it. I had to stretch to it, and actually kicked the ball as he stooped to it. I kicked the ball into his body. Frank Laidlaw yelled, 'Did you see that, ref, the dirty bastard.'

Meads remained convinced that Kelleher hadn't seen the incident but had been influenced by the histrionics of Laidlaw. When Kelleher told Meads he had to depart the game, the big King Country farmer was initially stunned. He began to walk off, then stopped when he heard Lochore's appeals to the referee. They, and additional protestations from teammates Ken Gray and Chris Laidlaw, proved fruitless.

With the Scottish crowd's boos spreading across the ground in sonic waves, Meads trudged off. At one point, he looked at the spectators and thought, 'I'd like to get hold of one of you.' But more than anything, he felt an overwhelming sense of shame.

To New Zealand rugby fans, this banishment of Pinetree was an outrage. In the Northern Hemisphere, many rugby writers and followers of the game thought it was something long overdue. One scribe wrote that for Meads to be sent from the field for that swinging leg, in his 11th season of international rugby, was like giving a burglar a parking ticket.

Meads was known around the world as a hard man on the field, a bruiser and an enforcer. For decades, most international locks were. Players wanted to test themselves physically against Meads and the All Blacks. Several of those who played with Meads have said it gave them great confidence having him in the side, and he was often asked to 'sort out' some of the opposing players who were trying things on in the scrums, line-outs, rucks and mauls.

When the Lions toured in 1966, Meads was punched in the stomach by cheeky fly-half David Watkins as he tried to charge a kick. In return Watkins received a 'back-hander' from Meads, and he fell to the ground like a shot extra in a war movie. One of the first on the scene was Scotsman Frank Laidlaw, who remonstrated long and loud with the referee that something should be done about Meads.

Then, a year later, at Murrayfield, on the scene again was Laidlaw, in the referee's ear. That time he got his way.

There were a couple of other incidents that helped build the 'case against' file for rugby writers who disliked Meads.

Playing against Australia in Sydney in 1968, Meads tried to clear the Australian halfback Keith Catchpole from a ruck by pulling his leg away. Unfortunately, his other leg was trapped under several other players, and Catchpole suffered severe injuries to muscles in his upper leg and groin that ended his international career.

In 1969, in the test against Wales at Lancaster Park, Meads broke the jaw of their hooker Jeff Young, who had been obstructing All Blacks by hanging on to their jerseys as they attempted to chase the ball.

The list of opponents faced by Meads in matches in New Zealand or on tour who tried to rough him up a bit is too long to mention. But there is one incident that stands out: on the tour to South Africa in 1970, Meads was seen as a key figure in the All Blacks' chances for a test series victory. In the early game against Eastern Transvaal, Meads was deliberately targeted. Just six minutes into the game, he had his forearm badly broken in a ruck. (Teammate Alan Sutherland had his nose broken and Jake Burns suffered a brutal kick to his back.)

All could see that Meads's arm was not right. However, on the sideline he was advised by a doctor that he could play on. After the match the same doctor cut away his jersey sleeve to examine the fracture. It was known as 'that dirty big break', and would keep Meads out of the first two tests.

'At least we won the game,' muttered a grumpy Meads.

Later in the tour he took to the field with a thin leather guard over the healing fracture. There was some opposition to this, with claims he could use it to strike other players. That was a ridiculous claim, unless Meads came up against someone allergic to leather.

In the late 1980s, the man who had told Meads he was taking no further part in that game at Murrayfield was one of the guests for the *This Is Your Life* television programme honouring Meads. Kelleher said he had no regrets about his decision, and still thought it was the right one.

*

On the All Blacks' 1976 tour of South Africa, one word that was frequently used in match reports was 'violence'. Every game — from those against lesser opposition in the midweek games to the test matches — had periods where thuggery from home players drew responses from the All Blacks, and matches descended into dockyard brawls.

In one of the more ridiculous encounters, against the combined North West Cape–South West Africa side in Upington, prop Billy Bush was seconds away from joining the list of sent-off All Blacks.

The match was played just 48 hours after the brutal 10–15 loss in the third test at Newlands.

The combined side were firing on all cylinders from the kick-off, on an afternoon when the temperature hit 31 degrees and tempers flared. All Black forwards, particularly, were copping it. Flanker Kevin Eveleigh was set upon shortly before half-time, and was cowering like a boxer against the ropes as punches were landed on his head and face. With blood pouring from a big cut under his eye, and looking slightly dazed, Eveleigh was escorted from the field.

The perpetrator stayed on and carried on using his fists.

In the second half, Bush reached the point where he'd had enough. Prop Hennie Coetzee had been 'the "villain" of the game', according to a contemporary report published in the *1976 DB Rugby Annual*. Having already been involved in 'several skirmishes', he suddenly went toe-to-toe, fist-to-fist with Bush. Referee Schübel O'Reilly blew his whistle and blew it again, but Bush wasn't stopping. He was giving Coetzee a dose of his own medicine, and it took several All Blacks to pull the big Cantabrian away — but not before one of his fists accidentally connected with the ref.

O'Reilly was on the verge of sending Bush off when the captain of the combined side, Herklaas Engelbrecht, implored him not to do so, hanging his own man by saying Bush had been provoked.

For a team that had set out to ruin the game, it seemed an odd piece of sportsmanship.

The All Blacks won the match 34–17, but afterwards coach J. J. Stewart wasn't even trying to hide how incensed he was at their opponents' tactics. 'You come halfway round the world to play entertaining Rugby, and your players get punched and injured — it's not Rugby at all.'

*

In 1980, the All Blacks were guests of the Welsh Rugby Union celebrating their centenary, when no-nonsense lock Graeme Higginson briefly joined the list of 'sent-off' All Blacks. Higginson was playing his 13th game for the All Blacks, one of which he had been captain for.

Late in the game against Llanelli, on a drizzly, dull afternoon that made the home side's red jerseys seem even brighter, Higginson set about freeing the ball from a ruck by way of some concerted rucking — which, incidentally, was against the prone frame of his teammate prop John Spiers. Scottish referee Alan Hosie had seen this, as had the crowd. With the incidents of Brigend two years earlier still fresh in their memories — when the sprigs of John Ashworth's boots had ripped open the face of Welsh hero J. P. R. Williams — the locals let their disapproval be known.

One of the touch judges, a Mr Inglis, had his bit to say on the matter, and Hosie spoke to Higginson. Then, greatly demonstrative, the diminutive Scotsman flung an arm straight out and pointed to the stands, while appearing to usher the All Black away with the other, much like a schoolteacher herding a recalcitrant boy out of his classroom. It very much appeared that Higginson had been sent off.

All Black captain Graham Mourie, highly respected for his diplomacy during his years as leader of the men in black, quickly engaged Hosie to plead for his player to stay on the field. Naturally, he was concerned for his teammate (and the subsequent reputation he would carry), but he was also worried about what Hosie's 'decision' would do for relations between the New Zealand and Wales unions and the Llanelli club.

Mourie later recalled that he was joined by the Llanelli captain, Ray Gravell, and Welsh legend Phil Bennett:

> ... highly excited and agitated, [Bennett] arrived in almost theatrical fashion and further confused the issue. The noise was deafening ... The shouting, the gesticulating continued, and many of the words spoken in the middle were drowned by the noise from the stand. Hosie finally got his message across and raised his right arm, spiralling it the way Scottish referees do to signal the end of a match, and blew the last, long blast on the whistle.

Game over? What just happened?

Hosie quickly retreated to the referee's room, followed by the two captains and a jostling pack of journalists. (Mourie made it a habit of calling on the ref after games to thank them, away from the hustle and bustle of the flood of spectators and attempts to swap jerseys with the other team. Many referees were quick to depart the field in those days. Job done, don't want to be seen fraternising with the players.)

In the referee's room, Hosie told the two captains that he had not been sending Higginson off, merely warning him that the next time he rucked like that he *would* be sent off.

The last minute or so of the game — won by the All Blacks 16–10 — had been a bit of a shambles. But perhaps the mind of the referee can be changed ... once in a century.

The other aspects of Higginson's play on tour were consistently impressive, and he was named in the XV for the test against Wales, bolstering the All Blacks line-out. Over the next three seasons he played five more tests for New Zealand, with injury and farming commitments gradually reducing his availability.

*

Fifty years after Meads had to make the long walk off Murrayfield, All Black inside back Sonny Bill Williams (SBW) became part of unwanted rugby history when he became the first player sent off in a test involving the British and Irish Lions. This in itself was something of a remarkable record when you consider some of the extremely rough play that had been meted out by the tourists on their various Southern Hemisphere tours. Exhibit A: the team call of '99', used to muster all and sundry to brawls when touring South Africa in 1974.

SBW also became the first All Black to be sent off in a test on New Zealand soil, something some rugby writers north of the equator said proved their longstanding arguments (also known as whining) that, up until that game, the All Blacks always received preferential treatment from referees. Unfortunately, the logic doesn't stack up when you look at the disciplining of New Zealand players when on end-of-year tours.

The 2017 series against the Lions had seen the All Blacks win the first test at Eden Park. Prior to that game, there had been some 'bear-baiting' of Lions coach Warren Gatland and his tactics by the New Zealand media. Much was made of 'Warren-ball', where a steady stream of forwards run off the halfback to get over the gain line. However, come game time, it was the All Blacks who ran the big men from close to the ruck, particularly big Brodie

Retallick, who had a storming game taking on the Lions forwards and making them do a lot of tackling.

They also took their chances out wide, with rookie Rieko Ioane nailing two tries.

The Lions did score the try of the night, from a counter-attack that started back at their 22, but otherwise couldn't capitalise or create opportunities the way the All Blacks did.

The All Blacks won the game 30–15, and the next few days saw what can only be described as 'traditional' complaints by the tourists' coaching and management team about the All Blacks' tactics. This, of course, is a great PR device that can be effective in two ways: first, to deflect any real inspection of your own team's failings, and, second, to indirectly get in the ear of the referee for the next test.

The venue for the next encounter was Westpac Stadium in Wellington, and the conditions were terrible. Wind and rain had the tourists rubbing their hands with glee. The last thing they had wanted was a dry night and a fast track. This game was going to be an arm-wrestle.

So it proved, until the moment that turned the game in the Lions' favour. With 25 minutes of play gone in the first half, SBW was shown a red card.

The crime he committed was a 'reckless but not intentional' shoulder charge, according to the disciplinary committee that sat to discuss his resulting suspension. SBW had joined Waisake Naholo in holding the tackled Lions winger Anthony Watson upright. The big All Black second-five's body position was all wrong, and his shoulder collided with Watson's head.

Referee Jérôme Garcès of France — whose officiating during the series from both in the middle of the field and the touchline suddenly made New Zealand rugby fans think that Wayne Barnes wasn't such a bad decision-maker after all — heard voices in his head from the television match official (TMO) and assistant referee. After a few words to SBW, Garcès quickly pulled a red card from his pocket and thrust it into the night sky like he was letting off a flare.

The All Blacks came desperately close to winning the match, despite playing the game a man down for almost an hour. Another decision of Garcès — that Charlie Faumuina be penalised for tackling opposing prop Kyle Sinckler in the air as the Lion jumped to collect a high pass — gave Owen Farrell the chance to win the game with a penalty kick. Which he did.

Lions 24, All Blacks 21.

While the journalists travelling with the tourists delighted in SBW's punishment and the Lions' win, there was a strange silence around two cynical hits on All Black number 10 Beauden Barrett, including a no-arms shoulder charge by prop Mako Vunipola, which drew only a yellow card.

Irish flanker Seán O'Brien appeared before the same judicial panel as SBW, cited for a swinging arm to the jaw of Naholo. It was deemed to have been a red-card offence, especially as it meant Naholo took no further part in the game, and had been 'missed' by Garcès and his fellow officiators. At his hearing, O'Brien was somehow cleared of the charge, after which Lions coach Warren Gatland said he would 'like to thank the panel for their professional and diligent approach'.

SBW was suspended for four weeks.

Twenty-six months after Garcès sent off SBW, his red card was shown to an All Black again. In the Rugby Championship/Bledisloe Cup test against the Wallabies in Perth on 10 August 2019, time was almost up in the first half. The All Blacks were struggling to get into the game but only trailed by one, 12–13. Then lock Scott Barrett went into a defensive ruck on the All Blacks' line, with his shoulder in much the same position as that which had seen SBW dismissed. Barrett's shoulder caught Wallaby skipper Michael Hooper on the head. The Australian yelled out in agony, causing Garcès to stop the game and refer to the TMO, Marius Jonker, for replays of the incident. Convinced of foul play, the dreaded card came out of the referee's pocket. (Perhaps Garcès would like to donate that infamous card to the New Zealand Rugby Museum when he retires from officiating.)

The absence of a fifteenth player on the field, much poor play of their own making and confident running rugby by the Australians saw the All Blacks lose by a resounding 26–47.

*

Other players who have played for the All Blacks and have been sent off in what is classified as an international match include Laurie Knight and Paul Koteka.

Knight played for the All Blacks in 1925, and five years later was sent for an early shower during Auckland's convincing 19–6 win over Great Britain. The match had been played in good spirits, with the home side dominating. Knight himself had been playing a blinder.

As the second half progressed, several of the forwards had an exchange of words and fists. Referee Joe Moffitt, from Wellington, tried to cool things down, and warned both teams that there was to be no more rough stuff.

Knight, no doubt still with a bit of adrenalin flowing, thought the referee was talking to his younger brother, Arthur 'Bubs' Knight, who was also in the side. (Bubs played for the All Blacks too, 14 times between 1926 and 1934, while Laurie's son — Lawrie — played 35 games for the All Blacks in the 1970s, including against the 1977 Lions.)

Standing up for his little brother, Laurie said to Moffitt, 'Don't go nipping at him, nip at me.'

Moffitt showed him the sideline instead. The Great Britain captain, Carl Aarvold, asked the referee to change his mind, but he refused. The Auckland crowd gave Moffitt a very loud and prolonged negative response to the decision.

There was no ill feeling after the game. Moffitt's only comment was that Knight had not been sent off for rough play.

At the after-match dinner, the manager of the tourists, James Baxter, made this curious comment: 'It is satisfactory always either to win well or to be jolly well whacked, and we were jolly well whacked today.'

Waikato prop Tohoa Tauroa Koteka, otherwise known as Paul or 'Bam Bam', had the delight of making the 1981 All Blacks end-of-year tour to Romania and France, and the 1982 New Zealand Maori tour to Spain and Wales, overshadowed by two sending-offs.

The first came in Wellington's successful challenge against Waikato for the Ranfurly Shield in September 1981. There was ill-feeling in the match right from the first whistle, but with Wellington up 12–0, Wanganui referee Bill Adlam had a major impact on the result. Just before half-time he sent Koteka off, for either fighting or kicking another player. A man up, Wellington went on to win 22–4, taking the Shield to the capital.

Then 13 months later, when New Zealand Maori played Swansea in Swansea, Koteka and his propping opposite Gareth John twice stood up from scrums as though the bell for a boxing match had rung and started clobbering each other. Koteka and John were both sent from the field. Photos of Koteka jogging off on a dull afternoon appeared in most New Zealand newspapers.

Swansea won 15–12. Koteka later moved to Western Australia, where he captained the state side.

*

In the 1947 North versus South game at Rugby Park, Invercargill, two opposing prop forwards who had been teammates on the tour to Australia earlier in the season, Johnny Simpson (North) and Leo Connolly (South), were sent from the field in the concluding stages of the game. After a scrum had broken up near halfway, the two big men continued to grapple with each other. The referee tried to separate the duo, but they ignored him and continued their face-to-face discussion. So the man in white blew his whistle and sent them both from the field. As they walked off, they shook hands and then put their arms around each other's shoulders, which drew cheers from the crowd.

*

Wayne 'Buck' Shelford can probably be considered very fortunate not to have been sent off for his punch to the face of Welsh lock Huw Richards in the 1987 Rugby World Cup semi-final in Brisbane. Buck had stepped in after Richards had manhandled Gary Whetton out of a maul and threw a punch at his head. Quick as a flash, Buck floored the Welshman with one punch. (Alan Whetton also came in to defend his brother and Buck, who had copped a punch from Welsh prop Anthony Buchanan. Alan's blow knocked Buchanan off his feet.)

There was no dispute about Buck's haymaker. The only person who hadn't seen the fist flying was Richards, who fell to the ground like a toppled tree, sprawled across the sideline.

Application of the magic sponge revived Richards, and, as he unsteadily stood up, Australian referee Kerry Fitzgerald sent *him* off for throwing the first punch, based on a report from the touch judge. The big number 5 must have been feeling really confused by the time he sat down again.

*

And then there's 6-foot, 2-inch Richard Loe, who deliberately brought his forearm down on the face of the 5-foot, 6-inch try-scoring Wallaby wing Paul Carozza at Ballymore in 1992. Carozza later said that he didn't receive an apology from the All Black prop for the cheap shot, which resulted in blood streaming from his nose. But he added:

> He [Loe] said a really weird thing, 'Worse things have happened — out at sea,' as though I was a sailor ... He seems an okay guy off the field but I guess he had a bit of lunatic about him on the field ... The only thing that really got me mad was the excuse-making from the New Zealand camp. If they'd said he'd done the wrong thing, if they'd copped it, I wouldn't have minded so much.

Later that season, Loe's foul play was headline news again after television footage emerged of him eye-gouging Otago fullback Greg Cooper during the National Provincial Championship final. He was suspended for six months, and it seems something of a miracle that 'Dickie', as he was known to his teammates, never had to make the long, solo walk off the field to jeers and cat-calls.

*

Troy Flavell's behaviour on the rugby field was once described by *The New Zealand Herald*'s veteran rugby writer Wynne Gray as 'reckless, irrational and undisciplined'.

In 1997, as a 20-year-old, Flavell was suspended for three weeks, after an appeal, for eye-gouging. Season after season he saw yellow (cards).

Six years later, a report came from touch judge Kevin Rowe to referee Paddy O'Brien during the Blues–Chiefs Super 12 match in Hamilton, after Flavell had blatantly stomped on the head of Chiefs hooker Greg Smith.

'Five blue trampled on the head of two black.'

'Are we talking a red card?'

'Yes.'

Flavell was banned for 12 weeks. In sentencing him, the judiciary looked at the four-week ban that had been given to Chiefs and All Blacks lock Ian Jones for a similar offence in 1998.

Flavell's suspension ended any ambitions he may have had to play in the 2003 Rugby World Cup. He went to Japan on a million-dollar contract at the end of that year, then returned to the Blues and the All Blacks in 2006 'a changed man'. David Nucifora made him captain of the Blues, in the absence of Keven Mealamu, but Flavell was a marked man and referees were always on the look-out for his indiscretions.

He was also a conspicuous figure in pubs and clubs, where drunk boof-heads would like to have him on. Regrettably, if he had a few drinks under his belt he didn't always find the wind-ups easy to ignore. In one instance, he punched a man in the face, causing an estimated $55,000 worth of dental damage to the man's mouth.

In the end, Flavell, who was an impressive athlete, played 22 tests for the All Blacks from 2000 to 2007. Unfortunately, he made the news again in 2016 with a drink-driving charge.

'They can't do nothin' that I can't do.'

— young boy watching the 1969 Wales team train at the Waitemata club.

'These kids aren't going to learn much here this morning, except a lot of bad habits.'

— well-known All Black at the same training session.

HUNTER AND MYNOTT

Jimmy Hunter and Harry Mynott (always known as Simon) were Taranaki teammates who played for the All Blacks on the 1905 tour 'Home' and for several seasons after. Hunter was a wing and Mynott a five-eighth. This poem in praise of them was written by Ernest L. Eyre in 1919.

HUNTER AND MYNOTT

They played for the butter province when I saw them first;
They were strong of limb;
They were the best of all the men
Who fought in the Rugby battles grim;
My thoughts drift back and my eyes grow dim,
As I think of each clever dapper punter —
These two great five-eighths, Simon and Jim —
Mynott and Hunter
They played together for many years
Made they names big in the Rugby world;
Shared together the pleased crowd's cheers.
When their foes' attacks to the winds were hurled.
Their flags of vict'ry they oft unfurled
On scores of fields, and their fame shall die not;
The ball from one to the other whirled
Like a living thing — from Hunter to Mynott.

They knew more tricks than all the rest;
They were quick at passing; and on attack
Were just like eels; they dodged with zest,
And made a fool of the cleverest back;
Though the pace was hot, they'd ne'er cry a crack.
They were quick on their feet as a railway shunter;
They ran like a horse on the racing track —
Hunter and Mynott — Mynott and Hunter!
I mind they came to Auckland once
With a set of backs that were hard to beat;
(They had no time for a Rugby dunce),
And the game they played was a Rugby treat.
They were the talk of the pubs, and street,
For though their players failed to hold
The lead they gained, and had met defeat,
It wasn't the fault of these cracks of old!
When they went to England they sealed their fame;
Their names are household words there now;
Folk hailed them kings of the Rugby game,
And they were verily kings, I vow.
Oft, when I'm plodding behind the plough,
And a football fence in my dreams I climb on,
A picture comes to my ageing brow
Of Simon and Jimmy — Jimmy and Simon!
... Who shall say. 'For the old years sigh not,'
When the old years held both Hunter and Mynott!

OH, REF!

At Auckland's last home game of the season, an Eden Park gate attendant was arguing with two men who said they were season ticket-holders but had left their tickets at home.

One of the men said, 'Brian Thompson's refereeing today, isn't he? Send someone off to ask him if he knows us. We're great friends of his.'

'Now I know you're lying,' said the man on the gate. 'I've never met a referee with two friends.'

*

A particularly chirpy player and a frustrated referee were heard to have the following exchange during an NPC game.

'What's up, ref?'

'Nothing. Anybody interested in playing some footy?'

'Think so. You interested in reffing?'

*

The job of the man with the whistle has always been a tough one, and — in the age of repetitive replays on big screens and small screens, with viewers being able to record and replay matches — is nowadays all the more scrutinised.

Referees who have had a good game in the eyes of the players and spectators are barely remembered over time. In many respects, that is a credit to them: the man in charge hardly noticed because his influence on the game was regarded as minimal.

Referees who, as they used to say, 'blew the pea out of the whistle' were and are spoken of with derision, and their appointments to matches responded to with doom and gloom in some quarters.

Can you remember the referees from the following games when the All Blacks lost in the Rugby World Cup?

- 1991 v Australia at Landsdowne Road, Dublin, lost 6–16
- 1995 v South Africa at Ellis Park, Johannesburg, lost 12–15
- 1999 v France at Twickenham, London, lost 31–43
- 2003 v Australia at Telstra Stadium, Sydney, lost 10–22

They were Jim Fleming (Scotland), Ed Morrison (England), Jim Fleming again, and Chris White (England). It is the unexpected performances of the All Blacks and their opponents that are most remembered from those games.

Then, of course, came the 2007 quarter-final against France (lost 18–20), refereed by the very inexperienced Wayne Barnes, who has gone on to be the most-capped RWC referee. Oh, the irony.

*

When the All Blacks played Surrey in 1905, the referee's performance was roundly criticised. The newspaper item below described the game as the 'greatest football farce in history'.

HUMOROUS CRITICISM OF THE REFEREE

The *London Daily Mail,* commenting on the Surrey match, said it was probably the greatest football farce in the history of

> the game which has been enacted. The Richmond spectators expected to see some wonderful football, but they reckoned without the referee. This gentleman was a Londoner and a member of the Rugby Union Committee. He was evidently under the impression that everybody had come to hear him perform on the whistle. The fantasia commenced in the first minute and continued with brief intervals for respiration throughout the game. Rain fell in torrents and between the bars of the referee's interminable selections, the players nipped and flopped about on the slippery ground like seals on an ice floe, but there was no football. Twenty-five minutes from the start the referee showed the signal of fatigue and the New Zealanders seized the opportunity to cross the line and kicked a goal. Several explanations are advanced for the referee's extraordinary lapse, but the two most generally accepted were that he had either dropped the whistle or else the pea in it had stuck. Unabashed by his temporary eclipse he blew harder than ever for the remainder of the spell and football was out of the question. During the interval he was the recipient of congratulations on his sustained musical effort. Fears were expressed that the severe exertions would tell on him in the second half. This was only too true, as the whistle failed on two occasions. Scores followed but still there was no football in it. It was an exposition of the power of music to tame even New Zealand footballers.

There were those who defended referees, such as 'Another Spectator' who wrote the following letter to the *Manawatu Standard* in 1928:

> It is a case of a beaten section in New Zealand's national pastime attacking a referee as a last line of defence. Those

> gentlemen, who are called upon to keep the game in existence, are always laid open to comment, and without them (as many unions are faced) the national game dies. If the Rugby game in New Zealand is to thrive, then let the public and players alike have more consideration for the 'man in control', who probably knows more about the game than the hardened critic.

In 1936, there was a hugely contentious match in the Far North between Omanaia and Pipiwai. At stake was the Hone Heke Cup, the trophy of Maori supremacy in Northland rugby.

A newspaper report in the *Auckland Star* described the game as 'a farce':

> From the kick-off tempers were frayed, and it was not long before spectators and players were involved in practically what amounted to a free fight. The spectators were mainly Maoris, and feeling ran high, so high that a few minutes before the end the game was held up for 10 minutes, giving the players an opportunity to 'cool down'.
>
> The Omanaia team, holders of the cup, were considerably delayed on the trip down from the North and were not ready to start the match until 4.10 p.m. The Whangarei referee, Mr. E. Harrison, who was to control the game found that the Omanaia team had brought their own Maori referee with them and he was forced to stand down in favour of the native. This official apparently was unable to control the game and there were three brawls within the first 25 minutes. Prior to the 10-minute spell being taken the referee had awarded Omanaia a try, but when they resumed he reversed his decision, and gave Pipiwai a penalty kick.

> Spectators were continually encroaching on the field and joining in the melee, but the game was eventually finished, and resulted in a win for Omanaia by 17 points to 8.

On the All Blacks' 10-match end-of-year tour to Romania and France in 1981, much was stacked against the men in black. In Romania — a Communist country that had been ruled with an iron grip by Nicolae Ceauşescu since 1967 — several players nearly had their cameras and film confiscated for trying to take group photographs in seemingly public places; black marketeers offered local currency, both real and fake, in exchange for American dollars; and armed members of the military seemed to be everywhere.

In Bucharest, the All Blacks struggled to a 14–6 win against a muscular home XV, whose forwards spent a lot of time battering away at the All Blacks' line from scrums, mauls and rucks.

The arrangements for travel between the French games were circuitous and lengthy. A liaison man quit because he claimed the job had become too hard. The midweek matches against French Selections — described to the media by Andy Haden in perfect French as 'vermin' — seemed to be intended merely to soften up the All Blacks with all manner of physical play. The refereeing was often unfathomable and in favour of the local sides. Somehow, only one game was lost, against Alpes at Grenoble, 16–18, with the All Blacks winning both tests against a French team that openly spoke of the All Blacks being beatable.

Rugby writer Alex Veysey was travelling with the team, and the report he filed after the All Blacks had beaten the Charentes-Poitou French Selection 17–13 was headed 'Keystone Cop ref stars'. In the article, published in the *New Zealand Times*, Veysey didn't hold back on criticising the failings of the man with the whistle.

> A referee who left home in the morning to audition for the Ringling Brothers circus but took the wrong turning, a touch judge who couldn't l e straight in bed and a game of rugby which was somewhere out of Disney's Fantasyland ... And cavorting through the whole show, the referee, a Mr Jean-Claude Doulcet, whose mental acrobatics confused everyone, and finally, himself ... All Black manager Pat Gill described the referee's performance as 'wizard of Oz stuff'.

Referees suffer injuries, too. A pulled hamstring or calf strain has seen a touch judge or assistant referee (as they are now called ... often a misnomer) take the place of the original whistle-blower.

One of the stranger injuries to an officiator occurred when Dr Humphrey Rainey — an Upper Hutt doctor and anaesthetist who had controlled the punch-up that was the 1971 Canterbury versus Lions game — was running a touchline for the third test between the Lions and All Blacks that same year.

'Gareth Edwards was flung into me,' he said, 'and as he collided with me he suddenly lifted his head hitting me under the jaw, catching my slightly protruding tongue between my teeth and severing the tip in the process.'

The injury had to be painfully stitched, and remained swollen for well over a week. Perhaps that is the only time a referee has had to make himself unavailable for games because he couldn't blow the whistle?

‘What is it about halfbacks, Justin?’

— Grant Nisbitt’s question repeatedly asked over the years to comments man and former All Black Justin Marshall.

‘Position, possession and pace.’

— All Black manager and former player Charlie Saxton’s philosophy on how to play the game.

‘He must have spikes under his jersey, or else they wouldn’t be afraid to touch him.’

— comment from an Oxford undergraduate when observing the wing play of 1905 All Black Jimmy Hunter.

PRESIDENT'S MESSAGE, 1981

Saturday, 12 September 1981, remains the darkest day in New Zealand rugby history. The last match of the Springboks' three-test series against the All Blacks was played at Eden Park. Prior to the game, in the streets surrounding the park, protestors and police clashed as ticket-holders tried to make their way to the ground. Police and anti-tour demonstrators were injured, several cars overturned, and baton charges dramatically scattered those marching in opposition to South Africa's apartheid system and the presence of their rugby team in New Zealand.

Inside the ground, one of the most dramatic test matches in our history was played against a backdrop of barbed wire, flares and flour bombs dropped from a plane flying exceedingly low over the ground.

All Black prop Gary Knight, who had won a bronze medal in the wrestling at the 1974 Christchurch Commonwealth Games, was felled by one such bomb.

The message in the match programme from the president of the NZRFU, Jack Clifford, as you would expect, ignored the tumult that had surrounded the tour and that subsequently made many turn their back on our national game for some time.

After expressing regret that the tour had to come to end, Clifford thanked the visiting side: 'At all of their fixtures on this tour patrons have been thrilled by their performances on and off the field,' despite the fact that the public and even media were rarely allowed to interact with the team. He admitted that there were 'some isolated alterations to the tour itinerary' but didn't state the reasons: the match against Waikato was cancelled when protestors invaded the pitch, and the South Canterbury game was cancelled for 'security' reasons.

Clifford anticipated 'scintillating rugby, played in an atmosphere of traditional sportsmanship', but not the unprecedented, sometimes frightening, protests that accompanied it. He acknowledged the 'excellent arrangements made for the occasion' and the 'hospitality' shown by the Auckland Rugby Football Union. This was to include barbed wire strung around the ground, and the Springboks sleeping under a stand the night before the match.

With some defiance, Clifford stated that support for rugby in New Zealand had 'never been greater' and concluded by 'sincerely' thanking the New Zealand police force and hoping the Springboks had a safe journey home.

ODDS AND SODS

The now treasured trophy of Trans-Tasman supremacy was gifted in 1946 by Lord Bledisloe, Governor-General of New Zealand from 1930 to 1935. It is worth noting that he pronounced his surname 'Bled-sloe' rather than 'Bled-is-loe'.

*

On 7 September 1921, the visiting South African Springbok rugby team beat the New Zealand Maori in Napier, 9–8. Two days later a cable sent by a South African reporter was published in newspapers.

> Most unfortunate match ever played ... Bad enough having to play team officially designated New Zealand natives, but the spectacle of thousands of Europeans frantically cheering on a band of coloured men to defeat members of own race was too much for Springboks, who were frankly disgusted.

It remains the most distasteful report on a match in New Zealand by a visiting rugby journalist.

*

> The majority of our men are fairly heavy smokers, and … were to be seen pulling away at their pipes with great vigour in the dressing-room just before going out on the field of play. Suppose that for the sake of argument smoking does very slightly impair one's powers of wind and digestion, we are sure that any advantage to be derived in this respect from abstention would be more than counter-balanced by a lowering of spirits and irritation at the abstention. Pipe smoking is the best.
>
> (From Dave Gallaher and Billy Stead's *The Complete Rugby Footballer on the New Zealand System*, 1906.)

*

Before the advent of the National Provincial Championship in 1976, the rugby provinces worked out among themselves who would play whom and when. The annual fixtures meeting in Wellington, which determined the season's playing calendar (held on the day before the NZRFU's annual general meeting), was fondly known as the 'wool sale'.

*

One of the earliest pieces of sports commentary broadcast in New Zealand was experimentally recorded on film at Carisbrook by Jack Welsh of Dunedin when the All Blacks played the British Isles on 21 June 1930. The 42 seconds of commentary was spoken by A. L. Canter for radio station 4YA.

> And New Zealand have been awarded a free kick right in front of their goal … Napier preparing to kick. He misses the kick [sound of crowd disappointment] and the ball goes out of

> bounds. And the score is Britain three, New Zealand nil. It is in the middle of the paddock. Both sets of forwards struggling hard for possession. Now the British forwards are away, led by Jones and Hodgson. Jones and Hodgson are in the thick of it today and playing admirable games, especially Jones. Now it comes out to Murray, to Spong. Spong to Bowcott. Throws a kick up-field and finds a posse. Oliver [All Black wing], come round quickly, laddie! He's round and speculates and finds touch ... halfway ...

*

When Springbok teams toured New Zealand, they would often bring a mounted springbok head, to be awarded to the first provincial side to beat them. In 1965, it was presented to Ken Gray's Wellington side, whose forwards gave their bigger opponents a lesson in cohesive, aggressive play, resulting in a 23–6 win to delight the Athletic Park crowd.

*

In 1884, the Sydney *Telegraph* wrote about our team thus:

> The New Zealanders seem to furnish a type of the excellence required. They are a fine body of men, well built, and with their muscular powers fully developed ... Rugby football is THE game of New Zealand and cricket is THE game of Australia. There is a natural affinity between the climate of New Zealand and the robust character of this outdoor sport. It has taken hold of the youth of the Colony, and is played with enthusiasm through half the year ... They are an ocular demonstration of the physical manhood which is being developed in New

Zealand. If the intellectual development is correspondent, there will be a fine struggle for manhood supremacy between the continental and the island colonies.

*

When the players in the All Blacks headed away on tours prior to World War II, the photos used for their passports were the same as those used for 'media' purposes, such as match programmes and even cigarette cards. Taken by Crown Studios in Wellington, the players were in a mix of attire, from their rugby jerseys to 'Number 1's — suit and tie.

*

In the early 1930s, before the All Blacks left New Zealand, they had an unusual piece of paperwork to attend to. During the Depression, the government had introduced a system whereby working men paid coupon instalments during the year, which were collectively used as a fund for the unemployed. Each player had to have his coupon book certified, usually at a local post office, as being paid up to the date they were to depart New Zealand.

*

Dick Evans, the Wellington Supporters Club founder, often led the pre-match parades through the city in the 1960s.

*

On weekdays, often on Wednesday afternoons, before the turn of the 20th century, social rugby games would take place. We now call them 'business house' matches. How is this for a combination from 1886: Butchers against Publicans! Pre-match, *The Auckland Star* newspaper reported that the game was:

> ... causing a good deal of interest amongst persons connected with those callings. A charge of sixpence will be made and ladies will be admitted to the ground free. In the evening, the representatives of 'beef' and 'beer' will dine at Robson's Commercial Dining Rooms.

*

In 1899, the Otago Rugby Union interviewed 11 members of the Kaikorai team who were defending themselves against charges of 'rowdyism'. A church minister claimed to have been in the carriage of a train when said rowdyism took place. The players all corroborated the evidence of other members that there was no drunkenness and no rowdyism during the train journey, beyond choruses being sung of well-known songs and a rhyme asking for food and drink at a refreshment room.

*

In 1883, it was reported in a newspaper that:

> ... an excellent Parliamentary joke was perpetrated in the House yesterday by Mr Edward Shaw. A debate was proceeding on the Pacific Islands Annexation project. Mr Shaw rose with others to address the House; he commenced by remarking that not many weeks ago Mr Macandrew interrupted an important debate to announce that he had just received a telegram stating that the S.S. *Ionic* had safely

crossed the bar at Port Chalmers. He (Mr Shaw) had now to announce that a communication had just been placed in his hands to the following effect — 'Football match: Wellington, won by a try to nothing.' (Cheers and laughter.)

*

Napier was a busy place when Hawke's Bay held the Ranfurly Shield in the 1920s. One weekend in 1923, when boxing championships were also being hosted in the town, the manager of the Wellington rugby team informed a *Star* reporter that the day before:

> ... during the absence of the team from the hotel on Sunday afternoon, when they were entertained at a motor drive by the local sportsmen thieves entered the rooms occupied by the players, and systematically ransacked their bags. Many small personal belongings were stolen, but what the visitors resented most of all was the theft of three representative jerseys, a kewpie, to which great sentimental value was attached, and a football.
>
> After the match on Saturday, when the officials were celebrating in a bar, a man entered and removed a bag from under the manager's feet. The bag contained money and jewellery, the property of the players. The would-be thief took the bag to a corner and commenced to abstract the money, placing it in his vest pockets. The manager asked him if he considered it a joke to steal, and thereupon the bag rifler struck him a blow on the face. Despite the fact that the manager has but one arm, he very soon demonstrated that he was more than capable of taking care of himself, and the troublesome one was eventually given in charge of a constable, though no complaint was laid regarding the attempted theft.

*

Canterbury coach Frank Jack said in 1990 that:

> A lot of North Island teams have a lot of hype; they play music and have all sorts of other things going on. But I like it the way it is at Lancaster Park, more traditional, and we enjoyed Carisbrook, a brass band, like the old days and good old cheering and jeering, depending where you came from.

*

Eden Park's cheerleaders had begun, somewhat controversially, in the mid-1980s. By 1992, they were costing the ARU over $100,000 a season, and it looked as though the pom-poms would be put away the following year. New Zealand Cheese Promotions, who used Inga Tuigamala in advertisements, took over sponsorship of the troupe. As a result, the cheerleaders became known as the 'Say Cheese' Cheerleaders, and not only performed prior to Auckland's home games, but also the All Blacks games against Western Samoa and the British and Irish Lions.

The rugby programmes for those games included promotional shots and potted biographies of the dancers, whose favourite foods included the likes of nachos and potato skins, and who enjoyed watching *Shortland Street* and *Beverly Hills 90210*. Some of the black-and-white promotional photos were full-page — larger coverage than for most of the players.

Before the All Blacks test against Australia at Athletic Park in 1990, the Dallas Cowboys cheerleaders had performed. It was a wet day and the soft, muddy ground and ramshackle stands must have been quite bewildering for the Americans. But they did keep up their smiles.

*

Even more costly to the ARU than the cheerleaders was the Eden Park big screen, which had begun life in 1991 as a movable screen whose images could barely be seen in bright sunlight, even with the sun behind it. The screen cost the ARU more than $2 million, but who, apart from other large sporting events such as the 1992 Cricket World Cup, would hire it? As it turned out, not enough promoters to prevent it causing the ARU a $32,000 loss in 1992.

*

At the annual meeting of the NZRFU in 1938 it was decided New Zealand had to come into line with the rest of the rugby union countries by adopting spells of 40 minutes instead of the local standard of 45 minutes. The failure of the Wellington union to fall in with the decision of the superior body of which it formed a part, was described in the *Evening Post* as:

> ... an act not only of discourtesy but of disloyalty. Matches with visiting overseas teams are played in 40 minute spells and there has never been the suspicion of a complaint by the public that the duration of play in any of these games was too short. Are we going to have the absurd proceedings of the clock face at the park being altered from forty-five to forty minutes for next Saturday's inter-island game, then changed, back again for local competition matches, and finally changed again to forty minutes for the representative games which commence in a few weeks' time and which must be played according to the decision of the delegates assembled at the annual meeting of the New Zealand Union?

*

On the 1976 tour of South Africa, the All Blacks convincingly beat Western Transvaal, 42–3. Despite the best efforts of the home side's forwards to rough up the All Blacks, and a 27–7 penalty count against the tourists by the local referee Mike Kessel of Natal, including 19–2 in the second half, a section of the Potchefstroom crowd weren't happy. They showed their displeasure by throwing oranges at other spectators, an All Black supporters' tour group and even the touch judges, who had to receive police protection.

*

Frank Mitchinson was a Wellington centre who, with 10 test tries, held the New Zealand test-try scoring record from 1913 until Ian Kirkpatrick overtook it in 1973. After his rugby days, despite a heart strain that prevented him enlisting in World War I, he farmed at Raetihi in the central North Island.

In March 1918, a catastrophic wildfire engulfed thousands of acres of bush in the area. Mitchinson had 1000 wethers that were paddocked and ready to go to the works. The direction of the wind changed, and suddenly Mitchinson's property was in the path of the hungry, roaring fire.

He grabbed a woollen blanket from his small farmhouse, soaked it in water and, with a burst of speed reminiscent of his playing days, ran headlong for the nearby river which bordered his property. Plummeting down a high riverbank, he plunged into the water, where he sat through the night covered by the blanket as the fire consumed everything about him.

By dawn, the fire had passed on. Mitchinson climbed up out of the river bed. Before him lay an apocalyptic sight. Everything had been burnt, and was smoking and crackling from the residual heat. All 1000 of the sheep had been incinerated. The farm dogs were never found. As the farming neighbours came together, it was discovered that on a neighbouring property three people had been burnt alive.

*

Western Samoa first toured New Zealand in the winter of 1976, when they played eight matches in 25 days, including two games against the New Zealand Maori. They only won one of the tour games, a 24–10 victory over Buller.

Crowds for the games were small, but there were large events hosted by Samoan communities wherever the team went. It is worth noting that all of the tourists were players who lived and played in Samoa.

Fast-forward 17 years to the 1991 Rugby World Cup, where Samoa put in a stunning effort. Having had to qualify for the tournament, they reached the quarter-finals after they beat Wales 16–13 and ran Australia close at 3–9. This form, and much lobbying the NZRFU by the likes of Peter Fatialofa and Bryan Williams, saw Samoa finally play the All Blacks in Auckland, the home of the largest Samoan population in the world.

Of that 28-man Samoan squad, 19 played rugby in New Zealand. Two of those players, Alama Ieremia and Junior Tonu'u, would later play for the All Blacks. Again it was an eight-match itinerary. Two games were lost (to New Zealand XV and the All Blacks), but they notched up impressive wins, including a 128–0 romp over Marlborough.

The curtain-raiser to the All Blacks versus Western Samoa match was the annual clash between the New Zealand and Australian Under-21 sides. The reserve halfbacks for the respective teams were Justin Marshall and George Gregan. Starting ahead of them were Elton Moncrieff of Wellington and Rodney Hayes of the Australian Capital Territory.

*

One April evening in 1998, the Crusaders were hosting Northern Transvaal. The Canterbury franchise had started the Super Rugby season poorly, resting on the bottom of the table at one stage. But then they started to turn things around, and clocked up win after win after win, with some terrific come-from-behind victories.

But during the match against Northern Transvaal, the Crusaders were behind and not playing well at all. The large crowd on the western terraces started to get impatient, distracted.

All of a sudden, up one of the old Tannoy speaker poles climbed a young man. Clinging to the top of the pole he started to attract the attention of those below him, then people in other sections of the park. Play continued, but all eyes were on the man. He taunted some, saluted others, and had a few objects thrown at him.

Slowly the boys in blue made their way around the front of the terraces and up the stairs to stand under the pole-climber. For some time he didn't notice the police below and continued to preach from his perch. At one point he looked as though he was about to make his descent, but when he looked down he saw for the first time the two policemen waiting for him, much to the amusement of the crowd.

Being beckoned to make his way back to terra firma, the man started to slide down the pole, then stopped and climbed back to the top again. He repeated this a second time. Then the crowd joined in, sounding his descent and then his panicked climb to the top again.

Down. 'BOO!'

Up. 'HOORAY!'

The crowd's delight in this little piece of terraces theatre grew louder. By now the game was merely a background to the showman on the pole. Even several of the Crusaders players took glances to see just what was going on.

Had the crowd been watching the game they would have seen the Crusaders score a couple of tries and take the lead in the match.

The strength of the human possum on the pole had to be admired, but eventually fatigue set in and he slithered down to his appointment with the local constables. As the man was escorted away, a chorus of boos followed his exit. Just before he left the sight of the terrace crowd, he raised his hand quickly and jubilantly into the air. A final loud cheer farewelled him.

The crowd went back to watching the game. Crusaders 31, Northern Transvaal 20.

*

Ticket scalping has always been an issue for All Blacks tests. When Great Britain were here in 1930, there were reports that anyone could get a seat in the sold-out Lancaster Park grandstand, 'if they knew where to go'. It was reported that one scalper had six assistants in the ticket queue at Wellington. All six bought the maximum allocation of four seats, and within a day the tickets were for sale on the black market in Christchurch.

*

The 1929 All Blacks' tour of Australia was the least successful up to that point. Affected by an ever-increasing list of injured players, they lost all three tests for the first time. In what could be seen as something of a metaphor for that All Black visit across the ditch, when their train left Armidale after their match with New

South Wales County bound for Brisbane, it derailed. Six of the eight carriages left the tracks in the Black Mountains, and three collapsed onto their sides. It was early in the morning, foggy and very cold for the passengers who had to disembark. Fortunately, the train had been travelling slowly, as it was making its way up an incline, and nobody was injured. The only two carriages not to leave the tracks were the last two, in which the All Blacks were sleeping.

Such drama was nothing new to Taranaki forward Alf Kivell: when he had been making his way to Wellington to join the team before they sailed, the train he left Stratford on had also derailed!

On that same tour, one of the tests against Australia kicked off late. Of the All Blacks' 35 member party, 30 arrived at the same time in a charabanc and were admitted through the gates. A few minutes later a car containing the other five All Blacks pulled up. They were told by a gate-keeper that they would not be admitted as the real All Blacks had already arrived.

As things grew heated, the gate official was warned that if the five could not enter the ground there would be no match. Eventually, a compromise was reached: the car had to stay outside the gates, and the five All Blacks were made to walk through the turnstiles. The players were 13 minutes late in taking the field. The All Blacks manager, Mr J. McLeod, said his threat of 'no match' was only a joke. 'But we were so helpless,' he said.

‘I thought [referee] Barnes was frozen with fear and wouldn’t make any big calls.’

— Richie McCaw finally gave his thoughts on *that* 2007 Rugby World Cup quarterfinal loss to France.

AFTER THE FINAL WHISTLE

In his 1978 short story 'The Big Match', Dunedin writer A. P. Gaskell perfectly described what it was like to leave one of our rugby stadia on a Saturday evening in winter.

As the early darkness began to descend, the crowds shuffled their way to and through the exit gates, lit only by tiny flares as cigarettes were drawn on; the exhaled grey smoke adding to the gloom of dusk.

> After all the cheering the place seemed very quiet, and from the street outside came the noise of cars starting up and whining off in low gear, and a tram screeching round the corner under the railway bridge. Overhead the sky was clear with a promise of frost. A few small boys ran with shrill cries under the goalposts; the rest of the field lay empty in the grey light, and the smell of mud came through the damp air.

An apt conclusion to this volume.

SELECT BIBLIOGRAPHY

Pat Booth, *The All Blacks' Book for Boys*, Whitcombe and Tombs, Christchurch, 1960.

Dan Carter with Duncan Grieve, *My Story*, Upstart Press, Auckland, 2015.

Rod Chester and Neville McMillan, *Centenary: 100 Years of All Black Rugby*, Moa Publications, Auckland, 1984.

Rod Chester and Neville McMillan, *The Encyclopedia of New Zealand Rugby*, Moa Publications, Auckland 1981.

Rod Chester and Neville McMillan, *The Visitors: The History of International Rugby Teams in New Zealand*, Moa Publications, Auckland, 1990.

Rod Chester, Neville McMillan and Ron Palenski, *Men in Black*, Hodder Moa, Auckland, 2006.

Don Clarke and Pat Booth, *The Boot: Don Clarke's Story*, A. H. & A. W. Reed, Wellington, 1966.

Jerry Collins with Tim Castle, *Jerry Collins' Road to the World Cup*, Hodder Moa, Auckland, 2007.

Matt Elliott, *War Blacks: The Extraordinary Story of New Zealand's World War I All Blacks*, HarperCollins Publishers, Auckland, 2016.

Matt Elliott, *Kieran Read: Tribute to a Great Eight*, David Bateman, Auckland, 2014.

Matt Elliott, *Thorny Encounters: A History of England v the All Blacks*, Pitch Publishing, London, 2018.

Matt Elliott, *Dave Gallaher: The Original All Black Captain*, HarperCollins Publishers, Auckland, 2012.

Bill Francis, *Peter Montgomery: The Voice of Yachting*, Trio Books, Wellington, 2015.

David Gallaher and W. J. Stead, *The Complete Rugby Footballer on the New Zealand System*, Methuen, London, 1906.

Bob Howitt (ed.), *New Zealand Rugby Annual*, Moa Publications, Auckland, (various, 1971–1993).

Bob Howitt, *Paddy O'Brien: Whistle While You Work*, Hodder Moa Beckett, Auckland, 2004.

Bob Howitt, *A Perfect Gentleman: The Sir Wilson Whineray Story*, HarperSports, Auckland, 2010.

Peter Jones with Norman Harris, *It's Me, Tiger,* A. H. & A. W. Reed, Auckland, 1965.

Lindsay Knight, *The Shield: A Century of the Ranfurly Shield*, Celebrity Books, Auckland, 2002.

Robin McConnell, *Iceman: The Michael Jones Story*, Rugby Press, Auckland, 1994.

Greg McGee, *Foreskin's Lament*, Price Milburn with Victoria University Press, Wellington, 1981.

Greg McGee, *Tall Tales (Some True)*, Penguin, Auckland, 2008.

Terry McLean, *Cock of the Rugby Roost*, A. H. & A. W. Reed, Wellington, 1961.

Terry McLean, *Great Days in New Zealand Rugby*, A. H. & A. W. Reed, Wellington, 1959.

T. P. McLean, *New Zealand Rugby Legends*, Moa Publications, Auckland, 1987.

John Mayhew, *Doc Mayhew: Rugby's Medicine Man*, Hodder Moa Beckett, Auckland, 2004.

Mils Muliaina with Lynn McConnell, *Living the Dream*, Hodder Moa, Auckland, 2009.
George Nepia and Terry McLean, *I, George Nepia*, A. H. & A. W. Reed, Wellington, 1963.
Ron Palenski, *Rugby: A New Zealand History*, New Zealand Auckland University Press, Auckland, 2015.
Keith Quinn, *Quinn's Quirks: The Rugby Wit and Wisdom of Keith Quinn*, Trio Books, Wellington, 2007.
Wallace Reyburn, *Mourie's Men: The All Blacks Tour 1978*, Cassell New Zealand, Auckland, 1979.
Alan Sayers and Les Watkins, *Fred the Needle: The Untold Story of Sir Fred Allen*, Hodder Moa, Auckland, 2011.
Gordon Slatter, *On the Ball: The Centennial Book of New Zealand Rugby*, Whitcombe & Tombs Ltd, Christchurch, 1970.
Peter Snell and Garth Gilmour, *No Bugles, No Drums*, Minerva, Auckland, 1965.
A. C. Swan, *The Log o' Wood: Complete History of the Ranfurly Shield*, Whitcombe & Tombs Ltd, Christchurch, 1960.
Alan Torley, *Rugby: The Pioneer Years*, HarperCollins, Auckland, 2008.
Brian Turner, *Meads*, Hodder Moa Beckett, Auckland, 2002.
Roy Williams, *Sports Crazy: A Lifetime in Kiwi Sport*, David Bateman, Auckland, 2014.

Selected websites

audioculture.co.nz
ngataonga.org.nz
nzherald.co.nz
paperspast.natlib.govt.nz
rugbymuseum.co.nz
stuff.co.nz

ACKNOWLEDGEMENTS

My sincere thanks to Max Cryer for his list of early rugby songs and the item on the myth of William Webb Ellis; and to my good friend and neighbour, Dave Cameron.

Thanks to the following for permission to reproduce lyrics: Christopher McVeigh; James at Auckland Rugby; Judy Wong, Chair Auckland Rugby Union Supporters Club. Thanks to TVNZ and Katie Usher, Digital Production Library for permission to use quotes from *The Making of an All Black*.

Thanks to publisher Alex Hedley for offering me this project, and to the editors, Kate Stone and the very thorough Madeleine James.

Special thanks to my wife, Melissa, and son, Peter ('How many words have you done now, Dad?'), who went without a holiday while I worked to meet the book deadline; and to Murray, for his ongoing interest.

LeFroy's Castle

By JP Cline

Introduction

I started writing this story back in 2014, after a trip to Ireland, where I exhibited my paintings. One evening I went to a pub in Howth, it was very cold out and I felt like I was a character in a Gothic novel, in the sense that it was cold, dark and gloomy and I was off to a big adventure. On that trip I met the most interesting people, for example, someone who works in a castle. I actually ended up having breakfast in a castle once. Coming from tropical Mexico where we haven't got that many castles, I felt a sort of "wow" moment where I thought about how in my country nobody has breakfast in castles and here in Ireland, since you have far more castles than we do in Mexico, chances of being invited to see one are greater than one's chances in Mexico.

Every castle on earth is believed to be haunted and I decided to write a short novel about a haunted castle. I have a big imagination and I think about ghosts, goblins, monsters, etc when I am certain places, such as castles, thick forests and so on. I also make up stories about where I am, I imagine the adventures of a lunatic or a mad scientist, or in this case a haunted castle.

I have a theme in my novel about dreams. There is a room in the house where it is believed that anybody that sleeps in it will have a dream where they see their death. I have always been interested in dreams and have often wondered "what if you could see the future in a dream?" That thought is what inspired me to write about the power of dreams. We all love dreams, I suppose, some of which we want to come true, others we wish wouldn't. In this case the characters, as I mentioned before, in a dream they see how they die, they cannot do anything about it but just the same, a spirit within the castle shows them the moment they die.

As for the setting, Howth means a lot to me. I love visiting Howth. I have many friends there. Unlike Howth which has one castle on the top of a hill, Clongriffin never once had a castle, in so far as I know. However I had visited a few castles in 2014, when I started writing this story and I imagined one. I called it Clongriffin Castle, taking the name from what is now a suburb of Dublin, but was mostly fields in the XIX century.

I hope you enjoy reading the story as much as I enjoyed writing it. The last thing I have to say about it, is, I am an artist. I paint and that is how I went to Ireland, to have my art shown in Dublin. That's where I got the idea for my story. Anyway, in art you tell a fraction of a story, but you can not tell an entire story. For example, if you paint a boat in the sunset, you don't tell people where the boat came from and where it is headed, much less who is in it and what they are up to inside the boat. So, you just tell people that there is a boat in the sunset. I did the same thing with my story. I give you an image of something that happened, an anecdote as it were, but I do not write volumes and volumes about who everyone was and where they came from and where they are headed. Because this is a written painting in the sense that you get a part of a story, which gives you an idea of what happened, and you decide in your mind what the story was before and what happened after. Like you do when you observe a painting. The idea of my story is for you to dream. It is a fantasy. That is why I kept it short but interesting. Dear reader, feel free to decide for yourself who the characters were before the story and what happened to them afterwards. I am only painting a picture of a short period in their life. It is up to you to dream about what happened to them before and after these events.

Please enjoy by story and have fun reading it.

Thanks so much, JP Cline

Chapter 1

It was a very cold winter in Ireland, then. Colder than it had been in a while. The north wind was so strong that one could imagine a herd of Polar Bears walking through the middle of Dublin. Polar Bears outside Christ Church Cathedral, and Polar Bears near the Liffey. Polar Bears on the Ha'Penny Bridge and Polar Bears as far as the coast. It was so tremendously cold out that night that very few people dared go out, for fear of being turned into an icicle.

Heath Rochester, a man in his thirty's had just arrived from England that night. He made it to a fishing village called Howth, hoping to find food, and a place to stay for the night, and keep warm. As he walked along Howth Harbour, in his dark coat, his hair blowing in the wind, and his hand in his pockets to keep warm, he saw a light on in a pub. Our friend, Heath, could not have been more pleased to see the pub for the cold was so tremendously bitter: He was dying for some warm pub food and a drink. Heath had also been walking for some time. You see he had set sail from England in order to seek adventure. He was an artist and had been told that Howth is a village that is very much worth painting.

"Pardon me, sir, do you serve food here?" Heath Rochester asked a man who worked in the public house as he walked in the place.

'Yea, we have, I can get you bangers and mash, and a pot of tea if you like" He thanked the man and went to sit down. Heath looked around; there was only one other guest in the pub. Quiet night, he reckoned, which was funny, considering the fact that pubs were known for having people all the time, but he thought the cold kept everyone away. The other man who was at the pub (besides the pub owner, who was working there) was elegantly dressed, in a tailored suit, near him was a brand new top-hat, which was a bit odd for a fishing village, to be seen wearing something that fancy. The elegant man didn't look very Irish he had very dark skin, brown hair, almost black, and dark eyes. You expect the Irish to be almost white, red or brown hair and blue or green eyes.

Heath blew into his hands to keep warm. "Bit nippy out, is it?" said the posh, dark skinned man.

"I can't warm up. The cold has penetrated to my bones," replied Heath Rochester. Just then the pub owner came back with the pot of tea and the food.

"That will warm you up, won't it?" said the man.

"I hope it will, I'm frozen."

"So, what brings you to Howth?" asked the dark man who was sat near Heath.

"I am an artist, I was told I would find inspiration for a painting here, or a series of paintings. English people like Irish landscapes these days, they pay really good money for them, besides, my life was a bit boring, back in York, really, things don't change in York these days. I wanted an adventure. To be honest, I used to have a big social life, I used to go to London to all the clubs, and have countless friends, we would go to the theatre and balls, and play cards, etc. Things change. Now many of them are married and have no time for social events, others have gone abroad. One of my friends went to America and now they have a civil war over in America, don't they? I decided one day that I would go as far as Ireland so now I am here." said Heath. Rochester was a single man of somewhat large fortune, and by large fortune I mean that his parents have money, but it doesn't belong to him, the money belongs to his parents, however he never lacked in anything but having said that his family always encouraged modesty. It was best to have people think you have less money than you really do.

Life in England got boring for Heath especially since he would read about people going abroad, to places like India, or Russia, etc, and in York, it's not that not much changed, with railways it was easier to travel, but when you are single and more and more of your friends have time for there families and less and less time for you, it feels as if life was not changing, besides, as an artist most of York knew about his work, but nobody in Ireland did, and Heath wanted to be known beyond York. People back home would say things like "Don't bother going to Ireland, nobody has heard of you there." Or "How are you going to sell paintings in a country where you don't know a single person?" that sort of thing but none of those words could persuade him to stay put, quite the opposite, actually, for our friend Heath, Ireland was the land of opportunity, a place where nobody was going to say hi to him because he was a Rochester, but rather he was just another artist from England, and that is exactly what he wanted.

“Oh you are an artist. Grand! I love art. I could never paint. I admire those who can. I cook and bake, but I don’t paint.” Said the strange, dark man.

“Well I paint and I don’t cook,” said Heath with a smile.

“So, can I see your paintings? Do you have them with you?” Asked the man, wanting to know more.

“I hardly ever travel with my paintings, sadly, to much of a hassle. I have photos of them though and I’ve an envelope with a few watercolours, would you like to see them?”

“Have you? Yea, that would be grand.” Heath pulled out an envelope full of photos.

“Oh I like this one, so I do. The moon, you’ve made it seem almost as big as the mountains. Tell me, what medium do you use?”

"That one is a watercolour, though I prefer oils. If you make a mistake on oils, you can correct it, I always make mistakes." Heath was feeling excited, here was a man that looked very well to do, glancing at his paintings with keen interest.

"And that one?" Said the posh man, as he went through the photographs.

"Oh that's Leeds Castle. I love castles."

"As do I.," said he with a bigger smile than before. The posh man studied the photo of the painting for what seemed like quite some time.

"You know, I sold that painting, Leeds Castle, to an American, him and his family were traveling and they ran into me. His daughter, Daisy saw it. I wasn't entirely done with it, actually, the American was in a hurry, so he said he gave me what money he had, and took it unfinished."

"But it looks finished."

"Look at the foreground, it was March when I was there, the daffodils were in bloom, and I wanted them in the foreground, if you notice there is just grass there."

There was a moment of silence, as the man observed the photo more closely. Heath kept quiet, as his new friend started looking at the rest of the photos, then all of a sudden the stranger spoke. "Oh, a Wisteria, I love that flower. I used to have it growing all over my walls, but I had to cut it down. You see, the roots were growing too big, they can damage the walls, you know."

"That's a shame. They give such pretty, purple flowers, and I love the way they look on old buildings."

"And my house is very old, about as old as Leeds Castle, so it is."

There was something very mysterious about this man, he was far too formally dressed for a small, Irish, fishing village, and when he looked at the photos, he refused to come to the light, as if he preferred the darkness to the light, yet he carried himself like a count or a duke. There was also something in his smile. You know how with some people, you don't know what they are thinking when they smile? Was his smile hiding a frown or sadness, perhaps sorrow? Whatever it was, he did not seem happy.

"I love old houses. My house in England isn't that old, I wish I had an old house, like yours. Maintaining them must be a challenge, though." Said Heath Rochester. It was true. His house, though big enough, was not a castle. Close to where Heath lived, there was a castle called Castle Howard, which was one of the greatest in all of England. And north of where he lived, in Ripon, there was that place where the mad woman lived. When Heath was a child the governess would tell tales about a mad woman locked up in the attic. Heath lived in a somewhat old house in York, quite big, his house was, but it was not as interesting as Castle Howard, nor was it as astonishing as the castle in Ripon.

"You know, you must come and see my house it's nearby, it's called Clongriffin Castle."

"My word, a castle, and are you a or a lord or something?"

"No, I'm Eamon LeFroy, my family has been here since the Norman Invasion."

"Eamon LeFroy, pleased to meet you, I am Heath Rochester, from York. No title to my name, no castles, just Heath from York. And tell me, not to be rude, but on another subject, it's getting rather dark, and it's winter, as you know, do you happen to have an idea where I might find a place to stay for the night?"

"Well you can't go back to Dublin City Centre, not at this hour. There are no cabs to take you all the way to Dublin tonight. Stay at my place, you can have the grey room."

"No, I wouldn't want to be a bother, I mean I can stay in the village, and maybe see your castle tomorrow. Surely there is some place I could stay here in the village, or at a nearby one, just for the night. "

"There's no places in this village worth staying, not at this hour anyway, besides, I've a fire, and you would have a large room all to yourself, you wouldn't be in the way."

Just then the owner of the pub heard what was going on and said "Mr. LeFroy is right, it's too late at night, and there's no hotels here, not for miles. You'd best stay at his castle. I've stayed at it before, just, Oh I don't like the Grey room, not enough sunlight comes to that one room." One could tell the pub owner looked nervous when he heard about the Grey Room.

"Well if I must stay there," said Heath a bit thankful, but also a bit worried, yet thing is, he wasn't worried so much as he didn't really know Mr. LeFroy, and if you stay at a castle, they are full of antiques, and Heath was very clumsy, supposing something would break, he would be out on the street in the dead of winter. Then again, if he didn't go, he would also be out in the street anyway, for the pub was about to close for the night.

LeFroy answered to the pub owner's comment regarding the grey room, "Nonsense! Grey room has more than enough light. It has that massive window on the side and you can look out to a very small part of the garden from there."

The pub owner just nodded. He wanted to say, "Look Mr. Englishman, I've stayed there before, and it's frightening." but he did not have a chance. Our guests grabbed their things and left before he could say anything.

That said, Heath joined LeFroy and off they went to Clongriffin Castle. The ride over there was quite something, as back then, it was mostly wooded area, with not that many houses around, just farms, for the most part and forest, besides at such a late hour, everyone in the town was asleep.

The next day, Heath woke up, but he felt strange, like when you don't know if you had an experience that was a dream, or if it was real. "Am I in a castle? How did I make it here?" He had a lot of questions to ask. As Heath got up slowly, he looked out the window, there was a thick fog, it was cold out, as well, and he could sense that. Pretty soon though, he got dressed and went down for breakfast, although he really didn't want to go down for breakfast in the castle because his bed was warm and everything else was cold, but you can't be rude and stay in bed all day especially if you are the guest of someone you have just met.

"Hello." said Heath to a servant that was waiting for him downstairs as he walked down for breakfast.

"Oh, Mr. Heath, you are expecting Mr. Lefroy, are you?" said she, when she noticed that Heath was still as if in a daze.

"I was, yes"

"Oh, there's no use finding him here, he has gone down to the village early in the morning. I have had breakfast made for you, just the same, and you are to stay here for the day if you like. Mr. LeFroy has asked if you would care for a tour of the castle later on."

"If it's not a bother." Heath Rochester looked around the place. "So it wasn't all a dream then?" he thought He saw the furniture and antiques and thought it best not to touch anything.

"He insists, and besides, I suspect you like antiques, do you, Mr. Heath, or am I to call you Mr. Rochester?"

"I do like antiques, indeed, and I am sure there are several I would love to see. There are a great many stories in this castle as well. And call me Heath. My father, when he is tremendously angry with me, calls me Rochester, but I am dying to know all the stories and secrets regarding the castle." Said Heath with a smile. He was finally waking up now that they had brought his coffee and food, and he was realizing that last night was not a dream at all. "Blimey, I am in a castle, aren't I? How'd I end up 'ere." He thought.

The housekeeper got quiet for a minute, she nearly dropped a pot of coffee she had in her hand. When Heath asked about stories the castle had to say. There were several stories in this castle, not all of them lovely but perhaps she could hide those from our dear friend from York, actually, come to think of it, some of the happenings in the castle were quite scary, really, but as long as the guest didn't find out about them, all would be great.

Heath saw that the housekeeper was upset, so he said, "You know, I am sure I can wander the castle alone, a tour would be a bit of a bother, wouldn't it?"

"Not a bother at all." Said she in a quiet voice.

The housekeeper and he left for the tour after breakfast, which started, actually, at the dining room, where breakfast had been served. Heath looked at the antiques, and the art. "Ah a Francisco de Zurbaran painting." He said, as he stared at the big painting in the room.

"Not an original, though, although I am glad you recognize it. You are an educated man." The housekeeper was surprised, because most people don't know much about foreign artists, much less 17th century Spanish ones.

"Yes, a Spanish painter, I know his work well, although this is a still life, he didn't paint many of them. I am astonished, actually as this is a copy of one of his lesser known works"

"There is an artist in Dublin that does copies of works, mostly Baroque art." said she.

"Copies of original pieces of art? Is that legal? I mean, wouldn't the artist dislike the idea?"

"He doesn't do copies of art from *living* artists, not that I know of, only of artists that are now dead and whose art is now quite valuable, for example if you can't afford an original work by a seventeenth century artist he will gladly paint a copy of it."

"Well he is talented, regardless, and by the way, so art from dead artists, is it?"

"Yes, thing is, the originals, for the most part are in museums or in stately homes, and people want art that looks like what they saw in the museum. This artist has made quite a name for himself"

"My word, has he indeed? I am impressed," said Heath as he thought about the famous artist that did very good copies of art that is now found in museums.

There were other antiques in the dining room, though, like the old chandelier brought from Bohemia, and the fine china or the incredibly old pieces of furniture, but nothing as grand as the painting. The furniture looked incredible as well, but some of it was new. For example, the table must have been from the Georgian period, and the chairs were quite recent. Eamon's grandmother, when she became a widow, sold a lot of the furniture and bought new pieces, which were brought to the castle upon her death. See, not all of Eamon's family lived in the castle. His grandparents from his mother's side lived as far as Derry, but when his grandfather died, they brought his grandmother to Howth and then upon her death the furniture that she had bought was added to the castle's collection. Other pieces were old but the painting was by far the masterpiece of the dining room, even if it was a copy.

After staring at the dining room they wandered into the next room, "I see Mr. LeFroy has art from India, not everyone does."

"There was a lady that my sister used to mind, an elderly English lady who had traveled to several countries. She knew Mr. Lefroy's family well and when she died, her children, well they didn't like Indian art, it was not at all their style, you see, so they brought it over to the LeFroy family as a gift." Most of it is from India, but not all of it. Some of it is Persian art."

"Well I think it's all beautiful. I've never been to India, must be very hot there, and quite noisy, I hear, but this collection of Indian Art is quite impressive, I must say, what are your thoughts on it, Miss…?

"Victoria"

"Ah, like our current queen"

"Yes, well, one day Ireland will separate, and she won't be my queen." said Victoria, in a stern voice. "let us not discuss politics though, as, you and I would never agree on anything when it comes to politics." She continued as they went to the next room. Victoria was right, though. Heath was an Englishman who rather liked Queen Victoria and the staff member, Victoria, hated the Queen and didn't trust English people at all. Not only that, but it was seen in Ireland that when the potato famine happened, Queen Victoria did nothing to help the starving Irish and that made people very angry to say the least. What the housekeeper did not know was, Heath was a modern man, a liberal, and very much a forward thinking person and he agreed that the way The Crown handled the Irish holocaust was very badly done. However, he couldn't talk about the subject because he could tell that the housekeeper, Victoria, still had strong feelings on the subject.

"Ah, several religious paintings, I see Mr. LeFroy is a Catholic." Said Heath trying to change the subject, and noticing the other works of art.

"Yes, everyone here is."

"I am glad you are. It is important to believe in something, isn't it?" York is mostly protestant, but Scotland has Catholics. Have you been to Scotland?"

"No, I can't say I have been there. I don't think I would like to go on boats. I prefer dry land, you see, and one does need to take a boat in order to get to Scotland. Besides, I wouldn't know what to do if I went."

"Oh I'm going to have to disagree with you, there. Scotland has plenty to do, like visiting the ancient castle of Edinburgh, for example. Or you could go to Orkney. I love Orkney. Ages ago, I had a watercolour teacher, his sister lived in Orkney. Besides, it's not that long of a boat ride to Scotland, and people there are friendly, for the most part, very welcoming."

"I wouldn't know, I try not to think of wandering beyond Howth. Wouldn't want to get lost somewhere. And, truth is, I get an upset belly when I travel by boat.

My father once took us to the Isle of Man, my sisters and I, that is. I was unwell the entire trip. Something about the sea makes me unwell."

That said, they walked, through the castle, looking at all the works of art, and all the antiques, all the sculptures, etc. Victoria would mention stories of the LeFroy family, and how they had come to possess such works of art. Little did our friend Heath know though that some of the works had a dark secret to them, so when he asked about who brought what to the castle, and what there lives were like, Victoria would avoid saying things like "that's haunted" or "that's cursed". Thing is, you don't say those things to your guests, do you? There were things that had happened in the castle though, like the gas lamps turning off on their own, or objects moving about without anyone to move them, or, the scariest event was when all the paintings on the walls fell without explanation. It was one night when LeFroy had guests over. His friend Dolly was in town and they were playing cards. It was late in the evening when they heard bang, bang, bang and looked around, and there were all the paintings on the floor. It happened so fast it was hard to explain. Dolly and Lefroy walked through the entire castle that evening and saw that every single painting had fallen on the floor. Nobody knew how that happened, and nobody dared speak of it to anybody but Victoria, not even now.

The tour did end after a while, and Heath thanked Victoria for her time and wondered when Mr. LeFroy might be back, to which he was told that after six he would be, and he would meet him then at that time.

Let me tell you, dear reader, the story of a few of these works of art. There was, for example, the sculpture of Christ, brought from a trip to Spain by Mr. LeFroy;s father on a journey that he made before Eamon was born. An artist under the reign of Queen Isabel, the Catholic Queen, made the Sculpture when she wanted to convert the Muslims in the 15th century. Behind it there used to be an ancient cloak that was worn by Spanish priests hundreds of years ago, but it was no longer there, as it had burnt in a fire. The statue of Christ was never damaged, but the cloak burned till there was nothing left. The fire started when Eamon (about two decades ago, now) was going to visit his brother in Derry. Back then there was no train from Dublin to Derry and the roads were in a bad condition, so the journey was long and difficult. Heath's mother was a devout woman, went to mass every day, and she said a rosary by the statue of Christ, while her son was traveling. The problem was, she lit a candle right next to the cloak and it went up in flames, the cloak did. Mrs. LeFroy was frightened, and had the staff take out the fire. Some thought it was a bad omen, a fire burning a priest's cloak during a rosary session, People believed in bad omens in those days, but alas, there was nothing to it, the fire was put out, the cloak was burnt and was tossed away, and the statue of Christ was miraculously untouched by the flames. People did speak, however, about the statue of Christ being unharmed by the fire. Imagine this: the priest's cloak was burnt until nothing was left of it, and the statue which went up in flames as well, was left as if nothing ever happened to it. In Howth people claimed it was a miracle, and for a while everyone wanted to see the statue that was never destroyed by fire. People talked about the statue for a very long time. They were puzzled about how it looked as if it had never been on fire, yet the cloak behind it went up in flames and not a bit of it could be rescued. Some folk said it was a witch had caused the priest's cloak to burn, others that it was a demon, but in reality it was only that a candle had been kept too close to it.

Among the other works of art were three John Constable paintings, which were given to the family by a man who owed them money and had bought the paintings from Constable, back when he was an art student. Now that Constable had died, the paintings had gone up in value, although Eamon had no desire of selling them. People that came to the castle though would frequently ask how much he wanted for the paintings, but Eamon really liked the works of art and you don't sell something you like if you have no need to sell it. People wanted to buy everything, though. Just the other day a lady that was well known in Howth and knew how much the castle itself was worth wondered if LeFroy was interested in selling it. But he thanked her for her time, and he told her that he had no need to sell the castle. Sadly not everybody had been as nice as this lady, when she was told that the house was not for sale, she left but others had asked about the value of this or that artifact and when they were told that it wasn't for sale they found ways of taking certain objects, later on to have them sold in the black market.

Back to the art that was in the castle, there was also a drawing of the Virgin Mary in one of the rooms in Clongriffin Castle, done by a Spanish artist, during the time of the Inquisition. The monarchy in Spain invested a lot of money in paintings and sculptures with religious themes to them, in order to convert their subjects throughout the kingdom. This particular drawing was small, but beautiful. It was an image of the Holy Virgin, dressed in 17th century clothing, and with baby angels all around her. The drawing of the Virgin was kept in a small corner. Heath asked why, and was told that since it had been a family possession these last two centuries, at least, were it to go missing, LeFroy would never forgive himself, so he keeps it in a dark corner, in hope that very few people well see it, and thus not feel the need to steal it. The painting had gone up in value because it was now viewed as a Spanish Baroque piece worthy of being in a museum and since it was very small and amazingly well done it was considered a rare piece.

Other works of art included antique and out of print books. The library was enormous, with thousands of books on many subjects, but I don't want to bore you, dear reader, with the stories regarding every single item in the castle.

Chapter 2

Six pm came, and soon afterwards showed up Eamon LeFory. “How was your day?’ he asked his guest, as Heath Rochester sat by the fire, holding a whiskey on this long winter night.

“It was good. I got a tour of the house. Victoria was kind enough to show me around. I love your castle I do not stay in castles often. ”

"And you saw all the paintings, did you?" asked LeFroy as he sat in a corner of the room, away from the fire, his clothes still wet from the rain. Heath Rochester wondered why Eamon had no sense to get changed into some dry clothes before coming to say hi.

"Yes! You have a great collection. I hope to become a great painter one day. It is difficult for artists to get noticed, especially nowadays that there are so many artists and sadly, not enough buyers. You almost have to make yourself ridiculous to be noticed". What Heath Rochester said was true, the art world was changing rapidly then. People were buying art that was seen as less perfect, and more badly done or with more mistakes, and hanging this imperfect art in grand hotels and such. You see, before, art had to be perfect, structured, organized and it needed to have a theme to it, say Greek Mythology or the life of a saint. But now there were artists that did not have the skill that other artists before them had. Some of them were doing things like paint a pile of pancakes with no story behind it besides the fact that it was a painting of pancakes. Sometimes there were even a swiftly done paintings with obvious mistakes, older people hated this new art, but younger people loved it.

Heath heard once about a man, perhaps in Paris, but he could not recall where. This artist had taken a canvas and covered it in black paint with no detail to it at all, just the black paint, then put a horrible title to it. But, in reality Heath doubted that such a thing had ever happened, because there is little merit in that. However, he did know of a man in London that had made a painting of a donkey and called it "self-portrait". Well when London Society saw it, folks nearly fainted, some even threw their hats at it in protest. Heath was not that ridiculous, he took his art very seriously indeed, but he did not know how to sell it to people that were not his friends. See, there are two types of artists: those that no matter how good or bad they are, they are they have all the right contacts that they sell everything they do, but then there are 90% of all artists that can be extraordinary, but not have the contacts to become known. And this was Heath.

When it came to selling art, Heath knew some people, back in York, but what happens is the following: If you go to York and want a painting, there are only a handful of artists there, and they all know each other, so you either buy art from one artist or another, but your options are limited. However, if you go abroad, chances are you will encounter more artists, so although Heath Rochester was known in York, as one of the most celebrated artists there, he was not known beyond York, and the big art centres of the world were not—sadly-- in York.

"Well your work speaks wonders to me. You must let me show it to some of my friends in Dublin, that is, if you don't mind?" said LeFroy to Rochester. And LeFroy was right, Heath's art was incredible, the thing was, only a handful of people knew about it.

Heath couldn't refuse that offer, since, wanting to be noticed is his goal, and the thought of having Dublin's elite look at his paintings was a serious matter to him. Imagine, having paintings in castles, or large country houses that would be a dream come true. But that's not all that was on his mind, as the two of them sat by the fire. Our friend, Heath also thought of the castle he was currently in. He had never been a guest in a castle in Ireland before. Gather, he had been a guest in a castle, but not in Ireland, and the feel to it was slightly different than to castles in England. Rochester could not explain it, but everything felt different, and besides, the furniture and antiques and works of art fascinated him, and how old everything was. Heath felt hypnotized by it, in a way. I don't know if any of you, dear readers, have had that one fairy tale moment when you walk into a room or a very elegant hotel and it just oozes elegance, far greater than what you are used to? That was what Heath was feeling. Heath Rochester came from an upper income family, but although they had valuables in his home, they were considered new rich and grand castles were still foreign enough to him.

Heath and Eamon talked for hours, about what it was like to own a castle, and about what life was like in old York, and all sorts of things they talked about, until it was well past bedtime. Victoria had left a couple hours earlier as she had work in the early morning and was no longer needed that night. Finally, when Heath could not possibly stay awake, he asked to be shown to his room.

The room was a magnificent one. Why they called it the grey room was beyond him because everything was in bright colours. In reality it was more like something you might expect in Spain or Peru than in Ireland. The walls were a bright lemon yellow, there was an old birdcage of rococo design made about a century or so ago in the corner, then there was the wardrobe, a French Baroque one, and a bed, which was lavish and elegant. Above the bed was a painting of Christ, which-- as pretty as it was-- it seemed to not fit well. As if the person who put it there did not think of the size of the wall or the decorations which would complement the painting. But no matter, it was a very beautiful painting. See, the painting was very small and the wall was quite big, so the painting looked a lot smaller than it actually was. Had the same painting been put elsewhere, or with other paintings, it would not have looked out of place. But lesson for us all, don't put a miniature painting all alone in a massive wall and not centred properly because one's mind will wonder what's going on.

That night, as he lay in bed, Heath Rochester heard the most awful noise, a Banshee, he thought. He had heard that in Ireland there existed such a creature, and although he didn't believe in them, he clearly heard the cry of one. Heath couldn't sleep that night, thinking what a horrible noise that was. It was a terribly cold night as well. Heath wondered if the unbearable cold and the loud scream were related to each other in some way. The Banshee is a strange creature, and it is said to do unheard of things. Imagine yourself in bed in a strange castle in a country you have never been to, trying to get a good night's sleep when out of nowhere you hear a scream as if someone were in severe pain, that is what our friend Rochester woke up to that night. He did go back to sleep however he wondered what the noise was.

The next morning came, though, and Heath was at breakfast when Eamon and he were talking. "Eamon, my friend, did you hear that noise last night? That horrid noise, almost as if someone had been murdered right in front of me."

"Oh it was just the cats, screeching," said Eamon. "You know how they are"

Heath knew very well what cats are like, and he also knew when he was being lied to, and that was one of those moments. Cats, indeed, don't make that deafening noise. See, for those of you not aware, when felines fight they do make an awful sound, or when they cry, but this was high pitched and nothing like a "meow, I am frozen please let me in" sort of cry. It was more like person, perhaps a woman going "Oh Dear God, I am in horrible pain" sort of noise, and nothing at all like a cat would make. At least not the cats in England. Alas, if LeFroy wouldn't talk about that horrid noise, perhaps Victoria would.

Rochester hurried with his breakfast and asked if he could see Victoria because he wanted to borrow a book. Eamon LeFroy rang for her, and she came at once. Eamon apologized that he could not help Heath look for a book, but he said he had to go to Dublin again, on a matter of urgent business, so he grabbed his things and left.

Eamon was a strange man indeed. He was very friendly, but he always seemed to be going somewhere and always in a hurry, yet when you asked him where he was headed, he never said where. LeFroy would only answer "yes" or "no".

Victoria was now alone with Heath, as soon as Eamon left, and they were finally able to talk.

"A book?" asked she "any subject in particular? We have thousands of books" They did have thousands of books. Actually, the family of LeFroy used to love to read, so they had collected books for centuries, and they rarely threw any away. The LeFroy's also had a habit of collecting books that people in Dublin would discard, so when you have centuries collecting books, in time you have a very huge library. Eamon himself loved to read, as did his father before him and between the two of them, their already large collection grew enormously. A little bit about the books, though. The collection began several centuries ago and back then getting certain books to Ireland was difficult in part because Ireland was considered so far away but also because back then not everybody in Ireland could read so there was no point in importing books from abroad, unlike now, where everybody in Ireland reads. The thing is, the LeFroy family for hundreds of years went through great lengths to get books. That is in part why books were rarely tossed out in the castle, but that was a good thing because now, centuries later, there was a collection of thousands of pieces of literature on countless subjects.

"Anything on ghosts, goblins, spirits, demons? That sort of thing?" asked Heath, inquiring about the books.

"You heard her scream too, then?" Victoria asked Heath "I told you, even the furniture had stories, when I gave you the tour of the castle, yesterday. You see, in the early years of the last century, Mr. Lefroy's ancestors, one of them, he shot himself here in this house, at a Christmas party. They say his ghost wanders the place, and the cries you heard are his cries from hell."

"But that sounded like a woman, did it not?" Heath didn't believe for an instant that somebody's ghost could be heard from beyond the grave. It was absurd; once you are dead, you most certainly do not make noise, much less shout at people as they slept, it is not proper to shout at people while they were at rest. What Victoria had read though, was that the Devil, or a demon can take any shape. They say that one day it can be a school boy, the next, an old person, and so on. Plus, it can trick you. Demons love tricks. One trick it does is to make you think you hear a child or a woman but you turn around and see a man. Or, for instance, you think someone is calling you, then you turn around and nobody is to be found. At any rate, the sound was that of a woman screaming and Heath wanted to find out why.

"It could be his wife, or perhaps one of his daughters. Tragedy has been in this house for a long while, but it's about time you know the story, let us sit down". As they sat, she began talking. "You see, many centuries ago, the family of LeFroy came over from France when the

Normans came and they were penniless then. You always hear about the grand Norman invaders, but along with them there were people whose lives had not amounted to much, and they saw opportunity abroad. Some of the members of the LeFroy family were highwaymen, others were prostitutes, and so on, but one day, someone became very wealthy, very fast. They say there's a golden treasure hidden beneath this castle. No one knows for sure, but what we do know is that the family is full of lunatics, and such. Not Eamon, no, he is perfectly normal. But some other relatives, some say the spirits from Hell wander these walls, and protect the gold, others, that it's a banshee, that guards the gold, while others say the story of the gold was made up. I don't believe it, however, some people have found priceless treasures on the hill in Howth. Another thing, whenever anyone is going to ask about the treasure, she appears, the woman with the horrible screams."

"Well I don't want it; I have enough money, thanks, and have never had need for more. I have learned that money doesn't provide happiness. A whole bunch of gold, I wouldn't know what to do with it, to be honest. I want to be happier, not wealthier."

"I doubt it's YOU, she is worried about, but you see, I can tell you are a very kind, innocent man and it's no accident that Mr. LeFroy found you in Howth, let's just say he needs an innocent, good hearted friend."

"Found me? "

Heath thought about everything, why was he at the castle? I mean besides the fact that he needed shelter that one night. But he felt in a way, that he was meant to be there. He was also enchanted by the whole experience. Thing is, here he was, an English man, in faraway Howth, in Ireland, in a castle called Clongriffin Castle, also known as LeFroy's Castle, and it all seemed strange, yet familiar to him at the same time. Everything did. Like when you happen to go to a place you have obviously never been to, yet you already know your way around? Or when you meet someone for the first time, but you feel like you had been friends forever? That, dear readers, is what Heath Rochester felt when in he was in the castle. Heath also thought about LeFroy, because you see, Eamon kept as many secrets as he did antiques, and he had a large amount of both.

"I see you are in deep thought, Mr. Rochester, Sr. Are you frightened by ghosts?"

"No. I don't think I believe in them, at least I didn't until now. I mean, I do remember when I was a child my mother took me to a house that she claimed was haunted. She said that in the castle there was a man that had married a lunatic, so he locked her up in the attic, but I never heard nor saw anything, so I thought my mother was trying to scare me, really. I heard that other people in this place called Ripon would mention the mad woman in the attic, but I just thought it was all made up. Really, I have never actually seen a ghost."

"Clongriffin Castle holds many secrets. Nobody is the same once they discover them, and if you think a story about a mad woman in England is scary hold on to your hat, this castle is far spookier than that."

Heath felt like he was already changed. One day he was preparing a trip to Ireland, the next he was in a mysterious castle that was seemingly haunted. Heath felt the urge to investigate the horrible cries at night, but he was also here to paint, though. And that afternoon, paint is exactly what he did, investigating mysteries would happen soon enough.

Regarding painting, Heath Rochester did not have a lot of materials with him but he had enough. And he was given access to a room where he could look out at the trees and paint them without getting wet. It was very cold and rainy that day. A wind had blown in from Russia over Scandinavia and had caused the weather in Ireland to turn painfully cold and wet. Heath did not know what to paint at first. He looked out the window and saw the grey clouds and the rain, so he painted that, but he had trouble concentrating, as his mind would wander constantly.

Night came, though and Heath was back in his room, reading a book about cursed objects, wondering if the banshee, or whatever that thing was, would come again, when he heard a nock at his door. Which startled him. "Who is it?" he asked.

"Hi, Heath, it's me" said Eamon LeFroy. "Listen, I wanted to ask you if you wouldn't be bothered by another guest in this house? You see, my cousin is coming from Galway tomorrow morning, Jane is her name, and, I think you and her would get along quite well. She is twenty, and has no friends in these regions. I was wondering if you could keep her company?"

"I haven't got many friends here either, so yes, not a bother at all."

"Grand, then, she arrives after breakfast, so." Breakfast, Heath had come to learn, was served early in LeFroy castle. Back in England, Heath Rochester was known to wake up later than expected because he had no children and he had no reason to wake up early but he had noticed that Eamon LeFroy woke up quite early, so Rochester would make an effort to be at breakfast especially early the next day.

Eamon left Heath for the night, and then the darkness came. There was the horrible cry of the Banshee or spirit, or whatever it was, but only once, although it must have played with Heath's mind, for he had the most horrible dream after the shout was heard. In his dream, he was in a park, back in England, and he sat, at a picnic with other people around him, when all of a sudden, he was staring at death itself. It was very strange indeed, because it started peaceful, a picnic, jolly good fun. He was talking to a lady and her child, when death appeared and took him away. Heath got up in an instant, he was nervous. It's like the spirit of death had followed him to England, but then realized it was time for breakfast anyway, and he needed to get dressed and go downstairs.

Heath Rochester was in deep thought as he got dressed, he thought about the dream of his death in a park back in England. He wondered who the woman was and who the child was. He was also taken by the fact that in the dream he looked older, not elderly but more mature looking, as if the dream were a vision of the future and that is indeed how he was to die. But then he tried talking sense to himself, as it were and said "It can't mean anything, the dream has to be meaningless."

Heath put his clothes on and went down for breakfast, where he saw Eamon and Victoria, who had just brought the tea. "Ah, your cousin arrives soon, doesn't she?" Heath asked his new friend LeFroy.

"Yes, one of my staff members has already gone for her at the train station. "Eamon wasn't in the best of moods, Heath thought, or perhaps he too had bad dreams. One could see in his eyes that something was upsetting him. Rochester decided not to chat for too long for fear of putting Eamon in a grumpy mood, so he ate his breakfast rather quickly. As he was about to finish with his meal, though, the door flung open and a youthful figure walked in, a gorgeous, young woman, dressed in red satin; red was *the* fashionable colour back then. The dress is worth talking about, though, it was, as mentioned, red satin but it went from a dark red at the top to a lighter red at the bottom and it was wide and gorgeous. Jane had blond hair and lovely eyes although from where Rochester was sat he could not tell if they were green or blue, but she had it in a fashion which looked like something that the Normans would have used. Jane also had a ruby necklace with black stones. Was it black jade, Heath wondered.

"Oh cousin" Jane said in a smile. "I must tell you all about my trip. Would you believe how fast trains go these days? I hate to think what could be invented that could go faster." She was going to say more, when she saw Heath, His brown eyes glancing at her captured Jane's attention. Her eyes sparkled and looked like some jewel or elegant crystal when she glanced at him.

"Hello, I'm Jane, you must be Heath. My cousin told me you are staying in the grey room. I find that room boring, not much to look at besides an old birdcage. Is that birdcage in the corner still there? Our auntie brought it from Italy once, or was it Spain? I'm in the next room, by the bye, the one that's near the library. I can sneak in and grab a book at night, something scandalous, I hope, like Tom Jones. Have you read Tom Jones?"

"Yes, I have read Tom Jones, indeed. And Are you not afraid of wandering these dark walls at night?"

"Not in my room, no, I stayed in your room once and had nightmares every single night, I can't tolerate nightmares, they frighten me. I sleep soundly in the other room, though."

"So, you had nightmares? I have them as well. Horrible, that room is. Isn't it?"

"I heard a woman was murdered in that room, like a century or so ago, and ever since haunts whoever stays in there." Said Jane

"Don't be silly" said Eamon who was hearing the conversation. "There's no such thing as ghosts." Eamon had been quiet this whole time, until now. He hated the talk of ghosts. LeFroy would get in the worst of moods when he would hear about ghosts, demons or anything of that sort.

"Oh I think there are ghosts. There's no point in owning a castle, if there's no ghosts or demons in it." Said Jane, to her cousin. "Gather, I could never afford a castle, I'm not wealthy, like you are, and castles aren't free these days, are they?" continued she. Heath was relieved to see Jane. Her energy was like a breath of fresh air in such a damp, dark place. Jane was like a bubble of glee.

Whatever the truth was regarding the ghost, now Heath was curious to say the least in order to find out what was going on in this castle but at least he had an ally this time. Both Jane and him could find time to search the castle for answers. Unfortunately though, that day there would be no time for searching the castle. Eamon LeFroy thought it best to have a picnic in the garden. Victoria called the rest of the staff of the castle, (which I had not mentioned much until now) to get to help set things up for the picnic. Eamon wanted his two guests to have tea near the forest area.

As the household staff was setting things up for the picnic, Heath realized he had not seen the gardens yet so he set out to walk in the garden. "My word, the garden is bigger than the castle." This part was true, the castle was big, but the gardens were huge.

"Oh and you haven't seen all of it, there's the woods beyond the garden, that are great for exercise and fresh air. You need to take a walk there one day, it's well worth it." Said LeFroy

"I am in need of exercise, aren't I?" replied Heath, as he grabbed another piece of the cake. "I also think I would like to paint this landscape. " but how big are the grounds, if you don't mind my asking?"

"Well, enormous but, before I forget, Heath, I was thinking, there's these men in town I happen to know, some friends of mine, and thing is, how would you like to show your paintings to them? I think someone has a gallery near Marion Square. I mean, you did come to Ireland to paint the Irish landscape, but what if I put you in contact with a few people..." Eamon wasn't done speaking, when Heath got visibly exited.

"WOW, a gallery in Marion Square? That's fantastic, yes; I would indeed love to go. Perhaps your cousin, Jane, would love to join us."

"Oh that sounds like fun. There's an antique shop nearby, at least there was, last time I was in Dublin. There's a portrait I like to look at there. I hope it hasn't sold. It's the one they used to put next to the window, the big one." Commented Jane.

"Grand! The three of us can go, day after tomorrow" said Eamon

"Why not tomorrow?" Asked Jane

"Well tomorrow I am in Howth all day. I've things to do, but you know, Heath, you were only in Howth at night, weren't you? You need to see it in the day, there's the train station that's about 20 years old or so, and the harbor. It was built before I was born, but not long before, and the abbey, Howth has an abbey as well. You need to go up and see it."

"Sounds like fun. I am sure Jane could show me around"

"I love Howth, such a small village, yet so near Dublin. The only thing I don't care for much is the walk form there to Sutton." Jane said.

"Listen, you will be grand, no one ever died, walking from Howth to Sutton." said Eamon

"I am sure we will be fine," said Heath, with a big smile.

"Heath, you mentioned how big the gardens were, well you won't believe it, when the castle was built, the nearby villages were incredibly small, only a house here and there, and some of them didn't exist until much later, so my ancestors bought an impossible amount of land, that's why there's far more garden than castle, really. Victoria has advised me to sell some of it to developers, but I couldn't think of anything worse than having suburbs in Clongriffin, besides, it's too far from everything, It won't happen in my lifetime." said Eamon

"I don't know." Mentioned Jane" The rest of Dublin is too far, but one day, it will grow out this way"

"As far as Clongriffin, nonsense! Next you will tell me they will put suburbs in Malahide. Don't be ridiculous, Jane." said her cousin. The idea of Dublin expanding as far as Clongriffin seemed ridiculous to LeFroy.

That conversation over and done with and the picnic came to an end, as it began to get dark and tremendously cold and Heath began to worry. He dreaded the nightmares.

When night came, Heath took his things off and went to bed and his fear came true. As he was in bed, he heard noises; at first he thought it was just the wind and rain, but then he wasn't sure. Our English friend used to not believe in goblins and fairies and such things, but those cries at night, it was like the cry of death. Perhaps spirits did exist and thing is, these cries did mean something, for some reason they seemed to only happen in this very room, but why Eamon denied them, was beyond him.

Heath heard the horrible cries, and he got out of bed and looked around. He knew he couldn't see the spirit but there was something there, he could feel it. Heath's spine was tingling as if someone was looking at him breathing on him almost, only there was nobody to be found. There were just old books and paintings in the room, and that old birdcage, nothing alarming. He knew, however, that he had seen a photograph of the same room earlier, perhaps in the morning he could look for it, maybe that could help. Sometimes photos can reveal secrets, or so Heath thought.

The next morning he rushed out of bed, and before he put his clothes on, he looked for the photograph. It was on the desk near his bed. Heath observed the photo. Where the painting of Christ is now, on the wall near the bed, there used to be what looks like a wood boat, why was it removed? And why was there an image of Christ now, where the boat was? That was the only difference between the old photograph and the way the room was currently. Heath Rochester did not know if anything he saw in the photo meant anything at all or not but he would soon find out.

After he looked at the photo, and got dressed, he went down for breakfast. Eamon wasn't down yet; apparently he hadn't slept well that night. Jane was down, however and she was looking very perky and Heath wanted to speak to her anyway. "Do you know the room I am in? "He asked 'I found a photograph of it and was there a statue of a boat or something before, a relief or wood carving, perhaps? You know, where the painting of Christ is?"

"The castle has a way of giving up its secrets. Eamon was worried you would find that photo, but, it was a wood carving of a ship that was destroyed, the real ship sunk, that is. Some of our family members drowned in it, or so I have heard. Some of our ancestors wanted to go abroad once, and they went on a ship that was supposed to go to America, anyway, the wind picked up and the ship sunk, but another boat was going by and found some people and rescued them. One of the ancestors had the wood carving of the very same boat with them, but when they came to Ireland and placed it on the wall, strange things started to happen. Gather, strange events always happened in this castle. I don't know if the boat had anything to do with it, but people said so."

"I knew this house had secrets, Victoria warned me about it."

"But how did you find it, the photo?"

"It was on the desk, couldn't have been easier to find, really."

"Oh, because last time I was here, that photo had been hidden away."

"Well it's not hidden now, is it?"

"Well I don't go into your room, no matter what." Those words being said, Eamon walked into the breakfast room where everyone was waiting. Heath was sad because he wanted to ask why the room was called the grey room, but with Eamon around, nobody would be able to chat.

"Sorry I slept in, I had a headache all last night." Eamon Lefroy did know about the spirit in the Grey room in Clongriffin Castle, he just didn't want to admit it, since he was ashamed that one of his ancestors haunted the castle. Eamon was a proud man, and wanted everything to be perfect in his life all the time and a ghost, or spirit, or banshee, or whatever it was, did indeed have a dark secret from the past and he never wanted anyone to know that some of his ancestors had been horrible. Yet Heath, the English guest, was an intelligent man and the truth would be found out. Our friend from York meant well and did not want anybody to feel shame by having secrets found out but when you have nightmares about your own death and when you hear screams at night in the very room you have dreadful dreams in. Perhaps it is wise to investigate the cause, besides the family of Rochester had deep, dark secrets too but they were buried in old England.

Heath Rochester was given a book by Victoria that afternoon. It was about spirits. As he read it he realized that when you investigate a spirit you have to be careful because, if you wake the evil spirits, every bad thing imaginable could happen. Heath thought, as he read. There was a section on good spirits and Rochester was convinced that this was a good spirit, maybe even a playful one. Nobody that was alive today had dared investigate the specter but Heath thought the following:

#1 The spirit seems to want to be found out. For example, if nobody left the picture of the room Rochester was in, it must have been him or her, or whatever it was.

#2 The religious images throughout the castle made Heath think that perhaps somebody in the past did try to investigate the ghost and they must have had a horrible time at that. So by placing images of Christ all over the place they hoped that the specter might calm down or go away... at least that was the conclusion Heath came up with.

#3 One of the chapters in the book talked about cursed vs blessed objects. Since the family of LeFroy collected antiques from all over the world, there was a possibility that one of them could have been cursed, thus introducing a spirit into the castle but by bringing in holy icons, some even brought from as far as Palestine, then there was hope that the spirit should go away. I need to explain this last point further. You see if you have a cursed object that has brought with it a malign being, a way to have the ghost go away is by bringing in a blessed object, say a rosary or a bible or an image of Christ or of some saint perhaps. It was evident to Heath R. that the reason why there were so many religious images throughout the castle was that someone had in the past tried to get rid of the evil being which had been brought into the place.

As Heath began to think, he began to write his conclusions down on paper, he thought that maybe he could find out which of all the objects in the castle was the cursed one, if any.

Another part of the book that he was reading talked about haunted houses, like in Salem in America, where there was a haunted house where the witches had once lived, or the Cathedral in Durango, Mexico, where visitors to the Cathedral frequently saw a ghost of a nun. Now Heath had two hypotheses, either a) one object was cursed, and must be removed, possibly burnt, or b) the castle itself was cursed.

Jane and Heath Rochester talked about what could possibly be the case in this haunting, as both scenarios seemed just as likely.

Chapter 3

Jane, Eamon and Heath Rochester went to Howth on that day after they had breakfast. Heath and Jane went to the village for a walk, while Eamon went to see a friend, who lived just up the hill. The ride over to Howth village was a pleasant one. Jane, by the way, was curious to know more about her new friend, Heath Rochester and so she started asking him all sorts of questions.

"So, Heath, how did you get a name like yours, in all fairness, it's not a common name"

"My parents knew a man in York, where I was born, whose family had come from as far as the Ottoman Empire and they say he was fond of me when I was a baby. When my parents were away for whatever reason he would look after my siblings and me. A great man, he was. It was he that came up with the name

Heath. It was a name he heard, or read about somewhere. I believe it was a story he came across, about a man called Heathcliff, so he shortened it. This man used to travel a lot and would hear the most interesting names that aren't terribly common. He also loved reading, so he did, and several books that he came across had characters with rather exotic names. I also learned a lot, thanks to him. His name was Aaron. And how I remember hearing about far away lands." Heath was in deep thought as he walked with Jane. He remembered old man Aaron and all the stories he would tell.

"The Ottoman Empire? WOW, I have always wanted to travel to those far away lands but now I want to know, how did that man, your parent's friend, Aaron, how did he come all the way to York and why?" asked Jane, wanting to know the whole story.

"I have absolutely no idea. His daughter worked as a governess, I remember that. Gorgeous, his daughter was. He gave her an English name because he didn't want people talking about why she had a different name."

"Oh dear, what ever happened to her?"

"Emily, was her name. There was a family in Halifax that needed a governess to work for them. You know, I haven't heard from her since she left for Halifax. I presume she finds herself well, though."

"You must visit her. Wouldn't that be fun?" Said Jane with a smile. She had heard of Halifax, but she forgot where it was located, as she had never actually been there. Jane loved hearing stories of adventure, and she wished she could travel the world over.

Heath thought for a while. He wasn't sure what he would do once he got to Halifax were he to go looking for Emily. Would he knock at people's doors to see who had a governess named Emily? Nobody would do that, although the population of the place is smaller than most places in the world. No matter, though, why would he look for someone else, when he had gorgeous Jane to look at and today especially. She was wearing a violet dress and a black coat to keep her warm during this horrid, rainy season. Her bonnet was black as well, with violet ribbons. No woman in all of Ireland could look more beautiful than she on that day. Heath thought that doing a painting of her would be a lovely idea. When he was younger Heath had studied the works of

Sr. Joshua Reynolds and Thomas Gainsborough. He remembered what his professor would say about how Gainsborough was better at landscapes, but everyone would pay him to do their portraits, and Heath Rochester was better at landscapes than at portraits. However, Jane looked gorgeous that day and he wanted to remember that walk with her forever. Heath thought of Jane as they walked, but he also remembered Emily.

Funny, though, you know how life takes so many turns. I guess you could describe them as winding roads, really. For example, Heath's childhood friend, Emily. There was a time before she left to Halifax to be a governess, that Heath could have courted her and as pretty as she was, Heath did imagine himself with her indeed. But she was more interested in being a governess, so they were never engaged, they weren't even lovers or anything. But all these years later, Heath was still single, but now staring at very beautiful Jane. Life would have possibly been lovely with Emily, had Heath been serious with her, but now he felt that life with Jane could be quite nice as well. Gather, as they say, it was early days, but just the same Jane was beautiful, and her blond locks of hair made her look like an angel.

The pair walked from Howth Harbour up the hill to Howth Abbey as they talked about this and that. Both of them loved the view from the Abbey. As they walked the grounds, it started to rain. "You know, this reminds me of Whitby. Have you been there? It's a gorgeous place, there's an abbey and the wind blows really hard all the time there and, thing is, if you stand in the middle of the Abbey, the wind tends to blow on all sides, and it sounds like ghosts howling. Also, there is a graveyard nearby, just like this one, so you get a really scary feeling. Whitby's abbey is quite similar to this one in a strange way. It's much bigger but the architecture is similar. You need to go one day, I would love to show you it." Said Heath with a smile.

"Whitby? I've never even been to England, but is Whitby big? I have seen photos of some abbeys in England and they are enormous, aren't they? Someone back home in Galway, where I am from, went once to Fountains Abbey on a trip he made to England and the photo he took made it look enormous, it did. " Jane was going to speak more, but Heath interrupted

"Sorry, I have been rude, you never told me how you got the name Jane"

"Jane? Well, I was born twenty years ago and there were Jane's everywhere then, really. There are fewer Jane's now, aren't there? I wonder where all the girls called Jane are now, are they all hiding somewhere? "

"Well in all fairness, how many Heath's do you know?" Both of them looked into each other's eyes and laughed. Jane blushed, as she stared at Heath's penetrating, brown eyes and Heath turned red as he looked into her blue eyes. "Oh look, you can see the boats form here," she said, to change the subject, hoping Rochester wouldn't notice her blush.

"Yes, I can see one come in now. I wonder if it came from a warmer climate. I often wonder about boats when I see them. I would love to go to a warmer country, maybe the West Indies, or somewhere, maybe even as far as Timbuktu." Said Heath. 'There is a place back in England called Scarborough. There is a small shop there, and the owner is a mulata from Santo Domingo and she is always mentioning the climate back home. It's what she misses most. I've an atlas in my house in York and I looked up Santo Domingo, it is remarkably far, actually, but I hear it is really pretty." Continued Heath.

"Oh, I always dream about traveling abroad. Egypt, West Indies, as you say, India, China, most countries, actually. Well your friend who named you, the man from the Ottoman Empire, it's quite warm there, isn't it?" Jane commented.

"I believe it is, well the part he was from anyway. See the empire is huge, so some parts are hot all the time, but other parts have real winter and it gets to be really, really cold. I believe he is from Palestine originally, but he told us once that they had so much heat in his hometown that they longed for rain, especially in the hot, summer months. The winter, I hear is quite different though, in Palestine, they get snow at times, although he said that they had better weather than the Arabs, and that in lands further East of him, see there are several rivers in the Empire--the Nile in Egypt, the Jordan river, which is where he was from, then the Tigris and last the Euphrates. Old Aaron would say that if you go to Egypt it can be quite hot. If you go to the area between the Tigris and Euphrates, in what used to be Mesopotamia, that is where Adam and Eve were from, well that gets terribly hot as well, but he grew up near the Jordan river and he remembered cold nights and especially cold winters."

"Is that so? I never knew that. By the bye, should we go look for my cousin now? The cold is a bit much for me, really. He said he was with a friend, Eamon did, I know this man, right, he lives a block from here, they always have tea there." Said Jane, and off they went.

For those of you not familiar with Howth, it is a very small fishing village where most people live on a hill overlooking the sea. But don't think tropical sea with palm trees. This is the Irish Sea where it rains 867 days a year and when it does not rain, there is a drizzle, so one must always be prepared for more rain and more rain. The best clothes to wear when planning a trip to Howth, is anything that will not soak through and preferably something to keep warm in as well. The people of Howth are tremendously friendly but they have a half hour of sunshine a year, so do not think you need short sleeves when you go.

The population is small in this village and they all know each other. They all go to the same pub that is not that far from the Abbey and it has been there for quite some time. Modernity is reaching Howth, for Dublin City Centre is not that far from it if one takes the train, although when the first train arrived, people thought it was too big and too loud and that it would be a failure. However, just a few years later everybody loved it.

Howth has an Abbey as well, which is in ruins. I think the Abbey goes back to the Middle Ages. There is a harbour as well and there are a few houses on the hill, not many, though. I rather doubt one would want more houses. The more people there are, the more crowded things get. The rest of the hill is green due to the rain. It is funny, though, Heath R. is from York, so he is used to the rain and the astonishingly green landscape. However, if you think England is green and rainy, Ireland is in a league all on its own. It would be hard to imagine any place on earth as green or as rainy as Ireland. More about Howth, though: one can see deer on the green area quite frequently. There is a castle on the top of the hill as well, but hardly anyone visits the top of the hill, as it is a long way up. Once at the top, on a clear day, you can see several counties in Ireland. Since very few people go that far up the hill, the people of Howth village had quite a lot of stories about the place. One of the greatest things about the green area on the hill in Howth, though, is that many of the locals enjoy having picnics there and all the children love playing there and running about on Sundays after church.

And there we find our friends, up on the hill, just leaving the Abbey and walking towards a house that had been built for the family of O'Dell, Eamon's friend. The O'Dell family had originally come from Limerick but decided to settle in Howth not that many decades ago. Remember, the hideous potato famine, also known as the Irish Holocaust, the one that Queen Victoria shamefully did nothing about? Those were tragic times when many fled Ireland and wasn't all that long ago.

Many Limerick families were very much affected by the tragic famine and were forced to leave in hoards. The O'Dell family wanted to go to England, because Martin O'Dell (at whose house everyone was now currently in) had a cousin in England and when his cousin found out that Old Martin O'Dell and his wife were suffering. He wrote to Old Martin and told him to go to England, where he and his wife would be looked after.

Life takes you places you don't expect and when the family of O'Dell was in Dublin, finding a way to get to England, one thing led to another and they ended up in

Howth, which they liked a lot, actually. Here, my readers, is where we find the current Mr. O'Dell (his wife now deceased). You see him there, with his friend Eamon LeFroy, discussing what's to be done with the garden. The rain was too strong for anyone that was indoors to dream of going out, but one can see the garden from the window, so no need to be outdoors and plan what's to be done regarding the gardening when you can be inside and decide. So there were Lefroy and O'Dell looking out at the weather, when there was a knock on the door, and in came our wet friends, Jane and Heath.

"Ah, Jane, I'm glad it's you, did you show Heath the village?"

"Yes, we got to see the Abbey, the harbour and the new train station, but it's getting dark and there's no time for the castle on top of the hill, or the tower and with this rain. "

"The Abbey was good enough for me." Said Heath with a smile, as he looked at Jane and her gorgeous eyes.

"Please, you are both cold, let me make you a cup of tea" said kind Mr. O'Dell "You must be sat by the fire to warm up." Continued he. Our friends, Heath and Jane were tremendously cold, actually, so the fire was very welcome.

The cup of tea was as lovely as was the present company. Heath was sipping his warm cup, when Mr. O Dell said "You know, Eamon has been telling me all about your paintings, you are an artist. He wants your paintings shown in Marion Square. You notice he seems to disappear quite frequently, doesn't he? That's because when he met you at the pub he got exited and wanted to show the whole world your paintings. Eamon could never draw or paint. He is good at running a castle, though, but in any case, he saw your paintings and he knows you will be famous, but you could use some help. No artist can become famous on his own."

I pause here to say, Eamon LeFroy always wanted to be an artist but he got rejected from all the great academies in Europe. However, he loved art and made it one of his goals in life to have other artists become famous. And that is why he was so taken by Heath's art-- he saw an opportunity to take a little- known artist from abroad and make his art known throughout Ireland, possibly throughout Europe as well.

"Eamon has been very kind, and truth be told, I was lucky, because I was looking for an adventure and he just happened to be in the right place at the right moment; it was cold, raining, I was frozen and walked into this one pub that had the lights on. And I think we got on well and I was more than happy to stay at his castle, gather, at first. In the beginning I was nervous. Imagine a man that you have never met in your life tells you to go to his castle. Have you heard of that man, Blackbeard, didn't he chop women up to bits, or was that Bluebeard? Either way, I did have that in the back of my mind, but LeFroy seemed so tremendously friendly and to be honest, I had no option, as there are no hotels in Howth currently and with such cold weather, I don't know what I would have done. Not only that, but I have met Jane now. She showed me around Howth, she has been so kind. I daresay I could not have had a nicer companion than her, really." Rochester looked at Jane and smiled. She sat in a corner, by the fire, looking as if she had never had a bad thought in her life.

"Oh, by the way, I stayed in Clongriffin Castle once, when I was new here, he found me much like he found you, Eamon did, my friend. But tell me he didn't put you in the damn grey room, did he?" said O'Dell.

"I am afraid so."

Mr. O Dell took a sip of tea and stared sternly at Eamon's eyes. "Heavenly Jaysus, Eamon, are you determined to put all of Europe in that room?" Eamon got upset at this, but he found nothing to say, besides, castle owners never show when they are upset or angry, it's not proper.

"I have stayed in that room a time or two, and I don't like it either," said Jane. "Everyone has nightmares, I think it's a spirit from the past that wanders there," continued she. Everybody the world over knows that all castles have spirits and goblins.

"Jane, I am miles ahead of you there. I did my own investigating and realized, there are several types of spirits, some are good, some bad, but they are real. Eamon has had a dark family history, suicides, shipwrecks, lunatics, highwaymen, prostitutes, murderers, heaven knows what else. The spectre of LeFroy's Castle is clearly one of his ancestors that's in torment in the afterlife and I often wonder if it could be someone that died there. You have had dreams there, no doubt, we all have" said O'Dell, looking at Heath.

"I saw my own death, in a park, many years from now. I was in England, but not in York, where I am from. I was in London. London was different though, I can't describe it, and it was much bigger. I keep having different variations of the same dream, and other nonsensical dreams but in this one, queen Victoria is celebrating something big, I'm old, but not very old, perhaps in my fifties or so. Anyway I go to a park, and then death stares me in the face and that's when I wake up. In one version of my dream, there was a fire, but in another one it was much more peaceful, really. I have seen other things as well. I wonder if the ghost isn't trying to tell me something. Thing is, it's more complicated than that, I'm afraid. In this one dream I was lying in a coffin in my own funeral in a medieval church that looked sort of like St. Margaret's Church in London, you know the one by St. James's Palace? But it was not like I was in my coffin all nervous like, no, it was actually quite peaceful, as if I was sleeping but I could see everybody mourn me. I also saw myself floating about the place but I was not remotely sad. Anyway, it's like I'm in my own funeral, and there's all these people there, I recognized some of them as well. Some people in my funeral are people I know quite well, but others, I have no clue who they are."

Jane got exited as she heard the story. "Oh I saw something similar, when I stayed there, in the same room, I saw myself, very far in the future though, I was very, very old, and I was with a friend, here in Howth, when suddenly death approached me. I nearly screamed when I had that dream. Only in my dream, Victoria wasn't queen anymore, and there was a fire or something in City Centre, at the GPO building in Dublin. I feel like something is going to happen there, but a very long time from now. I also remember the number 16 reappearing in my dream." Jane thought for a moment, could the ghost allow us to see the future? What was the point of it? I mean if you know how you die, is there a point in knowing the date of your death, you can't prevent your death, you just know that's how it is going to happen. Is there a point to knowing how it happens if you can do nothing about it?" Jane thought about all this.

Eamon got cold, very cold, but spoke "As you know, my family didn't always have money and the castle wasn't always ours. I came to live there when I was four years old, after my grandfather died. He had lived there before us, my parents, my brother and I, that is. Thing is, my parents put me in that very same room and my brother was in the next room, the one that Jane is currently staying in. My brother loved reading stories to me and scaring me before I would go to bed. I had nightmares for years, but thought they were just my brother's stories, until my family decided to put visitors there and change me to another room. The visitors would hear noises or have strange dreams, or hear the screech of death, not everyone could bare it. Priests came, tried to do exorcisms and everything, they even bought images of Christ and our blessed mother and put them throughout the castle, you know, Heath you were asking about the small painting of Christ above your bed? There was a relief of a wooden boat there, but it was a relief of a boat that shipwrecked when one of my ancestors was trying to reach America and when the village priest came and I told him the story about the shipwreck, he told me to get rid of it. It was a gorgeous wood carving, but I gave it as a gift to my old friend Dolly. In the end nothing worked. We got rid of the boat on the wall and the dreams and screeches kept happening. I reckoned time passed and I got used to living in a haunted house but I get lonely and I can't sell the castle as all of Ireland knows about the spirit. Nobody would buy it and besides, it is a bit far from Dublin City Centre, isn't it? At any rate, I have upset myself now. O'Dell, do continue, what have you discovered?"

"Tonight, something happens tonight. Heath, take note, it's past eleven and I am tired, but I will say this, you will wake up the earliest of all of us tomorrow, you all need to stay here for the night, the rain hasn't stopped, and besides, I already have your beds ready, I knew all three of you were going to stay here for the night, because when I stayed in the grey room I saw tonight's events unfold exactly as they are. I saw the rain and you, Heath, whom I have never met and Jane, I saw your violet dress and your black coat in my vision. We will be packed like sardines tonight but you can take the train to Dublin City Centre tomorrow morning. Remember Heath needs to show his art in Marion Square and it is important he goes. Back to my story, though and Heath, listen well: I repeat, I had a dream as well when I stayed in that room and I know I won't wake up tomorrow, I have also seen my own funeral, I'm not scared. I am seventy and it is my time to go."

"Nonsense, O'Dell, you seem in perfect health" said Heath.

"I've heart problems, I think. I don't feel wonderful, from time to time. I repeat, I am not scared, but I know I'm not waking up tomorrow. In my dreams I saw myself reunited with my loved ones, what greater pleasure could there be for an old man?"

This statement frightened everyone except O'Dell, nobody could speak a word after that, but it was late and they all decided to go to bed anyway.

It was true, though, Heath was the first to wake up and O'Dell had died in his sleep. It was a shocking moment for Heath, not only finding O 'Dell dead, but, the way he said it would happen. Beside his body, though, he found a note, which seemed to have been written the night before. The note read:

Dear friends:

First of all, please do not be sad for my death, I lived to my seventieth birthday and that's long enough for me. I was a very happy man in life, so no need for tears, my wife is waiting for me in heaven now, and...

The note stops there, as there was nothing else written in it. A Garda did come to investigate, however, just in case of murder or whatever but he found nothing suspicious and as he asked questions, which everyone was happy to answer, he came to the realization that O'Dell had no known enemies, and for the most part, people liked him dearly. Not only that, but Martin O'Dell was one of the most respected men in Howth. You know the people that absolutely everybody likes and nobody can say anything bad about at all, well that was our friend from Limerick, all of Howth liked the guy a lot. The Garda also said that his note could not have been a suicide note, because there wasn't a suicide. Martin 'O Dell had apparently just stopped breathing. There was a longer examination just to rule out any wrong doing but basically, his heart stopped, really.

In time a funeral was had and people came from as far as Limerick to say a last farewell. O'Dell was buried in the grounds of the Abbey in Howth, as was known that he wanted. There is a headstone that reads "Here Lies Martin O'Dell, born 1795, died 1865"

There was a party on the evening of the funeral. Well not entirely a party but since Martin's family had come in from as far as Limerick, they all decided to get together and have a night to remember him. A big dinner was had and a lot of drink. People sat throughout the house and talked all sorts of stories, like:

"Remember when Old Martin didn't know about the trains and we told him that we were going to Dublin and he had got the horses ready?" said one of his oldest friends.

"Really, he hadn't heard about the trains?" asked another, one of his nephews, who was quite young.

"No, you see, they were very new then and not all of Ireland had heard about them. It was tremendously funny because we told him to show up at the train station, so he did but with horses." Said the wife of his oldest friend. "He said he was ready to go to Dublin and we replied that we were as well but we were going by train. He asked what a train was. We all laughed so hard," continued she.

Similar stories were told throughout the night. Everybody got to know each other a little better then and what was great was the fact that Martin O'Dell had touched everybody's life in a very different way but yet they all remembered a happy man. It is funny, though, as the night carried on, people got louder and louder. There was a woman, must have been a relation of

Martin O'Dell, she might have had quite a lot to drink, or perhaps she is just a noisy person, but she began to say jokes about people and laugh when they would say tragic stories. The poor woman made everyone uncomfortable but some of the stories were funny, although nobody seemed to remember much the next day but that is because at some point, somebody got out the Absinth and everyone started telling stories of Old Martin, even Health told stories and he had only met him once in his life. The good thing about Absinth is the next day, you don't remember a thing and whoever says they do is lying.

Since Martin had everything planned for his passing for years, he had, all this time to think about it. The funeral was not a sad one, as O'Dell would not have liked that. There was a priest, he spoke beautifully about O'Dell and there were flowers and then there was the wild party, but I already mentioned the party.

Life did go on for everybody else, by the way, all of Old Martin's family went back home quite happy that they got to say goodbye to him. See, dear friends, when a young person dies, it is quite sad but when an older person dies, especially an old widower with no children to speak of, it is always expected. But enough sadness for now, let us move to happy events.

Chapter 4

Regarding Heath, though, he did go to the gallery in Marrion Street but not on the day of O'Dell's death, because he didn't think it right proper, to do so. He went afterwards, once things had settled down.

There were days in between the funeral and the visit at Marrion Square that Heath Rochester was creating art and everyone knows that artists have good days when everything goes right, and bad days when by accident you ruin a painting. Rochester had a bit of both. One day, he was finishing a watercolour. He had three next to each other, superb pieces of art, but stupid him, took his coffee into the studio and dropped it on the watercolours. Which were ruined beyond repair. Jane, who was nearby, heard him scream "Damnit!"

"Heath, are you all right?"

"I'm not, look, my coffee has ruined my paintings and even the paper has ripped, I worked so hard on them, I did." Heath was really sad.

"Well it's not the end of everything. You can make new ones."

Heath was in no mood to argue but Jane could see he was upset. He wanted to say "How would you know it's not the end of everything? I need to turn these in tomorrow, now I've nothing to show.' But he was calm, very angry, but calm and he said, "You are absolutely right, it can be fixed." You know those moments when something tragic happens, like a painting being ruined and someone tries to help, but they are only making you more upset? That is what Heath was going through. Heath Rochester was a great man, but he had a flaw. When he was upset he would say horrible things to the wrong person, and the wrong person to be upset with, was Jane. Heath knew he could not say anything rude to Jane, in spite of the fact that on other occasions he would have, although she had nothing to do with him spilling coffee on his paintings. This time he kept quiet, but she could see that he was visibly upset.

Jane was right, though, it was not the end of all things. Sometimes with art, things that you spend a very long time at are discarded as being "too perfect" and things that you spend a half hour at and in a bad mood at that, people love and are willing to pay good money for. Heath Rochester learned that lesson in time, and even though lessons can cause heartache, they become valuable to us. The coffee accident, although it did ruin some superb paintings, made Heath rush and since it was going dark and the next day he would meet very important people in Marion Square, he had one choice, which was to produce as quick as possible, paintings which went as follows:

Painting#1: A seascape, with a sunset, but Heath got the lights and shadows all wrong, so nothing made sense. He was nervous and angry, so he paid little attention to where the light was coming from and this where the shadow would be. That painting is a great one because the sun is setting on one part and the light is hitting the boat on the opposite part, with an unexplained shadow at the bottom, making everything technically wrong, but in time these mistakes were what made Heath Rochester famous.

Painting #2: A landscape with people in it, but things like someone's arm wasn't painted because he forgot to do so and a dog in the foreground was left unfinished. That painting was in time seen as the greatest thing since sliced bread.

Painting the last: The Liffey River, which by the bye would have been superb, had he finished it, but at this time he had painted so much, he was exhausted, so he left it almost as a cartoon, one could say, that done, Heath R. took his things off, went to bed and slept like a baby.

The next day was his big event in Dublin, meeting the fancy people. Heath woke up later than he should have, but he got dressed rather quickly and went downstairs for breakfast and nobody noticed he was tardy.

Heath's trip to Marion Square went well. Jane and Eamon LeFroy and the painter went on the train to city centre and from there, they walked to Marrion Square. It snowed that day, and you should see the snow in Dublin, it's just gorgeous. The whole of Dublin was covered in beautiful, white powder, the parks and gardens looked like a winter wonderland. So, our three friends walked across the Ha'Penny, and stopped to look at the Liffey River as snow fell on it you could almost see the water freeze. The snow falling on all the buildings in the city was a gorgeous sight. The way the snow covered the brick buildings, it made them look like something out of a fairy tale.

For those not familiar with Marrion Street, it is mostly a residential area with wonderful, Georgian houses and very few businesses, hardly any businesses, actually. But there is an art collector that can be found there and he exhibits other peoples' work, as well as his own. The house looks like a private residence from the outside but all the neighbors know that if you want to buy art, this one particular house, is the place to go.

There were our three friends, waiting for the art collector on Marrion Street West at this one gorgeous, Georgian house. They looked around at all the art on the walls, when a tall man walked in. "Ah, Heath from England, is it?" said the man. "LeFroy told me all about you and your paintings. I recognize you, due to your dark hair."

Heath shook his hand. "Yes, thank you, I am the artist, yes. I brought some samples of my work, most though, is photographs of my paintings that I have in York. But I have some watercolours and sketches as well. I do mostly oil landscapes, but I haven't got my oils with me and watercolours will do." Said Heath nervously as the tall man inspected his paintings. Heath was going to tell the tall man about his ruined watercolours but Eamon had advised him earlier not to, for this man in particular likes his artists to not expose any flaws. You see, dear friends, there are two types of art lovers, those that don't want to know when an artist has made a mistake such as spill coffee all over there art (such as the case of the tall man) or those that do and that love hearing stories from artists. This one particular man was not very chatty and could not be bothered with too many stories about how the art was created.

"Hmm, where is this?" said the tall man, holding a painting of a castle that he was examining.

"It's a Norman Castle, close to York, I am from York and this is not that far from my home, sir."

"Oh for an instant I reckoned it was Clongriffin Castle."

"Well both of them are Norman Castles, aren't they? I guess Norman Architecture, thing about it is, it's all quite similar, in a way, isn't it? It is all very imposing. I suppose the idea of the Normans was to make you feel as if you have really been conquered." Said Heath Rochester with a smile.

"I hadn't thought about it, but I suppose you are right. But tell me, I see two mistakes on it, first of all, the tree in the foreground, if you think about it, it is illogically big and second, the grass near the tree, where on earth did you find such green pigments? I find the green almost not natural, some of my clients might not be pleased with it, they would find these two mistakes to be too shocking and however, I doubt they are mistakes. Thing is, I think you made these errors on purpose, first of all, I think the story is not that this is a castle near York, but that there is an enormous tree, and behind it, there is what could be a castle, so, you are thus, telling us the story of a very big tree, as for the green grass, I think you chose to shock the viewer by making unnaturally green grass. I had a teacher, ages ago, she called it Poison Green and that is what you have done, instead of it being calm and soothing, we are frightened by such colours, as if the castle were perhaps scary in a way, the garden with the massive tree and the poison green, my word." The tall man was very dramatic, he loved exaggerating everything, so he did.

"You do not find it to your satisfaction then?"

"Nonsense, I love it. There is an Italian man I happen to know that will be thrilled with this painting, what else have you?" He glanced at the rest of the paintings "hmm, some sheep at sunset. I love this one; you used sepias on this one did you not? Oh and a small watercolour of a lake, people like miniatures these days, I am sure you could produce more if asked. Oh, I recognize this, it is here in Dublin, and my word, you captured the urban landscape perfectly." The urban landscape the tall man was referring to was the Liffey River scene that Heath painted the previous night, when he was tremendously tired.

The tall man was very pleased with Heath's work, he decided to have five of his paintings, which is just as well, for Heath hadn't brought much more than five paintings with him. The agreement was, five for now and were they, with luck to sell, then more were to be fetched later, but were they to not sell, then the tall man would keep these for his private collection. Heath could not have been a happier man, so off he went, after saying goodbye to the tall art collector, down to a nearby pub with his two friends to celebrate; not only that the tall man would keep five paintings, but that he seemed to have overlooked the badly done watercolours. See the art world was changing then, old people wanted something classical, either about a biblical scene or a historic one, etc, but young people were bored with perfection, and liked imperfect paintings because we live in an imperfect world, so there was no need to have things done flawless, and Heath was exactly the man the new, young professionals wanted. His art was not always accurate, but it was pretty, it was very colourful and the people of Dublin loved that, because it was a contrast to the grey skies of Ireland.

Heath, thanks to the promotion of this tall man, would become the biggest sensation in Dublin.

Heath and his friends were at the pub having drinks, watching the snow out the window, they were all smiling.

"Well done, you" said Jane. She was happy because she felt that Heath was going to become a famous artist and this was his first step towards that.

"A toast to Mr. Rochester, the artist." Said LeFroy with a smile. Everybody raised their glass to Rochester. "So, I've a question. Your artistic name, what is it going to be?" continued Eamon. He was wondering, was it going to be Heath, or Rochester, or H.R. or something else? Artists can even invent a name for themselves, can't they?

Heath thought for a minute, he didn't like the sound of H.R. it was too empty, no feeling to a name like that, he reckoned. When he was an art student he signed his paintings as Rochester, or H. Rochester, but as he got more experience he began signing them as Heath or H, so he said "I will remain being Heath." Everyone was pleased with that answer. There is more to the story, though. When Heath was a student there was already another Mr.

Rochester and in the art world you can't have two people with the same name, it's not proper, so that is why Heath decided to keep signing his art with the name, Heath.

Jane was a very sociable woman and not shy at all, so she got up and started telling other people at the pub that she was sat with a man that would one day be a famous artist. People replied things like "my word" or "oh, is that so?" Heath got embarrassed when folks approached him and said things like "So, an artist, is it?" Fellows asked about his art and what style he painted. Some people said that they knew other artists as well, but then people would say names of artists and ask if Heath knew them and then he had to say that he sadly didn't. You see, Heath knew very few artists back then, none of which were famous.

As everybody was talking about Heath the artist and about how his meeting had gone with the tall man, Rochester realized that he did not know his name and that it was very rude indeed to not know the name of the person promoting your art.

"Dolly" Said LeFroy.

"That's Dolly?"

"Yes indeed, my good friend Dolly, he was at my castle once when all the paintings fell from the walls, he has witnessed the spirit first hand. His name is Adolph but he prefers to be called Dolly." Continued Eamon.

Heath R. sat there a bit puzzled, He had heard the name of Dolly being mentioned but somehow pictured the person to be remarkably different and not at all a very tall man, but he did agree that if your name were Adolph that Dolly would do.

As everyone was talking in the pub, they noticed that it had stopped snowing. Everybody was happy because now they could leave and go about there activities. Jane was especially happy, but then everything made her happy. Heath loved the fact that she was so entirely cheerful. Let me describe Heath Rochester's feelings for Jane:

Rochester, like all good artists was a sensitive man. But he had struggles in life, so he knew that the right woman for him would have to be a kind, friendly one, preferably religious, although what religion she practiced was of no consequence. You see he was a Christian, and supposing Jane had been an atheist, then they would just argue all the time, so he was pleased to know that she was a

Catholic. Heath also liked her youth, she was barely twenty, and acted fifteen, but Heath really liked that, because it meant that she was in no hurry to grow up, although he knew she was not stupid, because she would say remarkably intelligent things at times. But then she could be childish as well. Jane was pretty, but not an astonishing beauty, and Heath knew that he was more handsome than she was pretty, but her friendliness, and kind soul made up for her looks. And, see, she was not remotely plain, she was actually pretty, just not VERY pretty, whereas Heath Rochester carried himself like an aristocrat, and sometimes acted like one. At the end of the day, Heath thought "there is no better woman on earth for me than sweet Jane."

After they left the pub and went back to LeFroy's Castle that had recently been covered in snow, Heath went to his room where he was contemplating his life as an artist. He thought of many things, first of all, how lucky he was that an art collector agreed to show his work to those that might be interested, because for someone to show interest in an artist's work is not easy. Second, he thought of his adventures here in Ireland, but he also thought it time to go home for now, although he did not want to. He had only just arrived and his adventures in Ireland (though many) had only just begun, although he had a lot to tell his parents and siblings when he got home. He was starting to realize that he was in love with Jane, even though they had just met. Heath had realized this one thing above everything else, that he would think about Jane every second of the day. When she was away he would wonder where she had gone, and when she spoke with someone and smiled, well he loved that smile. He could not leave her without saying what he felt about her. Heath lied in bed that night, all these thoughts going in his mind, and more. You know those nights when you are in bed and one voice tells you "time to leave Clongriffin Castle" and the other voice says "no, it's to early, there's more adventures ahead". That's the sort of night that Heath had. In the end he decided to just write to his family back in England and tell them that he had decided to stay longer in the castle.

Jane also thought all night long. She thought of Heath. She also thought of the Ghost in Clongriffin Castle for she knew for certain now that it allowed you to see the day of your death and that for some reason it seems to only haunt the grey room. The question was, who was this spirit and why was it specifically in that room? She also wondered if the ghost, or whatever it was, could show you pleasant things, like the day of your wedding, or an image of your children, or the houses you would own in the future, that sort of thing. Imagine, if you know what's going to happen in the future, then you are well prepared for it. Mr. 'O Dell was very well prepared for his death because he had seen it in a dream all those years ago, and he believed his dream to be a vision. Jane remembered that when she had stayed in the grey room before, just like old O'Dell, and like Heath, she too had seen images of her death, although she knew it was many years from now. But she also remembered other dreams that she had in the past in that specific room. She remembered having dreams of things that would later be talked about in the newspapers, or of people that she would meet. She now remembered a specific dream where she was in England, specifically in York, and there was a man who looked astonishingly like Heath, and a voice said, "He will be important in your life". Jane had forgotten that dream, as she had it a long time ago, but she all of a sudden remembered it now, and she thought "goodness me, how could I have forgotten such a dream?" It was obvious that she was to meet Heath and that he was to be an important man in her life.

But Jane also thought all sorts of things about Heath, as she lay in bed. It is not proper for a decent girl to think of a man, when they have just met only a few days ago, but she saw something in him, something magical, in his eyes.

LeFroy, on the other hand, didn't think of anything, really, he fell asleep and woke up the next morning, with instructions to give to the household staff to start breakfast for everyone. Breakfast was ready when everyone woke up. At breakfast, LeFroy said that he had received a letter from a relative of his now deceased friend, O Dell, saying that if Eamon could take care of selling the house, as there was no one to inherit it due to the fact that Martin O'Dell had no children and his siblings in Limerick did not want a house in Dublin. And what's even more so, Howth was too far from Limerick and, besides, a house there would be too expensive to keep, and none of his relations reckoned they could afford it. Old Martin had relations, but they all lived miles away and not one could in reality afford to live in his house. Besides even if they could, most of his relations were his brothers and sisters and they were not of age to move to Howth, as they were now elderly. That said, there was no option but to sell the house, as there was nobody to inherit it to.

Victoria had already been advised about the situation of the O'Dell house, by the time everyone woke up and she was already writing an article for the local newspaper regarding the sale of the house in Howth. Very few people are as efficient as Victoria; really, there is nothing she won't do and everything she puts her mind to is done to perfection.

"So, Eamon, how can I be of service?" asked Heath, eager to help with whatever was asked of him, when he was informed about the sale of the house.

"Well, thing is, the house needs to be left without furniture or any belongings if it is to be sold. I was thinking, do you reckon you and Jane could go and see what things could be brought to the castle, and what stuff could be sold?"

"Neither of us mind, do we, Jane? We can leave this instant, if you like"

"I hope you don't mind. The sooner the better, actually, there will be people wanting to buy the house soon enough, no doubt."

Neither Jane nor Heath minded, besides, it might be fun to go through someone's things, and see what is to be done with what. For this task, Victoria accompanied them. She had a good idea of what was to be done and knew that it would take a while, so she explained Jane and Heath in detail all the chores that had to be completed.

There was more to it, though, in reality, going through Martin's things, that is. You see, Old Martin had not kept his house in top condition in the past few years, so not only did they have to get rid of the furniture, but they would have to give it a bit of maintenance as well in order for the house to sell. O'Dell had good health, save for a heart problem he was not aware of, however, he had noticed that he got more and more tired the last few years. So his house had sadly been neglected.

Victoria had known for some time that the house would go for sale and that everything inside would need to be sold, so she had (with O'Dell's permission) done a list of what would go where, in the event of his death.

The belongings of the house were as so:

Antique furniture, dating as far back as the time of Cromwel,l was to be kept. The same went for the piano.

Clothing was to be given away to those in need. Some families had not recuperated from the famine and were in dire need of clothing, even old clothing. Anything would do. And there was lots of very old clothing, but it's better to wear something that's several decades old, than to wear nothing at all, especially in this cold weather.

Everything in the kitchen was to be divided; half was to be sent to the castle, the other half, to those in need.

Household decorations were divided as well. Those that were antiques were to be kept in the castle, as were newer decorations that everyone knew LeFroy would like. As for the rest, it was also to be given to charity. The subject of a sale was mentioned, but Old Martin was such a kind person, so generous indeed was he, that the thought of someone profiting from his chairs and tables seemed silly, especially when there are those that can't afford food, much less a chair to sit on. And Victoria knew that. So at the end of the day, nothing was to be sold and everything that was not sent to the castle was to be given to charity.

Our group of friends divided the chores: Jane went through things in the kitchen, sorting out pots, pans, knives, forks, etc.

Heath went through Old Martin's clothes, and Victoria sorted out all the furniture. She could not carry any of it, but she at least dusted them.

Heath was looking at O'Dell's clothes, putting them away for charity as he was told. Most of the clothes were what he called old people clothes, meaning it was not antique at all, just out of fashion. A few things were worn before Heath had been born so he thought, perhaps a theatre production would like them for when they do plays that take place a while ago. He asked Victoria about it, but she said: "No, Martin wanted absolutely everything to go for those in need."

Then there was Jane in the kitchen. In her house back in Galway they had a kitchen, but it was a very small one, whereas this kitchen had more pots and pans that she knew what to do with. There was also fine china, which looked very expensive, but she did not know what to do with any of it. She thought: "Do I put things away for the poor, or are they to be sent to the castle?" In reality she made one or two mistakes, sending a few things to the poor, which were to be sent to the castle, but at the end of the day, OK, so some needy families got fine china, the good thing is, they were able to sell what they got and use the money for things they needed.

Not all the finery was by accident sent out to the poor. Many things were sent to the castle, which was great because that way the kitchen staff could use new (or new to them) things to cook with.

As for Victoria, she had mentally separated what was for charity and what was to be taken to the castle ages ago, so now she had it easy. She was also very clever because she knew that she could not carry anything but she knew the neighbours here in Howth and she asked them to help her lift the furniture and send it to the castle. Gather, she did give a few things to those who gladly helped as gifts yet, several pieces were sent to LeFroy Castle in Clongriffin.

Just when everyone thought that they were nearly done deciding what went where they realized the house hand an attic. Not all houses in Ireland have attics, so they were not expecting to find one, but when they went to explore it, they realized that it would take almost an army to explore it well. There was old furniture, hats, old clothes from the 18th and perhaps the 17th century...

Everything was old, there, even letters that were from two centuries ago, some were. Cobwebs filled the room, as did dust and dead insects, it was not a pleasant site.

Our three friends sat patiently, deciding what to do with everything, when Victoria realized, some of these belongings used to be at the castle before. She remembered seeing them there. "I wonder why Mr. LeFroy would leave his things here," said Victoria.

Amongst the many belongings, were an old gun, perhaps used by the LeFroy family and several bullets nearby. The gun was perhaps made in the mid 18th century, even earlier. There was also medicine that appeared to have never been used, articles from newspapers and such. Why would Eamon hide things here, if there was plenty space in the castle, it just did not make sense. Everyone was fascinated about the gun, though, it was of a Baroque design, and was kept in perfect condition. It was obviously an old gun, because technology had progressed in the last two centuries, and this being in the 1860's, people had more sophisticated weapons, whereas a few centuries ago people were still using primitive looking guns.

"Look at this gun I found" said Jane

"Oh my, it's decorated with seashells, how strange," mentioned Heath

Victoria was not impressed. "Listen, some children from the area used to come visit the family of O'Dell all the time, since the O'Dell's never had children, they were more than happy to have as many children over as they could. If any of them saw the gun and thought it to be a toy, it could be very bad. Do hide it" Victoria was nervous when she said this and, in a sense, she was right.

She was spot on, Victoria was, regarding the children. Jane looked out the window and there was a group of youngsters staring at the house, asking if there was going to be any tea today.

"See, I told you, Martin O'Dell always had tea for them at this hour, and his wife always had biscuits ready. She would make them herself, and if she did not have biscuits, she had bread."

That said, the gun was put away in a box and placed on a shelf where nobody would find it. The children from Howth were allowed in the house, though not until the gun was put away. They knew that Old Martin was no longer there, but since they saw people inside they wondered if there might be tea, and there indeed was. No house in Ireland can go without tea, even when trying to sell a house that someone just died in, you still keep the kettle on. You see, this house was always a happy home, one where guests could come in and out as they pleased. The family of O'Dell loved telling stories of the good old days, before the famine. "Life was easier back then" Mrs. O'Dell would say "Everybody was friendly then," she would add. Martin would add how now everybody was more conservative and how before people were more confident, more open minded, that is according the O'Dell household. It was true, though, life does change and hardships did indeed make people more conservative.

That night, they all went to the castle for supper, and asked Eamon about his belongings in the attic at the O Dell house. LeFroy did not give a straightforward answer, but then again, he never did. He just said he got tired of seeing the things in the castle, and O'Dell did not mind keeping them. He did explain, however, that some things were best forgotten. The gun, for example, was the one that one of his relatives used it to end his life. He said that his great, great grandfather had shot himself dead one Christmas, many decades before he was born, and someone apparently had kept the gun, although why on earth would they do that was beyond his understanding. Victoria, who had full knowledge about the suicide, was also bewildered about why anyone would keep that weapon. Many times she had wondered why nobody sold it.

As for the medicine, well, most of his family (past and present) had needed some at some point, including his great-grandfather who died at the age of forty-one, and several of his aunts and uncles, which were prone to illness, but there was no point in keeping medicine. Times had changed and scientists were discovering new and more effective ways of curing people, so all the old bottles were of little use, and were thus tossed out. See in the 18th century, and the first half of the 19th century, knowledge of medicine was in it's early years, so what was kept in this box, by the 1860's was considered outdated, so there was no point in keeping old stuff that by now served no purpose.

Regarding the newspaper articles, they just mentioned events from his family, christenings, funerals, weddings, etc. Even Eamon's father's christening gown was nearby, and a few wedding dresses, including his mother's, and his auntie's. Some of the clothes, like baby gowns were kept, for memory sake, but the wedding dress that Eamon's mother wore was thrown out, because Eamon Lefroy had no wife and would thus have no children, and nobody would want to be married in an old dress from the times of King George. Little did Eamon know that one-day people would collect Georgian dresses and put them in museums, especially wedding dresses. They now have a certain value, where, people feel they tell a story, and if that story took place a long time ago, and if it was a romantic one at that, as some weddings tend to be, then people pay more because they go "here is such a dress with a very lovely story to it." The dress that Eamon's mother wore on her wedding day was just tossed out and lost and one day there was no memory of it.

Jane did see the dress one last time, though. She tried wearing it, but there was no point to it, as the dress was made for a much thinner person. "Look cousin, everything is so delicate, even the buttons. Is it Chinese silk?" But, oh how she wanted that wedding dress. There were several reasons why she could not have it, though. First of all, it was made during the reign of Mad King George, and fashion had changed so much since then, and if Jane were to have worn it, she would have looked absurd. Second, Eamon's mother was both shorter and thinner than Jane, so there was no way she could fit in that tiny dress, although she did love looking at it.

Our friend Jane imagined herself in her wedding, wearing a dress as beautiful as this. She always thought of her wedding, married to a kind man, the wedding would be in the prettiest setting ever, perhaps a castle or some great, country house, and all her friends and family would be there.

"Remember, dearest Jane, our great-grandmother made clothes. She was so good at dress-making that all the ladies in Dublin would go to her. When my mother got married, she made the dress for her from materials a man would bring from Paris." Said Eamon.

Jane had heard the story a million times, but she loved hearing it. Jane could not make dresses, you see. She once tried making a scarf, but it didn't go as planned. Like I mentioned, Jane is a big woman, and when she sat down to make the scarf, she realized she had done one for a person half her size. Then she tried making a purse. It was supposed to be in the shape of a pineapple, but it didn't come out the way she wanted at all. Just the same she felt happy that there was a dress maker in the family, once upon a time, and that people admired her work, even though they did not know what to do with any of it. Jane was a romantic in many ways, as she looked at the dress she remembered stories of their great-grandmother. See, Dublin was a smaller place then, and there were fewer places to buy gowns and such, so a good seamstress could make good money and she was the best in Dublin once, her and Eamon's great-grandmother was. It was an honour to be a descendant of such a wonderful person.

Eamon could not decide what to do with all the other things though. Some things were important but others were not. Here is the scenario, the castle of LeFroy was, as you know, filled with antiques, but the O'Dell family had a house full of things that were in some ways just as old or valuable. But they did not fit in the castle, and since Old Martin and wife had come from Limerick with no belongings, Eamon had thought it right to let the O'Dell's have quite a lot of furniture. I must say, though, I have now bored the reader by telling stories about random things that were found I should now move on. But before there is one last thing to mention. See neither Jane nor our English friend, Heath, had thought of the most important thing of all, the money. Allow me to paint a picture for you, as it were:

A piece of furniture, say a buffet, has been in the LeFroy family for three centuries, however, there are plenty of pieces of furniture just like it, so taking it from Howth to the castle in Clongriffin costs money and there is a risk of the furniture being damaged. Eamon stressed about the idea of selling the furniture, vs keeping it. There was a lot to consider, like the fact that Ireland had gone through tough times recently, so very few people had enough money to pay for a tremendously expensive piece of furniture. So were he to sell it, it would have to be for a fraction of what it was worth, but were he to keep it, he would have to pay people to send it to the castle, and the road was bumpy, so the risk of things not getting to the castle in prime condition was a real one. Poor Eamon LeFroy did not sleep well at all. He told everyone to bring the furniture to the castle (what was worth keeping) but he wasn't sure it was the right idea.

Chapter 5

The next few days Heath went to the garden outside the castle to paint. He found a new technique, which was to do quick paintings, with swift brush strokes. He realized that people liked his new technique, whereas before he would spend days, even months at a single painting and he noticed that people did not like them as much, yet people adored his new ones. See, times were changing and not everyone wanted perfect art. There was a new, younger audience that wanted paintings that you create within hours, at most a day or two, as opposed to what was full of detail and elaborately done. Funny, Heath remembered when he was in the Art Academy, and if anyone has ever been to one, the art professors are very strict and do not allow for any creativity. Heath Rochester is very creative but his technique is not the best in the world. Our friend Heath remembered how when he was in the Art Academy, his professors would give him tasks, like painting something from Greek Mythology, or a scene from the life of a certain saint, but Heath felt that those subjects had been done over again for hundreds of years, and that the younger art market wanted something new, original and that wasn't a painting of Apollo, painted for the thousandth time. Dolly came over a time or two to see Heath's progress and he chatted with Heath about his swift, entirely non-perfect paintings and how he would find clients to purchase them, which happened indeed.

Dolly knew the right people. There was, for example, a couple that rented lodgings for visitors in Dublin City that bought several of Heath's paintings through Dolly's help. There was also a woman that lived towards Wicklow who put Heath's art throughout her house. Some people wanted art for a certain room or as a gift to friends for a Christening. Heath felt like an angel had come down from heaven and had come to tell all of Ireland about his art.

Anyway, there was Heath in the garden painting one day when he remembered his professors and how they would not allow his creativity to blossom. Now his creativity was finally flowing and people loved what he did.

Jane loved observing, as Heath would paint. She would put on her prettiest dresses and look at him, as he would create his art. "Pray, tell, what medium are you using now?" she would ask

"Ah, I asked Eamon the other day, where I could buy art supplies, and he pointed at a place in Dublin, so I took the morning train over and found what I needed, he is so kind, isn't he? I got everything I need to do oil paintings. You see, when I was an art student back in York, getting art supplies was a challenge. I pretty much had to make everything. However, now there are all these new art supplies stores that used to not exist." What Heath said was very true. You see, about fifteen years ago, when Heath started painting, art supply stores were tremendously hard to find, so he had to make absolutely everything himself, meaning he had to do the paints, the brushes, physically construct the canvas himself, etc. Now times had advanced and more and more people fancied taking up art since there were more art supply stores.

"Oh, you are working in oils, are you? I wish I could paint, but I was thinking you should do a portrait of me, I would pay for it." Heath was good at landscapes but not so good at drawing people, but he could not say no to sweet Jane, so he got out a new canvas.

"Sit there if you like, on the bench by the tree." Jane had on her red and black dress today, with her black bonnet she loved so much. Heath started with the sketch and remembered to include the bench and the tall tree. After the sketch he allowed her to relax and take refreshment while he painted the background. There were some grey skies, which he painted, as well as the garden. "It looks like it might rain," he thought.

Jane came back when Heath was done painting the background, and sat while he painted her in her red dress. "Oh it's getting rather cold," said Jane, the muse.

"It will only be a few minutes, then we can go inside." Said Heath with a smile. He continued painting. "Wait, I just need to put in some highlights."

When the painting was done, Jane got up. "Ah, wow, let us show Eamon, I am in love with it." Eamon saw the painting and Heath was paid very handsomely for it. Heath Rochester was in the library when the painting was shown to him; Eamon LeFroy had just received a letter from his auntie and uncle, Jane's parents.

"Jane, I have news from Galway."

"Oh, if its mammy, do tell her I am having too much fun, I can't go back home. I just sat for a portrait, besides, O'Dell's house has not sold yet and I need to help with that. I did promise Victoria I would help, what's more, if I go back to mammy she will only sermon me about some thing or another and I've no time for sermons."

"Oh dear Jane, they just worry about you, is all, and yes, they would like for you to go back, not for your sake, but because your parents just worry."

"Nonsense, I will write to them this instant and tell them that I find myself perfectly well. I can't tolerate Galway. Society is tremendously boring there, besides, there is not much to do-- no gambling, no balls, no plays to see,

Clongriffin is much more fun, really. Not only that, but, see, you don't know Galway like I do. It's a lovely place, it's my home, it's where I am from, but people there are more conservative than I am, I get frustrated there at times."

"See I disagree, I find Galway to be fascinating. Heath, you have been quiet, any words on the subject?"

"I wouldn't know, I have never gone further west than Marion Square, really. On that note, I should write to my parents and siblings as well, they would be worried, but when it comes to tremendously conservative people, Jane might be right. Where I come from not everybody agrees with my point of view. Jane, you and I are similar in that aspect, we are forward thinking people."

"Thank you, and see I get frustrated by a lot of things, like the fact that as a woman I have no rights. All men want is for us to look pretty and not do anything. If I had my way, I would write travel books. "

"You write?" asked her cousin. He had never seen her write a word in his life, but that is because Jane is the sort of person that can only write when nobody is around. She finds that her creativity comes when she is alone. Jane has a secret diary and a few short stories and poems about this and that, but beneath all her flirting and putting on fancy outfits, she is insecure, and her writing is very personal, so were people to read her work, she would blush. She did have a dream, though, which was to write travel books and obviously to travel the world and write about her adventures.

"I do write" she answered her cousin.

That night while Jane wrote her letters to her family in as she put it "boring Galway", Heath wrote to his family.

Dear Parents:

You will not believe the adventures I have had. I found my way to some fishing village and there is a castle not far from it, actually, full of antiques and everything. The castle goes back to the Norman period and the antiques, many of them are from the Tudor period, however the owner, his family had traveled the world, so there's loads of stuff from other countries. We went to Howth, which is the name of the village. It rhymes with "both". Anyway it is not far at all from the castle called Clongriffin, the villagers also call it LeFroy Castle. Anyway, this nice old man passed on, a good friend of the owner of the castle, a Mr. LeFroy, though he insists I call him by his first name, Eamon, but I always pronounce his name all wrong, as it is not a familiar one to me. I don't think there are any Eamon's in York. I can never get his name right. By the bye, he has got the loveliest cousin, Jane. The day I met her she had this gorgeous satin dress, entirely red, she looked like a vision, like some sort of angel, really. She has no idea how much I think about her and I rather feel as if a witch has possessed me for I cannot stop thinking about her. Regardless, I have agreed to help with the selling of the house of the man that died, will write soon.

Your son, Heath R.

Heath got a reply soon enough, but his parents only asked about Jane and if he was actually in love with her, to which he replied that he was. He was astonished at how quick the reply was from his family. He was under the impression that post from England took ages, but the letter from his parents and siblings came much quicker than he ever imagined. Heath thought of the speed in which letters arrived by then, and how incredible it would be if messages could be received within an instant. He thought "imagine if you could write to anyone in the world, regardless of where they were and they would receive your message straight away?" He thought that before 1900 someone was bound to invent a machine that could do that. The telegraph was in a sense that, however, Heath always felt that something could be improved on a telegraph... well Heath was always thinking about this and that, but his thoughts often times bored others when he spoke his mind, so he kept his thoughts to himself, for the most part.

After Rochester answered the letter that he had recieved he put his clothes on and went downstairs. He was happy because the night before he dreamed about York. Heath Rochester had a strange idea about being a North Englishman. He thought of people from the south as barbarians, really. He even went so far as to say once that people from the north were prettier people and far more civilized, so for him, there was nothing better than to be a northerner, and when he dreamed of York, de dreamed of the place with pride. I must add as well that so far as Heath was concerned, being a Northerner was so great that he reckoned the North of England must have been created by Jesus himself. Not everybody shared his point of view but just the same Heath loved

York and thought it superior to any place in southern England.

It was a cold morning, Eamon was reading with Jane by his side, as they were discussing her trip back to Galway. Heath had gone out for a walk since early in the morning and was not around. Jane finally had a chance to tell Eamon LeFroy that she was starting to feel something for Heath.

"Does he speak to you about me, when you are alone?" she asked

"All the time. All I hear is Jane this and Jane that. You wore a red dress once and he was quite impressed by it." Eamon was going to continue when Heath walked in.

"You won't believe it. In spite of the cold and rain I found some flowers. They are starting to bloom, Jane, you must go to the garden with me. I did a painting of them, look." Heath showed the painting to Jane and Eamon.

"Oh I love flowers. Do sit, I am nearly done with my coffee, can we go after I am done?" asked Jane with a big smile.

"Oh please, I shall have some myself."

A staff member brought the coffee and then Heath and Jane went to see the flowers. Eamon needed to go back inside the castle so he did not accompany them this time.

"Daffodils; they came early this year, Jane." said Heath as they walked in the garden. "I need to go back to England to see my parents soon. I can't convince you to come with me, can I?" I have a house in York. Not as big as this but it hasn't any ghosts. No premonitions, no nightmares about death, but you must meet my family, it is a large one, both my family and my house. I have many brothers and sisters, and I know that although you aren't fond of England, because the English are too stiff, as you once mentioned but my family would welcome you. Thing is, I can't stop thinking about you. I know, it's not Ireland, but please visit."

It is a truth universally acknowledged that single women aren't supposed to travel alone, much less with an unmarried man, for it might cause a scandal, but Jane was dying to go. "Let me think about it" she said, with a smile. See, Jane couldn't say 'yes I will go" because of what her cousin might think. Thing is, she knew Eamon well and he might think that were her cousin to be seen with a man that she was not yet engaged to it would be her ruin. On the one hand he was right, leFroy was, for proper Irish girls don't travel with men that they aren't engaged to, much less if they have to stay at a hotel for a night or two. What would people say?

They were speaking, silently when LeFroy approached them. He had apparently forgotten something and came back when he saw his cousin and his artist friend. "Oh cousin, you won't believe it, Heath needs to go back to England and has invited me to go with him, imagine, York." You could see her eyes shine bright when she said those very words.

"I think you would like York. You read a lot and you like history and, you know what, Jane, there's many castles there and abbeys and all of them are haunted. I think you would enjoy a trip there," said Eamon.

The rest of the day was spent discussing the trip. Heath told them all about things to do there, and about his large family, and how they had been settled there since longer than he knew, etc. They talked about all the castles worth seeing, and the shambles, and nearby ruins and things. Jane's imagination went wild. She especially loved hearing about York

Minster, and the stories about how it was built and who is buried there, and so on. She also wondered if there were ghosts there. Heath told Jane how the current York Minster was done in a style called Perpendicular Style and how if you look at the ceiling, it was like looking at a lace gown. People in York say that the Perpendicular ceiling was similar to the fabrics that people used in the Middle Ages. Jane imagined herself a queen back then, in the 1400's wearing lace from head to toe and with a knight fighting other people for her love. She also imagined herself to be the Faerie Queene except, unlike in the books, she imagined all sorts of terrible things like her fighting demons and dragons and a haunted, dark forest where a dashing prince with brown eyes would come rescue her.

That night, as the three were sitting near the fire, dozing off, Jane realized she was nearly done with her book and would need another one for her trip. "Cousin, I'm going to the library, I need to see what book to take."

Off she went and while she was away, Eamon and Heath talked about her trip, and how she would be well looked after. Eamon would have loved to go as well but, like always, he said he had business to take care of. Pretty soon, though, Jane re-entered.

"I found the perfect book: Fanny Hill."

"Fanny Hill? Yes, one of my favorites" said Eamon with joy. Everybody loves the story of Fanny Hill, a woman of pleasure.

"Well I would love to hear about it, but I'm tired," Commented Heath. And off he went to bed. Heath was very tired, it was late in the evening and he had blood shot eyes.

That night, Heath had another strange dream. This was to be his last, though. In his dream he saw a man by the name of Neill who had died a violent death in this room, but he also saw something else. He couldn't tell if it was another man or a group of people in the room. There was something like a cloud in the room and he could see what seemed to be another person or group of people but he knew not how many. Neil was dressed like people did in the late 1700's, he was sat in this very room and he shot himself.

The next morning, Heath asked his friend who Neill was "My great, great grandfather, why? What have you found out about him?"

"He died in my room, didn't he? And most violently so… He is the man you were telling us about, is he not? You know, your great-great grandfather that shot himself. He is without a doubt the ghost that for some reason warns us about our own death. Jane and I were talking about him, she wondered why you can only see the day of your death and why only in that room. Jane asked why the ghost wouldn't show you your wedding day, or the day you buy a house, or your future children, etc. I think your great-great grandfather, Neil, his soul is in torment for ending his life in the grey room and he doesn't want anybody to suffer the same fate as him, am I right?"

"He committed suicide there, and after he died, they found a letter, saying that he would come back t haunt us. It was worse than that, actually. My great-great grandfather, Neil, he shot himself at Christmas. He was an alcoholic, and a most violent one at that. He never treated his wife kindly, my great, great grandmother. While Neill lived his wife and children suffered a great deal but after he died, certain things started happening. My great grandfather died shortly thereafter, of an illness. Nothing alarming except for the fact that he was quite young. My grandfather inherited the castle, but he lived alone for the most part. He is the one that decided that the grey room should look more uplifting. It was too dark and perhaps a change in colour would brighten things up. Anyway, about him, I mean he had my grandmother with him, but long story short, I doubt it was an ideal marriage. My grandfather was not violent in the sense that he never hit anybody, however he did get angry quite frequently. He had a violent, grumpy temper and my poor grandmother suffered a great deal because of it. I remember things like, well as you know, there are no shops here so if they needed anything they needed to go to Dublin. And the trains did not exist then, so it happened more than once that when they were on their way back and my grandmother would say "Oh I forgot this or that" my grandfather would get tremendously angry. Even with Jane, we once went to Howth to see the deer, and Jane was a child and had a fall and cried, as is normal for a child. Well, grandfather, God bless him, got tremendously angry at Jane for falling and for crying. I remember it well, we were all scared.

When my father inherited the castle, he and mother actually had a normal life, besides the nightmares, and they both died the way great-great grandfather Neil predicted. My mother was a sociable person, always entertaining people. When they lived here in the castle they had huge balls and parties of all sorts and everyone in Howth was invited. My father was less sociable, he was prone to being stern and when he tried to make a joke, he would get it wrong and then would have to explain it. Nobody found that funny, really, but bless his cotton socks, he tried telling jokes.

When I met O'Dell, I tried convincing him to get rid of any evidence that Neil had ever lived. There is a book on the family history that one of my aunties put together. She is still alive, though very old. You would love her, such an extravagant woman, reminds me of Mrs Havisham, really. You had it in your hand when you went to the attic, her book, you just did not know what it was."

"Well that solves that problem. Now I know perfectly well who the ghost is. It's Neill, your ancestor. Now, how do we get him to stop haunting whoever stays in the room, and how do we know why he killed himself, and who was the man in the room with him? I've a million questions, I don't know where to start," said Heath. Heath Rochester's head was spinning. He had heard about a suicide or murder in the room he lived in, then of a man that died shortly thereafter, of an eccentric woman and of all sorts of things. He needed to relax, maybe see if Victoria could get him a soda or a brandy, or brandy with soda, or whatever, really.

"If you need to know, Neill, had five mistresses that we know of, plus he never treated his wife with any respect, and was an alcoholic. He would get enormously depressed when he drunk and one day he grabbed the gun you saw and he shot himself. Thing is, put yourself in his shoes, imagine you are in this very castle shortly before 1770, your wife hates you, your children can't look at you, and your five mistresses all know that their children they had with you will never inherit the castle. What's more, many of his bastard children have worked here before. One still does. That is why he killed himself. He would spend all his money on loose women and drinking and he was going to lose the castle. I have thought about it before, he was such a tremendous wreck that had he not shot himself, one of his mistresses would have done so. See, back then men were allowed to hit women, now almost nobody does. Anyway, at first everything was fun, then he would get bored of one, treat her horribly and move on to the other one."

Victoria (who was walking in with soda) was a descendant of Neill and his affair with a maid. Her family had stayed in the castle since then. Victoria never saw the suicide, she knew about it, but she never saw it as this was the mid 1860's and she was in her fifty's so she could never had witnessed the event as it happened years before she was born. Victoria looked younger than her age. But I will tell you her secret: she died her hair and used cosmetics to cover up her wrinkles and she was also fond of high heels and walked like a queen, thus looking younger altogether. Eamon also dyed his hair. He had gone grey about a decade ago and hated it and eventually found some dyes to cover up his grey hair.

"Are you sure your great -great grandfather was not murdered?"

"Positive, he did it in front of his friends at a Christmas party."

"That is gruesome. I couldn't imagine anything worse, but hang on a minute, why was everybody in that room that night? It was Christmas, shouldn't they be out at church or having dinner? Didn't you say there were others in the room?" asked Heath.

"He called them to the room, he had been drinking heavily, and made an absolute ass of himself, but he always did. Everybody followed him up to his room, but in hope that he might fall asleep. They started to undress him, but found a gun in his pocket, he grabbed it and right then and there shot himself dead. So, now you know. My cousin, Jane, thinks we should sell the castle. I don't want to torture the future owners with a ghost. I don't know what to do. I would be honored if you could take Jane with you to England while I decide. Don't worry, I don't drink, and I am not a depressive sort, and Victoria has already given the gun to my friend Dolly. He is fond of old guns and he absolutely loved the seashell decoration it has on it. I will be fine, just so you know. The ghost has showed me my death in a dream and it's not for a while now. I just, don't want Jane to be burdened with, well with my having to choose what to do with the castle, and perhaps having to move everything. Besides, she is a happy person, if you remind her of her family's past, it might torment her. We can't ruin her happiness. I would prefer her to go to York with you for a few weeks. I could meet you there, if you like. By the way, this is of utmost importance, what is your address in York? I think that in a week or so I will come visit, if I may?"

"Are you sure you don't want a priest to see the house? And I must warn you; I don't own a castle. I own a big house in York, but it's not a castle. You are free to visit, but I've fourteen siblings. We would be tight, having said that, you are more than welcome to visit. "

"Many priests have come to bless my house from as far as Rome. One said to have fire be put out with fire. I know what he means, but the house is too beautiful to be burnt. See I even had a group of demonologists study the castle. They live in the north. It was about a month before you came. Remember Dolly, the man that buys your art? Dolly is a friend from Dublin, as you well know, well he heard about these people that study demons, they came to the castle and tried to get rid of whatever was haunting the place, but since there is no satanic being in the castle, just a tormented spirit, all their conjuring was for nothing," said Eamon LeFroy.

"But the furniture is even more beautiful than the castle itself. Look, I've an idea. Take the furniture out, put it somewhere else. It is all yours, and after all, the furniture is. Buy another house, maybe not a castle this time, but we are in the 19th century, there are so many gorgeous houses all over Ireland, you would be bound to find one. Move elsewhere, and lock this old castle up. Meet me in York; I will in the meantime entertain your cousin. Does she like nuts? I've a walnut tree, I could show her my nuts, she will love to harvest them."

The plan was agreed upon and Heath and Jane left the following day.

Chapter 6

Jane was welcomed with open arms in the house of Heath's family. All of Heath's siblings were tremendously interested in hearing all about Ireland.

"Tell us about the castle." One would say.

"Is it old, is it scary, is it dark?" another would say, then someone else would go "is it true that Ireland is quite green?" Everybody knows that England is very green, but Ireland is much greener than England, because it rains more. See, English people, when they travel abroad go "my home town is so green" but Irish people go "you don't know what greenery is until you have been to Ireland." England is gorgeous and is very green, but Ireland is far greener.

There were many, many questions, and many stories that everyone wanted to hear about Ireland. The family would stay up by the fire every night to hear the stories. Jane did indeed feel at home, she was afraid at first, that she would not like England, since it is very different to Ireland, and because her family had always said that it was better to be single for ever than to marry someone from England, so she grew up with this idea since she was a girl. But Heath and his family were far kinder to her than she ever dreamed they would be. She liked this family, and they liked her. She also liked the fact that they showed her all the sites in York. She soon grew to love the place, although she thought frequently of Ireland. Jane loved going out for walks as well. Jane's favorite thing of all the sights she had seen though was York Minster. It is quite impressive how such buildings were constructed so many centuries ago. Jane was an optimistic person and that helped her enjoy her journey in York.

Jane loved stories about York Minster and how the central tower once fell in the Middle Ages, or how an Anglo-Saxon king was once baptized there. She also learned how the church was once made out of wood, but was now out of stone, which was great, because stone buildings last longer. Although, having said that, in the year of 1840, the church did catch fire and she wondered if that happened again what the result would be, would they rebuild it or would they put another church in it's place or whatever?

One day, not long after they had arrived in York, Heath took Jane to a nearby town, Whitby, for a picnic where they had tea in the park. For those that don't know Whitby, it is small, there is an abandoned abbey and the wind howls there all the time. The town is charming as well. Jane and Heath walked there, in the town first and then they went to a nearby park for tea and food of all sorts and loads of tea. Heath's family did not join them on this trip, for he asked to be left alone with her.

"Jane, I was wondering, you seem very happy here indeed. Would you, that is, we are both single, and you have seen how I live. It is not glamorous, but it is what I have to offer. Would you love to be my wife? Do say yes." Heath was tremendously nervous, and struggled to say these few words.

"Yes. I was beginning to wonder if you would ever ask."

"I am so glad, what a relief! Had you said no, I don't know what would have become of me."

Heath got down on one knee as he spoke, and put a ring on Jane's finger. The ring was one that had been handed down from his family, and was nothing new or impressive, but Jane did not want anything new and fancy.

Heath's mother, Elizabeth was the first to hear the news upon their return from Whitby. "My son is to be married, and to this beautiful girl, look at you, luv. Oh dearest (to her husband, Henry) Let us tell our friends, and oh Jane, I know a dressmaker, and a cake, you need a cake. Oh my word, how much excitement."

Poor Jane, though, she liked her new mother-in-law, but she was realizing that with her involvement, everyone in the north of England would go to the wedding, and they would have her wear the biggest dress anyone had ever seen, and it would probably end up being in The Queen's House, the wedding would be, down in London or something huge like that, and the thing is, Heath's mother, although she didn't have a tremendous amount of money for something as big as that, she had some money saved in the bank for her children's future and she did want something huge. However Jane had always wanted something small, maybe close friends and family only and nothing beyond that. Jane had dreamed of a wedding in a garden with only the closest of friends around, but she could tell that her new mother-in-law wanted the biggest event ever. Jane also worried if she could get her family over from Ireland for the occasion. She also needed to set a date, have a menu, have bridesmaids, she wanted a white dress, white flowers, perhaps an early morning church service followed by breakfast for the guests. She also wanted her husband to show up in blue, he looked good in the following colours: blue, violet, green and grey, but every time he wore blue she would nearly faint at the sight of him because he would look amazing.

As for what Heath wanted, he didn't care if they got married in York or in Ireland or as far as India, or wherever, really, or if it was in The Queen's House in Greenwich or in his parent's garden, all he wanted was to show up and that's it. Heath was a kind man, sensitive, but he wasn't into weddings, but he knew everybody would help organize it. To be honest, Heath liked weddings as much as people like cockroaches. He tried to avoid them at all cost and whenever he got invited to one he found a reason to not go and would send one of his siblings to represent him. There is a reason behind Heath's hatred of weddings. See, as an artist he had spent years and years painting and selling art when he could. One day, shortly before he left for Ireland, he realized that most of his friends were married and had children and he was still single. But really for years he had avoided weddings because once there people would ask when his turn was to get married so he decided not to go, instead what he did was to save his money and go to Ireland where nobody knew him. Now Heath is back and has brought Jane along with him.

The entire family of Rochester helped with the wedding invitations and everything, so they did. One day, though, as the family was talking about the wedding, after they had gone to see Heath's grandmother, who was in charge of making a white dress for Jane and a blue suit for Heath, there was a knock on the door as they were all together, sat by the fire. One of Heath's sisters got the door.

"A man in an Irish accent has come."

"Oh do let him in, surely it's one of Jane's relations." said Henry, Heath's father. Jane looked puzzled, she hadn't written to her family yet, she had been so busy with flowers and dresses and choosing what to give everyone for breakfast after the ceremony that she plumb forgot to write to her relations in Galway and to her cousin in Dublin and tell them about her wedding.

"Hello, I've come from Ireland, does a Mr. Heath live here?" Heath went to see the man.

"Yes I do."

"Oh grand, I have a message from Clongriffin Castle, I traveled all the way from there. Thing is, tragedy has happened there. LeFroy, I think he went quite mad, really."

"Mad?"

"Well he acted strange when you and Jane left. You see, Victoria, my cousin, she called on me when you left, and she had me help with taking all the furniture and art out of the castle. We were not told why, but were told to do so Dolly came over to help as well. We received a good payment for removing all the furniture, so I was put on a boat to England after that, told where to reach you, and here I am. Now if I am allowed to sit and have refreshment, I have been traveling for ages, I have." The man sat down, and was handed water. Then continued the conversation. "Poor Eamon, I heard he is selling the castle, though, for what little money anybody was willing to give."

"I've a little bit of money," said one of Heath's brothers, a small boy. The boy did not comprehend that a small bit of change in his pocket could not buy a castle, as he was too young to understand the conversation.

Everybody discussed what to do with the castle, they also wanted to talk about the antiques, but Victoria's cousin insisted there was nothing to be done, that they had been sent somewhere, though he knew not where.

"Perhaps I should go see him." Said Jane as they talked.

"Well he is your cousin after all, if he is quite unwell, then you should." said Henry. Jane did go to Ireland.

The trip to Ireland was uneventful the sea was actually much calmer than one expects it to be. Jane arrived in Dublin and took the train to Howth, where Victoria. met her. "Eamon is well, do not worry, it is the castle. We were moving all the antiques, and the grey room caught fire, but nobody was in the room then. I can not explain it, because see, it was a long day, we had taken everything out of the castle, to have it sent some place you will soon find out, and we had come to Howth to have some food and had all left the castle, we were all very hungry. The strange part is, not a single person was in the castle at the time, nor were any candles left on or any lamps of any sort. It was last Sunday, and all the staff was given the day off. We came to the castle, and saw the flames. A man came to investigate, he did a great job at it, and although he found no arsonist, he did find evidence that the fire had started in the Grey room, how they figure these things out is beyond me, but anyway, poor Eamon is in shock."

"What nobody knew yet was: remember when old Martin died, and the antiques they found in the attic? One of them was cursed, we don't know by whom. Legend has it that at some time in the seventeenth century a witch came to Ireland from across the sea, and she stayed at the castle in the very same grey room, but she felt she was not treated kindly so she cursed the place and every object in it. Nobody in Ireland today believes in witches, but what is true is that some of the objects such as mirrors broke without reason, paintings from the entire castle fell from there walls, that happened even until some days before Heath arrived, not every day, but once every couple of years or so. Also, doors would slam and windows would open and close for no reason and knives had been flying through the castle... there was a lengthy investigation and to not bore you, here is what happened, as they say, in a nutshell:

"A woman did come to the castle from abroad in the 1690's and the then-owner was a grumpy man. His children had left and gone to Galway to live for they could not tolerate his foul temper. One of them was Jane's ancestor, so it was no surprise that the house guest was mistreated. She did curse the castle, beginning with the very room she stayed in, and she stormed out and left the castle, never to return, but she left some daggers in the room. The daggers were said to fly through the room without anybody moving them, until one day around 1850, Eamon gave them as a gift to Old Martin. When Old Martin heard about the witch he had them locked in the attic. When he died and everyone went to pack his things, nobody thought anything of the daggers, not even Victoria. She was more worried about the old gun they found than some old knives, so she brought them back to the castle and that is when Eamon began acting like a mad man.

"There was more to the story, though, you see. For generations the family of LeFroy was cursed. At first it was nothing major, just someone having a stroke of bad luck, say, but then things got worse. It got to a point where whatever the LeFroy's tried to do, it would come out wrong. Many family members lost all their money and took to working in the streets, others had businesses that failed and left them in ruin, while others yet felt darkness everywhere they went. One day Eamon's great-great grandfather, Neil ended his life in the room that the witch had cursed. His life had been a disaster from start to finish and it was not going to get any better ever. He did not know of the curse or the witch but he knew that no matter what he did he could not be happy. When Neil died, the power of the curse got weaker. Neil's son (who was now married and with children) died the next year but of sadness, not of a curse, and Neil's grandchild (Eamon's grandfather) grew to be a grumpy man. But the witch's curse could have no power beyond just making him ill tempered. You see, the curse would lose strength when a person would die in pain in the very room that the witch stayed in, and that had happened upon Neil's death-- although it did not go away, it just was not as strong. The witch had also allowed people to see their death because it is what she wanted, for anyone that would stay in that very room to see the day and hour of their death and to not be able to do a thing about it."

Jane arrived to what remained of the castle, and there she saw Eamon, unhurt physically, but mentally quite shaken. "What happened?" Jane asked and that is when she was told about the curse of the daggers.

"Our ancestor, the one that shot himself one Christmas party, decades ago, I don't believe in the supernatural, but there is something you must know, dearest Jane. On the night of his funeral, guests said that they smelled something burning, when asked where the smell came from, it was from his room, the grey room. A lot of strange things happened right there, items showing up in random places, and clocks stopping for no reason, even paintings falling off the shelves. Remember the one painting in that same room the painting of the boat? It fell once, and broke. A man tried to repair it, but could not, so I bought a painting of Christ and put it in that room. Things stopped falling and breaking without reason, I didn't know if it was because I brought a blessed painting into the room or because I gave every cursed object to old Martin to have locked up. But the dreams continued. When it was obvious that the dreams were a prediction of what is to come, after Old Martin died the exact same way he dreamed it when he stayed in the room, it was obvious to me that it had been my great-great grandfather, the one who died there, whose ghost was doing all this. I don't know how the fire started, I may never know, but I have no doubt it was him," said Eamon, only he was wrong about one thing. It wasn't his ancestor that killed himself that caused the terror, it was the witch that cursed the place, and whose curse caused him to run mad and kill himself, but thing is, nobody alive remembered the witch, but how could they? Nobody's memory went that far back. Things were discovered in time, though. Even burned down places leave clues of the past.

Eamon did not then know about the witch, he only knew about his great-great grandfather dying in that very room, but in time the entire truth was found out.

"First of all, I have a lot of questions. I have stayed there, and have seen the date 1916, ever since then that number has appeared multiple times, I think I die then, but no matter, I would be an old lady. Second, where will you live? Are you going to rebuild?"

"My cousin, I can't rebuild this, it is a pile of grey and black rocks now, who wants to buy them? And besides, I have written to Heath, he knows everything I just told you and I am in luck, there is a new house in York, Heath's parents were building it for when either him or one of his siblings would get married, that they could live in this new house. My furniture has already been sent to England," said Eamon.

"I know that house, it's not one house, it's two, across the street from each other, really pretty ones, Heath showed me them the other day." Said Jane in deep thought. Hang on a minute, if you go to York, what will happen to dearest Victoria?" continued she.

Victoria was not at that moment with Jane and Eamon as she thought it right to let them have there privacy, so she had gone off to walk, and was unaware she was being talked about. "Victoria", said Eamon LeFroy, "Remember Dolly in Marion Square? I had some paintings that were worth some money, actually quite a lot of money, and I sold them to him. Every penny I got from selling the paintings went to Victoria for her decades of loyal service to me, she is a wealthy woman and can do whatever she wishes to do with her money."

"And the art dealer in Marion Square, Dolly, does he want to see any more art? Heath has an entire room filled with art that has not sold." Inquired Jane. This was very much true. When Jane was in England, Heath had showed her a room full of art that although was some of his best work it had failed to find a costumer. Dolly was the right man to sell Heath's art.

"Well we have to stay at his place tonight, nobody can stay here, it's all in ruins, the entire castle is. Why don't you ask him?" said Eamon. Just then Victoria appeared. Our three friends went to Marion Square, to where Dolly was waiting for them with open arms. Dolly was a very friendly man who loved company so he had already made dinner for Jane, Eamon and Victoria.

"Eamon, I heard what happened to your castle. Tragedy, isn't it?" Said Dolly at dinner.

"Yes and no. I mean it's sad to see the castle go up in flames, but way I see it, at least none of the furniture was in it, and now I can sell the land. I finally have buyers interested. But listen, thanks for letting us stay here for the night, you are grand." Said Eamon

"Am happy to do so," replied Dolly.

Victoria and Jane went to the kitchen while Dolly and Eamon talked in private after dinner and they chatted about all sorts of things, and Eamon talked to Dolly about a possibility for Heath to show his work somewhere in Dublin. There was a neighborhood, not that far from Dublin Castle that had a place for Heath to exhibit. Dolly the art dealer just needed to see when space would be available.

Dinner was now over and done with as was their chat, and the men joined the women. "Jane, I've good news, I am going to write tomorrow to a man I know, he has a place near Dublin Castle and he can show your friend Heath's work if you like, we just need to see when," Said Dolly the tall man.

"Oh is that so?" Jane's eyes lid up as she said that. "But, how can he bring his paintings from England? I was mentioning to Eamon earlier, or was it you, Victoria, I can't remember who I said it to anyway, he has a room filled with art that has not sold. All of his art is great, thing is, all of his friends in York already have paintings he made, but he needs to have more clients," continued Jane.

Everyone thought for a moment, because yes, bringing art over from England was not going to be easy, they discussed what was to be done, when Eamon remembered he knew somebody quite well that ships things regularly between England and Ireland, he could call on him tomorrow and ask how to get the paintings over.

Drinks were served as they talked and then everyone went to bed, quite peacefully so, and the next day they all woke up with quite a lot to do. Eamon looked for his friend and arrange for the paintings to be brought over, Jane wrote to Heath and told him the news, and Dolly the art dealer took the carriage over to visit his friend. Dolly had room for Heath to show his art, but not for a few months, which was great, because that would be in the middle of spring anyway, plus the wedding could be postponed so far as Jane reckoned, she knew that Heath would rather show his art than go to his own wedding.

The next day Jane went with her cousin to Clongriffin to get rid of all the stones and rubble of what was once a castle. They woke up early and made it there before ten in the morning. It was a very windy day, very, very cold but Eamon and her had talked about clearing out as many rocks as possible before they would sell it.

Jane was standing in what used to be the entrance of the castle when she saw a door on the floor, one that neither she nor Eamon had ever seen before. Jane opened the door, which led to a basement. She did not have a torch to see where she was going but she reckoned so long as she left the door open she would be able to see where she was going.

The basement had several things from the seventeenth century, pieces of furniture, old candles, &c. She went to tell Eamon about it. He was beyond words. When he inherited the castle not a word had been mentioned about a basement. The place was very dusty, but since he was pulling rubble from other parts of the castle, he had a rag with him anyway, so he just started dusting everything.

"Look." He said "A letter" continued he. The letter read as such:

Dear owners of the castle:

I write to you on this day, June 1st on the day of our Lord 1693. I, Morgan of County Wicklow stayed in this castle last night. It needs be said that I was treated with scorn and violence. I, a traveler was tired and although I was offered rest the owners and staff called me a harlot and a wench. A pox on this house! I curse thee, whosoever might live or visit here from now until the end of days. The only way the curse will be broken or weakened is through love, I curse that word, love, wretched word. Finally, those without love, but yet with hatred I will come for their souls but not without tormenting them in this life first.

Morgan The Red of Wicklow

Both Jane and Eamon read the letter, they talked about what they read and came to the conclusion that it was she who cursed the place and she no doubt haunted many people that lived and visited here, but when Heath's great-great grandfather died it must have sufficed for her because most of the torments (though not all) stopped after his death. Neil was a very unhappy man who never knew that a witch had cursed him. When Neil died he was mourned even though he had been cruel with those around him and the seed of love was beginning to be planted. Later on Eamon (who had seen darkness) sought the light and found it with Heath who was a pure soul and with his cousin Jane.

There was still an enigma, though who caused the fire in the castle if there was nobody around? Was it Morgan's spirit, was she the cause of all this, or was it just an act of nature? The answer to that question will never be known, however, it is known for a fact that the fire did start in the grey room and it did spread quickly as well one should remember that nobody, not one living person, was in the castle then.

As evening settled Eamon and Jane went back to Dublin to Dolly's house where Victoria and he waited for them with some tea. During tea Eamon showed his friends the letter and asked their opinion on the matter. A lot was discussed, such as who was Morgan The Red and why had Heath's family been cruel to her. It was sadly concluded that nobody knew for sure who this witch was, however they knew that there was once a story of a woman who had once escaped life in Dublin and had gone to live in the mountains in Wicklow, far from everyone, and that she was believed to have been a witch that could curse people she did not like. Nobody believed in the story of the Wicklow witch and not one person knew for sure what her name had been however it was assumed that it was the same person.

Another subject that was talked about was that of Heath, Dolly had been in contact with him through a letter or two and had encouraged him to come at once and bring as much of his art as he could with him to Dublin.

Chapter 7

Heath came back to Ireland and just in time too. His paintings had shown up in boxes before he made it to Ireland which was easier, really. That way he did not have to carry them with him on his trip, so he had time to see how they had made it, and if they were damaged. Some had been but not tragically so. The paintings were sent by boat but a wind had picked up which caused the box that they had been placed in to move about, thus damaging a few of the paintings. Everything was fixed just in time. In art nothing is beyond repair. Invitations were sent to all the important people in Dublin, some as far as Galway, including Jane's parents and siblings. People came to see Heath's swiftly done paintings, and to have a drink and admire his work.

When it was time to give a toast to the artist, Heath said "Dearest Jane, without you this would never have happened, I am sad that we had to postpone the wedding, but I finally get to meet your family."

What went on in Jane's mind when they discussed the wedding was: First of all, a new life in York sounded nice, I mean let's face it, it wasn't Ireland and Jane loved Ireland, however she loved Heath, and could not imagine being away from him. Furthermore, she got along with his family quite well, so she knew that even though she would miss Galway tremendously, she would be able to visit from time to time, and she did, actually. She knew that she would miss the little things about her life in Galway, such as the way her mam's kitchen smelled when someone was cooking, or the cats that she had, she would miss them more than words could express, but she knew that life with a man as good as Heath would not be bad at all, because he was kind to her and his kindness and gentleness towards her would never stop, and she knew that more than anything in life, she wanted a man that would treat her right, so long as she lived. Jane was worried, though, because her parents saw the English as the conquerors that brought nothing but misery to Ireland and to see their daughter marry an Englishman was not what they had planned for her. A bit on that, though.

Jane's mother and father always dreamed that they would marry Jane to a hardworking Galway man and Jane met several of them, mostly older men that had made a good living for themselves in spite of the hardships in life. But she did not want any of those older, more mature men. She always wanted a youthful, sensitive, more artistic man and with Heath she got exactly what she wanted. Jane's parents, when they met Heath were sad that he was not exactly what they would have liked, but they could not deny the fact that Heath was tremendously kind and loving towards her so they talked in private with dearest Jane about what they were worried about, and she told them to stop worrying. But an Irish parent can never stop worrying and in time they grew to accept him as part of the family.

I will not spare you, my friends the ever so boring detail about the planning of the wedding since I already mentioned some things before, but there was one, detail you must know, which is that the wedding took place in Whitby Abbey one morning. It took ages to decide where to have the wedding. Some people suggested Fountains Abbey, others thought Castle Howard, while others reckoned York Minster would be a good idea. But after a long look at each place, Jane chose Whitby Abbey because that is where Heath proposed to her.

Jane looked stunning, as did brown eyed Heath, her in a white dress with white flowers and him in a blue suit. They did have a baby some time afterwards, named Daniel, and Eamon was the best of all uncles for him. Eamon provided everything that little Daniel needed, and showed him much love and affection.

Eamon had all of his furniture brought over from Ireland and settled a new life just across the street from Heath and Jane, where he visited baby Daniel every day, and told him stories about a haunted castle and of ghosts that once terrified the people that stayed there. Daniel, when he was no longer a baby, and could now comprehend everything, said that the stories must have been true, because he had a cat, and the cat would frequently stare at the wind and would get scared to death and hiss at it. Daniel was aware that there were many days when there was nobody there but the cat, and it would stare at nothingness as if something were moving, then the cat would run and hide in fear and hiss at the nothing. Cats are that way, though. They see things that we cannot see, such as beings from beyond the grave. Daniel's grey cat obviously saw spirits and was more than obviously terrified of them and would do anything possible to let Daniel know when a spirit would walk by. Since it was only a cat, it could only hiss and scratch, but that was enough to let Daniel know that something was in the room.

As for Victoria, Eamon had left her enough money for her to never need to work, and with that money she bought a small house in County Meath, where she attended her garden every day. Victoria did not need more than her garden in order to be entirely happy, and when she moved into her cottage with a large garden she was very, very happy.

Dolly kept in touch with Heath, and kept promoting his work, until in time he made Heath a very wealthy man. Heath did not become wealthy immediately, actually, you see he found that as time advanced and the nineteenth century came to a close and the twentieth century was born, the art world changed drastically, one day people in the art community wanted one thing, the next day it was out of style, and it was not always easy for tall, Dolly to find clients for Heath. But every year he found enough people interested in Heath's work that in time articles were being written about him in the papers, and such. Heath always had a dream, though, which was to show his work in places like Milan, Paris, etc, and in time, thanks to Dolly's help he did.

The End

POEMS

Exploring

When was the last time

That you went exploring,

What hill did you climb?

I expect it wasn't boring.

When was the last time

That you walked in the woods;

From the top could you climb

To unknown neighborhoods?

Have you learned something new,

Or re-discovered something old?

Did you have a clue?

You could be so bold?

Say, what did you learn?

That it snows in the desert,

And the arctic can burn,

Or you can get cut by a gentle fern.

Next time you are out

I ask you to observe

The hills and trees about

Nature is a teacher we deserve.

Kittens (a thought)

I wonder:

Do kittens have a soul?

Thing is, kittens cry, they smile, and kittens play too, they get angry, they get happy, they feel. I believe kittens do have a soul. Furthermore, regarding kittens, each one is different, so thus kittens must have a soul.

THE HOUSE

There is a small, brick house
On the road to a lake.
What beauty one can create,
Such a gorgeous house.

The place looks ancient, however
Were the owner's poor or rich,
Were they Davis, Williams, or Flinch?
Most gorgeous, small house ever.

I see chickens around it,

and a cow and two dogs.

They play in nearby bogs,

But the house is not lit.

Now you've heard of the house

Made out of brick,

Now empty and sick,

Who will buy this old house?

Will they repair it

Or will they tear it down?

Will they paint it orange, blue or brown?

No doubt a new light in here will be lit.

THE RIVER

There is a river,

don't you know,

It has a rainbow

of a rosy glow.

I took my shoes away

And wet my feet,

Felt my heart beet.

My feelings I did obey.

Listen to the song

the water makes

as a fall it makes

The drops fall long.

There is a river

And it flows just for us

You can hear it, thus,

it's sound can make you shiver.

Virgin Girl

Ode to thee oh virgin girl

Though you are so humble,

A God still came

from your womb.

I praise thee, Jewish, virgin girl.

You obeyed your heart and did not stumble.

It is because of your faith

We all have hope.

Old Man

How is life, old man,

Now that you are in heaven?

I hear a dove

singing in my ear.

If the dove sings, you are O.K.

You know, old man?

I heard your friends are angels.

I bet you tell them jokes.

I can see the angels laugh

Thank God you are at peace

And that you are able to

Make the angels laugh.

Cupid

Can a cupid wander through the fields of love,

wandering through gardens of hearts and of roses

and fly across the earth like a beautiful dove

to touch lovers with his arrows full of roses.

For sometimes love hits like a shock from up above.

When love strikes, we trust not our heads nor our noses.

So love brings happiness when life is indeed tough.

Love's strength is epic, like Hercules or Moses.

But love can break into countless of small pieces,

So be true to your heart and never let it go

even if you find yourself in awkward places

So always be gentle to your one and true love

whom as time flies by, you will love day by day

and never let go of that one whom you most love.

If love was not so... (a quick thought)

If love was not so TOUGH

If love was just a GAME

If love would not HARM

If love would not BURN

If love would not leave a SCAR

From Boy to Man

I

Once upon a time
A boy went for a walk
Without a dollar or a dime.

Beyond this world and time
Did our young boy walk,
Without speaking, like a mime.

II

Once our boy had left

His home, which was so new,

His family he as well left.

He went to conquer with no debt

Upon the rocks, mud and dew,

Going north, south, right and left.

III

The world was his,

And he was the world's

When he learned and saw bliss.

Only after learning, did the world become his

His arms, his face, his ears,

Everything now, with him is.

IV

Now our boy has grown into a man,
No longer a child is he
Proud is he of the life he ran,

And of how he became a man,
Of lessons life brought him,
From China, Iceland, to Iran.

During a Walk

I went for a walk today.
The sun was shining, the wind was calm.
There was a slight breeze, yet...
It bothered me not.

I believe it is a magic day
As if I was in the golden pot
At the rainbow's end;

So much peace to be got.

What's better than my sunny day,

Is the fact that I spot

Some bunnies at my foot's end.

"This must be a carrot," they thought.

A Thought

I wake up before dawn, people are still asleep. It will be a very busy day. I think of all the people in there beds, some of them barely climbing in them, yet my day has started...

I had a break around noon. Nobody to boss me around or tell me what to do, even if it's just for a little while. I'm off for a walk, and enjoy the day. I am not making e-mails or phone calls for just this peaceful moment. I will only look up to the trees and flowers, before the crazy day continues.

A Wet and Windy Day

Some people say

Cold weather brings gloom.

They hate the cold winds

Of one month, but love

The heat of May

I like a good windy day,

When the leaves of the trees

Move about like

Dancers prancing

Throughout the day.

When rain falls today

Upon the leaves

Flying through the air

I can not happier be,

Than upon that wet and windy day.

Happiness (a thought)

To me, happiness is not how much money you make in a day's work. Nor am I happy knowing what I own or what I can buy. No!

To me, happiness is waking up every morning to the song of a bird. I am also happy when I take a hot shower, and feel the drops on my body. As I walk I feel joy as I see a plant grow strong. A plant can be the greatest thing I see. Rain and sun is all a plant need to grow.

These are the joys I see in my life, not fancy cars or big bills, just simple things, like a plant or a tree. I think about the plants. Funny, as I shower in order to look and feel better, I I see the rain falling on the plants, and know that they too must feel better. I need the water, as does the plant.